CRUCIBLE OF CONFLICT

Published by
Whittles Publishing Ltd.,
Dunbeath,
Caithness, KW6 6EG,
Scotland, UK

www.whittlespublishing.com

© 2023 John Sadler

ISBN 978-184995-542-3

Thanks are due to the following for allowing
me to reproduce their copyright images: Adam
Barr (Adamski), Bev Palin, Trevor Sheehan
(Defence Photography), Gerry Tomlinson &
Geoffrey Carter (UK Battlefield Trust).

Printed in the UK by Micropress Printers Ltd.

CRUCIBLE OF CONFLICT
THREE CENTURIES OF BORDER WAR

JOHN SADLER

Whittles Publishing

This one is for Bev Palin

'The landscape here is one of gently rolling hills of great natural beauty, and the area is rich not only in scenic attractions but also in great houses with an amazing store of literary, legendary, and historic associations. This was the front line of the centuries-old struggle between two warring nations, one comparatively rich and aggressive, the other poor and struggling to maintain her independence. It was the source of a great heritage of ballads, telling stories of feats of valour, love, and betrayal, and of supernatural forces. And it was the home and inspiration of such figures as Sir Walter Scott, James Hogg, John Buchan and Andrew Lang'.

LORD STEEL OF AIKWOOD

CONTENTS

ACKNOWLEDGEMENTS

Once again, in writing of the borders and border wars my heartfelt thanks are due to staff at the following institutions for their courtesy and assistance throughout the writing and research processes: Alnwick Castle Archives, Alnwick; Johnnie Armstrong Museum of Border Arms & Armour, Teviothead; Bamburgh Castle; Berwick Museum & Art Gallery; Bellingham Heritage Centre, Bellingham; British Library; Cumbria's Museum of Military Life; Douglas Archives, Drumlanrig Tower, Hawick; Durham County Record Office; East Lothian County Archives; English Heritage; the Explore Programme, Newcastle; the Friends of Harbottle Castle; Fusiliers Museum of Northumberland; Hexham Old Gaol Museum, Hexham; Hexham Partnership; Historic Environment Scotland; Green Howards Museum, Richmond, King's Own Scottish Borderers Museum, Berwick upon Tweed; Literary and Philosophical Society, Newcastle; Ministry of Defence (Otterburn, Redesdale & Spadeadam); the National Archive, Kew; National Museums Scotland, Edinburgh; National Records of Scotland, Edinburgh; National Trust for Scotland; Newcastle Central Library; Glendale Local History Society; Coldstream & District Local History Society; Remembering Flodden Project; Flodden 500 Project; Northumberland Archives, Woodhorn; Northumberland National Park Authority; Royal Armouries, Leeds; Society of Antiquaries, Newcastle upon Tyne; the UK Battlefields Trust; Tullie House Museum, Carlisle; Tyne and Wear Museums & Archives, Newcastle.

I have a great many people to thank, many who have knowingly and many others unknowingly contributed to this book which has been a long time in the making. These include: Max Adams, Dr. Lyndsay Allason-Jones, Fiona Armstrong, the late Alec Bankier, Adam Barr, Margaret Baxter, Stan Beckensall, Alix Bell, Barbara Birley, Peter Blenkinsopp, Chris Berendt, Steven Bogle, Liz Bregazzi, Robert Brooks, Colin Burgess, Chris & Barry Butterworth, Dr. David

Caldwell, Ronnie Campbell-Smith, Dr. Tobias Capwell, Geoffrey Carter, Doug Chapman, Beryl Charlton, Andrew Cochrane, the late Ian Colquhoun, John Common (senior), Marjorie Common, the late Tom Corfe, John Dale, John Day, Terry Deary, Ruth Dickinson, Andrew Dineley, Gordon Dixon, the late Wilf Dodds, Keith Douglas, Ulfric Douglas, Colin & Lindsay Durward, Margaret Eliott, Flora Fairbairn, Janet Fenwick-Clennel, Ann & John Ferguson, Tony Fox, Alistair Fraser, Jane Gibson, Bobbi Goldwater, David Goldwater, Dave Grey, Julia & Alan Grint, Anna Groundwater, Jane Hall, Tony Hall, Clive Hallam-Baker, the late Robert Hardy CBE FSA, Jim Herbert, Rob Horne, Philip Howard, Andy Jepson, the late George Jobey MC FSA, Chris Jones, Terry Kowal of the Scottish Parliament, Jennifer Laidler (for verse extract), Sue Lloyd, Stephen Lowdon, Paul Macdonald, May McKerrell, John Malden, Kath Marshall-Ivens, Paul Martin, Dr. Xerxes Mazda, Major Sam Meadows 2 RGR, Margaret Mitchinson, Brian Moffat, Glenda Mortimer, Peter Nicholson, John Nolan, Colm O'Brien, Geoff Parkhouse, Harry Pearson, Phil Philo, Aiden Pratt, Baroness J. Quinn, Stewart Rae, Sarah Reay, Julian Reynolds, Joe Ann Ricca, Peter Ryder, Pearl Saddington, John Scott, Trevor Sheehan, David Silk and colleagues at Newcastle Keep & Black Gate, Barbara Spearman of English Heritage, Alex Speirs, Lord Steel of Aikwood, Derek Stewart, the late Jock Tate, Anne Telfer, Paul Thompson, Neil Tranter, Graham Trueman, Anne-Marie Trevelyan MP, The Honourable Christopher Vane Chester Herald, Jenny Vaughn, Philip Walling, Sir Humphrey Wakefield, Charles Wesencraft, Bob Widdrington, Peter Woods, & Dr. Paul Younger.

My heartfelt thanks to all of those who took the time and trouble to offer a viewpoint when asked to do so; I am deeply obliged for your contributions and apologise for having had to edit some of these down, due entirely to space constraints. Thanks also to April Jackson for the original drawings, Chloe Rodham for the map, another fruitful collaboration, Julia Grint for editing, and Beverley Palin for the indexing.

I owe a particular debt to my first-rate agent, Tom Cull and to the team at Whittles, and as ever to my wife Ruth for yet another bout of my writer's self-absorption. All errors remain my sole responsibility and should any agency, organisation, or individual find they have not received accreditation or have been accredited in error, please let the publishers or me know, and I'll ensure future amendment.

John Sadler
Spring 2022

TIMELINE

AD 79–84: Agricola campaigns in the north, establishment of the Stanegate Line

120–128: Hadrian's Wall is constructed

367: Large-scale 'barbarian' incursions south of the Wall

383: Magnus Maximus withdraws bulk of remaining Wall garrison

573: Battle of Arthuret/Arfderydd

590 (circa): Battle of Catraeth (Catterick?)

634: Battle of Heavenfield

685: Battle of Nechtansmere (Dunnichen?)

793: First Viking raid on Lindisfarne

832: Battle of Athelstaneford

865–866: Ivar's Great Northern Army conquers Northumbria

870: Siege and taking of Dumbarton by Ivar & Olaf of Dublin

918: Battle of Corbridge

937: Battle of Brunanburh

1018: Battle of Carham

1093: Malcolm III killed at Alnwick

1138: Battle of the Standard

1174: Battle of Alnwick, William the Lion is captured

1258: First mention of Leges Marchiarum

1296: Sack of Berwick by Edward I

1314: Battle of Bannockburn, Bruce's defeat of Edward II

1328: The Treaty of Northampton/the 'Shameful Peace'

1332: Battle of Dupplin Moor

1333: Battle of Halidon Hill

1346: Battle of Neville's Cross

1388: Battle of Otterburn

1402: Battle of Homildon

1464: Battles of Hedgeley Moor & Hexham/Siege of Bamburgh

1488: Battle of Sauchieburn

1502: Treaty of Perpetual Peace

1513: Battle of Flodden

1523: Siege of Cessford Castle

1542: Battle of Solway Moss

1544: Hertford's devastating raid on Leith & Edinburgh

1545: Battle of Ancrum Moor

1547: Battle of Pinkie

1560: Treaty of Berwick

1575: Raid of the Reidswire

1596: Buccleuch's raid on Carlisle

1603: Union of the Crowns

1640: Battle of Newburn

1642–1651: Wars of Three Kingdoms

1644: Siege of Newcastle

1645: Battle of Philiphaugh

1650: Battle of Dunbar and the death march to Durham

1678: Crookham Affray

1707: Full union between England & Scotland

1715: Jacobite Rising in Scotland and Northumberland

1745: Marshal Wade begins his Military Road, having been wrong-footed by Lord George Murray

1761: Hexham Massacre

1771: Baillie John Hardy introduces stocking frames in Hawick

1815: Pringle brand of knitwear founded

1815: At Waterloo Sergeant Ewart takes the French colour

1819: Hogg publishes Jacobite Relics

1823: Scott builds Abbotsford

1847: Construction of the Royal Border Bridge, Berwick begins, castle remains are demolished

1890: James Paris Lee invents a spring-loaded column-feed magazine system for centre-fire cartridge rifles

1911: Lauder Common Riding revived

1915: Piper Daniel Laidler wins the VC at Loos

1935: William Joyce ('Lord Haw-Haw') addresses a meeting of the British Union of Fascists in Dumfries

1936: Jarrow March/Crusade

1942: Adam Wakenshaw wins a posthumous VC in North Africa

1950: The Anglo-Scottish border is closed for the first time in four centuries after students uplift the Stone of Scone in an attempt at repatriation

1960s: T. Dan Smith pursues his vision of a 'Brasilia in the North'

1966: Bernat Klein sets up business at Selkirk

1968: Jim Clark dies in an accident at the Hockenheimring in West Germany

1969: Launch of Esso Northumbria on Tyneside

1971: G. M. Fraser publishes the Steel Bonnets

1971: Release of Get Carter

1999: Scottish Parliament opened

2014: Independence Referendum results in a victory for the 'No' campaign

2016: Brexit Referendum results in a 'Leave' vote

2019: SNP calls for 'IndyRef 2'

Introduction: The Border Line

'Water can flow, or it can crush. Be water my friend'

Bruce Lee

The Border Marches were the furnace in which the identities of England and of Scotland were forged. That's my assertion anyway and if it sounds a bit Hollywood, then I'd say it deserves to be. What happened on the marches throughout three centuries of endemic violence and interstate, local, tribal, and family level, irrevocably marked the character of all of us who came next. It still does, we are unique.

I've been writing about the borders for a long time, so what's new? Well, the nationalist debate which, despite the 2014 Referendum, continues arguably more fiercely than ever. Will there be a 2nd Scottish Referendum and how does the cultural history of the borders fit? I've already spoken to a number of SNP 'activists' and this idea of a cultural identity, forged in the fury of those Border wars, is a thematic strand of their current push for a 2nd try.

Post Covid, the debate will intensify and the whole furore caused by Brexit will resurface. The two referenda, Indyref One and Brexit, have raised the spectre of the Saltire higher than at any point since the Union of 1707 and it's not going back into the sentimentalists' closet anytime soon.

But I'm focusing on history and how people and events have shaped and influenced their descendants. My main theme will be those reivers, the Steel Bonnets of dark legend. Much has been written, a fair bit of it by me, about them but virtually nothing by them. They relied on an oral tradition of balladry and had to wait for Walter Scott to give them a romantic makeover (one they probably wouldn't have even begun to recognise). But I'm going to start with horses. And if men and women were a different breed so too were their chosen mounts, without which reiving would have been nigh on impossible.

THE RIDER AND HIS HORSE

My version of a border horse or hobbler was called George and I rode him regularly from Redmire near Tarset across Upper North Tynedale. He was as near to a borderer's mount as you're likely to get, not quite 15 hands, deep chested and strong with a mouth like iron and a temperament to match. He looked like he could have been ridden by Kinmont Will. While he was about friendly as Will with a hangover, he was extraordinarily sure-footed, could be relied on to find his way home from just about any spot anywhere without putting a foot wrong and had tremendous stamina.

Horseback is the best way of seeing the border country, a damn sight easier than walking and while George didn't gallop, he could strain himself to a decent, if fairly sedate, canter. You had the feeling that riding straight at a group of snarling lances wouldn't have bothered him one little bit. Over that wide and empty sweep of border hills with wind brushing a celestial hand over a savannah of waving grass and peat, only the mournful, lilting cry of curlews as a theme tune, it's easy to project yourself backwards. The trees are all wrong of course, serried ranks of Forestry Commission pine, spruce, and larch as regular as a Red Army Parade and every bit as oppressive. But there are still almost no signs of modernity, just now and then the alien masts of wind farms, sprouting like the devil's asparagus.

In 2019, in the deep south-west and the pure Agatha Christie village of Painswick I was, of an evening as we say, at table with an Italian Brigadier, who'd formerly been defence attaché in both China and Mongolia. He was a lean, restless type, who reminded me of the actor Gian Maria Volonte, a charismatic baddie in the early Dollars films and latterly a brilliant Charles 'Lucky' Luciano. A keen horseman, he'd actually ridden along the entire length of the Great Wall but found his true Shangri-La in the cold uplands of the Altai.

A serious Genghis Khan anorak, he'd ridden solo for days with only a vast hunting eagle for company on a tireless Mongolian pony, a direct descendant of Genghis' fabulous and lethal cavalry. He rode without seeing anything that couldn't have been there in the thirteenth century. We get a taster of that here on the border fells (meanwhile he still hasn't worked out how to get the eagle, with a wingspan the size of a Lancaster, back into Italy or what his wife will say when he does).

As for the borderers' horses, the consensus is that these were what was called a Galloway nag or pony: 'The province of Galloway formerly possessed a breed of horse peculiar to itself, which were in high estimation for the saddle, being, though of a small size, exceedingly hardy and active. They were larger than the ponies of Wales, and the north of Scotland, and rose from 12 to 14 hands in height. The soils of Galloway, in their unimproved state, are evidently adapted for rearing such a breed of horses; and in the moors and mountainous part of the country, a few of the native breed are still to be found'.

'... This ancient race is almost lost, since farmers found it necessary to breed horses of greater weight, and better adapted to the draught. But such as have a considerable portion of the old blood, are easily distinguished, by their smallness of head and neck, and cleanness of bone. They are generally of a light bay or brown colour, and their legs black. The name of Galloway is sometimes given to horses of an intermediate size between the pony and the full-sized horse, whatever may be the breed' [1].

Once the riding days were gone, these ponies proved unsuitable for domestic and farming roles, so the specific breed evolved and the old lines gradually disappeared, so they were virtually extinct by the eighteenth century. It's hardly surprising that, as noted, King James VI and I when suppressing the borders, made it illegal to own a horse worth more than £30.00 Scots. Previously, the borderers' nags had been highly prized with a considerable investment in imported bloodstock from Poland, Hungary, and Spain so whilst one might look workaday, it was in its own way, a thoroughbred and priced accordingly.

Good horses were an essential aspect, not just of reiving but of cross-border warfare at all levels. A young Edward III of England found to his cost in the embarrassingly abortive Weardale Campaign of 1327, how knightly destriers were totally out of water in the mosses (pun intended). The light Scottish hobilers ran rings round them. Such prime and awfully expensive horseflesh, seen as the arbiter on any battlefield, was practically a liability on such difficult ground; chasing a will o' the wisp enemy who refused to stand and fight. Steel Bonnets had highly specialised needs, and their lives would often depend on their horses. Footmen were obviously at a huge disadvantage (not that this would deter them, most raids had their 'foot loons' following). It was said a good mount could cover 40 miles each way on a raid without resting. It could turn and manoeuvre either in a running fight or herding unenthusiastic four-legged spoils. This seems incredible and yet the evidence from many a foray supports the assertion.

Where a horse can go, a hound will follow. Just as well – fast-moving, long-loping border hounds called 'slewdogges' were highly cherished and highly priced, changing hands for £10.00 sterling (or £100.00 Scots) in the money of the day (you could likely multiply that by a hundred to get a current calculation, say £4,000.00–£5,000.00). It seems likely, as George MacDonald Fraser argues, that these were trail not blood hounds and the modern equivalent is the Cumbrian trail hound, but their ancestry probably goes back to the black and tan St. Hubert Hound from the Ardennes [2]. The name probably comes from 'sleuth' – track or trail, though possibly from those sloughs and mosses over which the animals pursued stolen livestock [3]. The dogs themselves were a handy bonus for any reiver.

Sleuth hounds seem to have originated in what is now Cumbria during the thirteenth century; an Act from the Scottish Parliament of 1289 bans any attempt to bar the passage of dogs when engaged in lawful pursuit. Robert Bruce was apparently tracked by sleuth hounds when on the run (one of which was his own)! A sixteenth-century writer describes the Cumbrian version as having a round thick head, short nose, large nostrils, long-hanging ears with a straight back, bushy tail, long, strong legs, well-clawed and padded feet [4].

In correspondence from 1526, James V wrote requesting sleuth hounds that could be carried pillion by horsemen and then set loose near their intended quarry [5]. We can rely on the well-informed Bishop of Ross: 'They are endowed with such great sagacity and fierceness that they may pursue thieves in a direct course and without any deviation and this with such ferocity of nature that they tear them to pieces even if they chance to be lying down with many others for from the first scent that they get they are never confused except when they come to a river, when they lose the scent. Nor have they acquired this art from nature alone, but they have learned it of man who, with much labour, forms them skilfully to this. Whence come it that among them as are particularly fine are purchased at a remarkably high price' [6].

RIDINGS

Lauder, Jedburgh, Peebles, and Selkirk are all Royal and Ancient Burghs and rightly proud of the fact. A tradition which they share is the Common Riding and these, in part, echo the importance placed on good horseflesh; as Bishop Ross affirmed 'a very poor man they deem it to be without a horse' [7]. The custom has ancient roots. Towns were granted charters to hold annual fairs and it was the custom of the burgesses (property-holders), led by the provost, to carry out a mounted inspection of the bounds.

Their purpose was entirely serious; to ensure nobody was encroaching on the civic lands which were sanctified by charter. This took place on the day of a fair and probably involved a very fair measure of serious civic imbibing. Such frivolity offended the dour strictures of the Kirk and the Scots Reformation made quite sure people were no longer enjoying themselves. In some cases, the Riding endured, while in others it was revived much later and the cavalcade was no longer led by the provost but by an annually elected candidate, the cornet (otherwise a junior light cavalry officer).

Genteel Peebles has a Common Riding and it's linked to the Beltane Fair staged each June. This had a long historic provenance but had fallen into disuse – it was revived to mark Queen Victoria's Diamond Jubilee [8]. At Lauder, the Riding occurs on the first Saturday of August with dozens of riders followed by hundreds of followers, and all accompanied by pipe bands. The town commemorates its Royal Charter, though, as Lord Steel points out, it was here in 1482 that Archibald 'Bell the Cat' Douglas [9] led a coup against King James III's coterie of catamites and made sure they dangled, en masse, beneath Lauder Bridge.

In the 'Auld Grey Toun' of Hawick, the Riding takes place in early June [10] and having lapsed, was revived during the interwar years as a potent symbol of civic pride and awareness. It's a serious business and this year's cornet undertakes some preliminary forays during the build-up. These are exhausting in themselves – traditionally he only summons male riders and the inclusion of ladies provoked a bitter rearguard action. He himself must be unmarried, like the 'callants' who bested the English in a sharp skirmish just beyond the town in the year after Flodden, just to show the men of Hawick still had teeth and weren't cowed. If you've ever played rugby against them, you will understand.

Older men are represented by the 'acting-father' while conventionally women were relegated to a strictly supporting role. The cornet's 'lass', in suitably demure attire with two dozen young women from the town, her maids of honour, attends to the de-bussing of the colours, tying ribbons to the standard (feminists are permitted to recoil). The cornet doesn't wear a dress, he's top-hatted and sports a natty green tailcoat, like some hard-riding squire straight out of Scott [11]. On the day, he's serenaded into the main civic hall by a fife and drum band, suitably martial with a lusty rendition of the old song cheering 'sons of heroes slain at Flodden' – potent mythology.

Selkirk Common Riding is backed by four and a half centuries of history and the 'Souters' [12] proudly continue today. Tradition insists that a company of fourscore archers, as Selkirk men were renowned bowmen, marched behind King James in his grand division at Flodden and 79 of them died there though not before, at such huge cost, they captured the banner of Sir Christopher Savage and his Macclesfield troop. I'm not one to debunk but it's more likely they stood as part of Hume's borderers opposite the Lancashire men on the Scottish left/English right and that their actual casualties would have been minimal. Still, the story is that a man called Fletcher, the sole survivor, rode back into the town, minus his comrades and overcome with emotion, couldn't speak of the trauma, just hurled down the captured standard. I wouldn't be the one to cast doubt in Selkirk, mind you.

On the Friday following the second Monday in June the ride takes place. The standard bearer is selected annually at a 'picking-night', some weeks beforehand.

All applicants are drawn from a group of young men who've acted as assistants for at least the last four years – most will have been riding since boyhood. As befitting such a key role, there's a long apprenticeship. At 04.00, the crack of early dawn, the flute band wakes the town, and their provost leads a promenade which finishes beneath the balcony of Victoria Hall by 07.00 where the civic party is waiting.

A suitable flourish of drums kicks off a long procession as the standard bearer carries high the banner won at Flodden. Scores of riders and many hundreds more spectators, today's foot loons, accompany him as he begins his solemn journey through the streets backed by massed pipes and the pennons of all the town's guilds, British Legion and even the expat 'Colonial' Society, (political correctness has, thankfully, yet to make significant inroads into the borders).

At full tilt, the horses blast across the foaming Ettrick, leaving foot loons on the bank. The ride traces the quite tortuous bounds of the town; Ridings really do demand significant equestrian skills since these horsemen only stop twice. First up is the grave of Tibbie Tamson. This unfortunate woman lived in the eighteenth century and the townspeople weren't kind to her. Today, she'd be recognised as having special needs; then she was hounded to suicide and dumped on the boundary where one citizen, more humane, buried her. This halt is by way of a civic apology. Then there's the three boulders 'Brethren' which mark the juncture with two large adjoining estates. Drink is consumed.

Then it's full on again back down to the water, foot contingent lining the streets in tense anticipation, that almost primal surge of horsemen spilling down the hillside, a magnificent spectacle but only the standard bearer approaches the square alone, as was Fletcher, to symbolically cast down the colours. All those other banners are waved in a prescribed, rather ritualistic pattern; played along to the tune of 'Up wi' the Souters o' Selkirk' [13]. More drink may now be taken, often quite a lot of it, this bit is probably historically accurate; let's face it, if you've just lost the battle of Flodden, you're bound to need solace!

Debatable lands

Godfrey Watson, when describing the Debatable Lands (there were disputed several areas), characterises the principal region in the west as a 'DMZ' – a de-militarised zone. He was writing in the early 1970s when the idea was well known, associated with a strip of contentious ground between what were then, North and South Vietnam, a 'free-fire' zone, fought over by both, controlled by neither. And the idea has stuck that these contested tracts between England and Scotland were dominated by anarchic violence and frequently they were. The Memoranda of the Borders from 1580 comments that 'the just bounds toward Scotland is in debate in diverse places where the two realms touch and have been the cause of great controversy between the nations. By means whereof there be certain parcels of ground upon the edge of the frontier doubtful as to whether realms they appertain, and these are called the Debatable Lands; in truth usurped by the Scots as well during the wars while our people retiring themselves into the country left the same desolate' [14].

Ridpath picks up the theme: 'As no authority was exercised in that tract by the kings of either nation, it naturally became a place of refuge for the most abandoned criminals after their expulsion or flight from their own country, from there they made their plundering inroads into the countries adjacent on either side ... and retired with their booty' [15]. The main chunk of real estate extended from the Solway in the west to Langholm in Dumfriesshire. Canonbie was the biggest settlement, and it encompassed the baronies of Kirkandrews, Bryntallone, and Morton. It wasn't a big space, ten miles (16 kilometres) from west to east and say just under 4 miles (6.4 kilometres) north to south. Boundaries were the Sark to the west and the Liddel/Esk in the east.

'Debatable' – in the border context, this does suggest some pretty sharp bickering, but the name quite possibly derives from Old English 'battable' which is simply a term for describing land suitable fattening up store cattle. Graham Robb in his recent absorbing study certainly favours this view which is most persuasively argued. I tend to agree and it's possible the strip was effectively shared grazing during the earlier medieval period, and it was Anglo-Scottish wars that poisoned the well.

A series of proclamations during the mid-fifteenth century – in 1451, 1453, and 1457 – sought to delineate the respective rights of both sovereigns and a further edict from 1480 attempted to prevent claimants from either or both sides from causing bother. It's here for the first time we get the word 'battable' and/or 'threap'. Thirteen years on and canny Henry VII of England, who wasn't looking for further trouble on his northern frontier, appointed commissioners to seek an agreed compromise though this didn't make any real progress. As the tempo of border hate spiralled after Flodden, Dacre, in August 1528, writes furiously to Wolsey complaining of: 'cruel murder and shameful slaughter', done to his servants because he'd not allowed the Armstrongs to settle in the Debatable Land [16]. It seems the agreed form was that both sides could pasture their beasts unhindered during daylight hours, but nobody could erect buildings or enclosures, so asserting rights of ownership. If anyone tried, then the gloves were immediately off.

In 1543 Henry VIII, who was never one to miss an opportunity, was laying claim to St. Martin's Priory in Canonbie on the grounds it was traditionally an English house

[17]. That's Henry of course whose idea of legality tended to be both highly subjective and entirely partisan. Nonetheless, the English were applying pressure which Maxwell, as Warden, was resisting and five years after King Henry's claim the first formal suggestion of an agreed split was put forward. The perceived alternative was pretty stark: by 1551 both wardens were ready to suggest – 'All Englishmen and Scots after this proclamation are and shall be free to rob, burn, spoil, slay, murder and destroy all and every such person or persons, their bodies, buildings, goods and cattle as do remain or shall inhabit upon any part of the said Debatable Land without any redress' [18]. Just in case anyone hadn't been listening, Maxwell conducted a sweep and torched any shielings he came across. Ridpath takes up the refrain: '... It was first proposed that .... The district should be wholly evacuated and laid waste, but it was afterwards thought better to make a division of it between the kingdoms' [19].

After the usual bureaucratic and diplomatic wrangling plus inevitable point-scoring, commissioners were appointed from both sides: Wharton and Sir Thomas Challoner headed up the English delegation; Douglas of Drumlanrig and Maitland of Lethington spoke for the Scots. Amazingly, both wanted the lion's share, and it wasn't until they agreed to invite the French ambassador to arbitrate that any significant progress was made. He, quite simply and with the Wisdom of Solomon, drew a line halfway through the rival claims, which made it hard for anyone to complain. The new line ran from the 'Sark to a point on the Esk, opposite the house of Fergus Graham ... the last and final line of the partition concluded 24 September 1552' [20]. This new frontier would be delineated by an earth and rubble mound, 'the Scots' Dyke' finished at both extremities with stone pillars. And so, the line was finally drawn.

What about the Grahams and Armstrongs, were they impressed? Not likely, lines on maps they'd never seen didn't matter much and it was soon business as usual with settlers, particularly from the Scottish side, encroaching. As ever, the Grahams could be relied upon to hold their own. A later survey, carried out a year after the Union, describes the English side as being well-stocked with those of their name [21]. Further east, a couple of small pockets of uncertainty were still causing trouble, as late as 1580 when Ridpath tell us: 'Certain grounds lying on the frontier, in the Middle and East Marches of both kingdoms, affording continual cause for controversy and strife, no decision having ascertained to which realm they belonged; the commissioners agreed to supplicate their respective sovereigns to appoint deputies for hearing the claims advanced ... and to cut off all occasion for further strife concerning them by making a division and fixing perpetual boundaries ... between the two kingdoms' [22]. And indeed, they did – the lines were finally fixed. So far, they've stayed that way.

GOD'S WORK

'If Jesus Christ were amongst them, then they would deceive him, if he would hear trust and follow their wicked counsel'.

Richard Fenwick 1597

Q. 'Are there no Christians here?' A. 'No, we're all Armstrongs and Elliotts hereabouts' [23].

'I curse them walking and riding; I curse them standing and sitting; I curse them/ eating and I curse them drinking; I curse them waking and sleeping, rising and/ lying; I curse them at home; I curse them away from home; I curse them inside/ their houses and outside their houses; I curse their wives, their children, and/ their servants who help with their evil deeds. I curse their crops, their/cattle, their wool, their sheep, their horses, their swine, their geese, their/hens and all their livestock. I curse their halls, their rooms, their kitchens/their stalls, their barns, their cowsheds, their barnyards, their cabbage/patches, their plows and their harrows. I curse all the goods and every building/necessary for their sustenance and well-being'. That's one very irate prelate ... [24].

The Bishop of Glasgow wasn't alone in condemning the borderers, and that's just part of his extensive 'Monition of Cursing'. While he might wax more lyrical, he was playing an oft-heard tune. Nobody wanted a parish on the Marches; it was the equivalent to a diplomatic posting to the Khyber Pass. There were clergy though, probably quite a few, who generally get a bad press that went 'native' to the extent they participated, perhaps even eagerly, in the crimes of their parishioners and needed strong towers, Vicar's Peles, as added insurance. Good examples still survive, such as Longhorsley, Elsdon and Corbridge in Northumberland. Many churches like Edlingham and Ancroft all had highly defensible towers.

This was a far cry from the earlier period where, in Bede's time, priests were regarded with great respect and status: 'Whence the religious habit was at that time in great veneration; so that wherever any priest or monk arrived, he was welcomed with joy as the servant of God; even when he was observed on the road, the people ran to him and bowing their heads joyfully received from him his benediction' [25].

That enthusiasm didn't survive the long wars and even the Reformation both in England and Scotland passed the marchers by. They rode out for the Pilgrimage of Grace in 1536, for the Northern Earls and Marians but that was business not faith. Bishop Leslie, who seemed to know a thing or two about the reivers and defined their convenient collectivism about the property of others also comments, along the no atheists in a fox hole line, that 'they never say their prayers more fervently, or have more devout recurrence to their beads and their rosaries, that when they have made an expedition' [26]. There's also the old tale of the 'unblessed hand', that a child's right (or if he was a Kerr, left) hand was excluded from baptism so he could be free to strike 'un-hallowed' blows on his enemies. This may be apocryphal, but the sentiment rings true enough.

No doubt the riding names were happy to be Catholic or Protestant depending on who was asking or, more importantly who was paying. On 29 May 1546, Cardinal David Beaton, who was seen as an obstacle to the reforming church, was murdered and mutilated; his mangled corpse was left hanging from a convenient window, just to ensure that their point was generally noted. Various borderers were implicated in the 'wet work' and later Black Ormiston, one of the fugitive earl of Northumberland's dubious hosts, was identified as the murderer, or one of them, of Lord Darnley, not that Queen Mary's repellent second husband was likely to be much missed.

As for the border clergy, they remain mostly in the shadows, itinerant preachers of dubious provenance and worse morals, unfrocked or never-frocked mendicants much given to drink and fornication. They are largely invisible from the written record; the Calendar of Border Papers only makes mention in May 1597 when Scrope writes to Burghley on the state of Scottish affairs generally and comments of the tricky relationship King James has with his ministers but doesn't refer to the borders as such [27]. There was however, at least one powerful exception and that was the truly remarkable Bernard Gilpin.

He was from the Kentmere Valley, of gentry stock with an uncle who rose to be Bishop of London and one of the executors of Henry VIII's will. An Oxford student and a gifted one, who took a dangerous path in opposing Bloody Mary's penchant for the mass production of Protestant martyrs, though he was no ardent reformer and spoke out for transubstantiation. Late in 1552, he gained the living at Norton in Durham. His preaching became so renowned William Cecil, (later Lord Burghley), granted him a general licence to speak from pulpits nationwide (a signal honour – John Knox was another upon whom it was conferred).

During Mary's reign, he judiciously spent some time studying abroad though he did come back before the Queen died and acquired the archdeaconry of Durham (his uncle at that time was Prince Bishop which clearly helped). Uncompromising and bold in his eloquent and sustained attacks on the abuses of the clergy, it was as well he had such a powerful benefactor. His enemies didn't give up and he might well have ended up at the stake if he hadn't broken a leg and if Mary hadn't, for once showing excellent timing, died when she did.

He became comfortable in his well-endowed living at Houghton-le-Spring in Durham even refusing the post of Bishop at Carlisle. He entertained well, endowed a grammar school (which survives today as Kepier School), and became well-respected. From there, he developed the mission for which he'd become famous, to take the Gospels to the benighted borders, something of a Sisyphean task which no one else had thought to attempt. Gilpin was fearless, refusing to be cowed or intimidated – when one contentious parishioner left a glove fixed to the door of one of the near abandoned churches he had rescued, he thundered out a furious sermon against the custom of duelling.

His legend grew – the 'Apostle of the North', the first clergyman to preach the reformed Church on the borders. In one he found another glove, this time a mailed gauntlet hanging impudently and threateningly above the altar. This was apparently the property of a local swashbuckler who left it handily around in case anyone dared take it down – thus triggering a challenge. Gilpin ripped it down and let everyone know he'd accept all comers. There were no takers.

In doctrinal terms, he'd probably be described now as an Anglo-Catholic, owing allegiance to the new faith but clinging to much of the old. Gladstone, writing in 1888, describes Gilpin (and his contemporary Colet) … 'as Roman in their sympathies; indeed, it would be truer to say of both that their tone of mind, as ecclesiastics and as educationists, was more what would now be reckoned as Anglican' [28]. Born in 1514 and living until 1602, his span like Sir John Forster's (which is where the similarity ends) covers almost the whole of the sixteenth century and if in that bloody cycle there was one man who always strove to do good it was Bernard Gilpin – God knows what Sir John made of him, I can't imagine they had much to talk about.

SACRED SPACES

'If thou wouldst view fair Melrose aright/ Go visit it by the pale moonlight/ For the gay beams of lightsome day/ Gild, but to flout, the ruins grey …'

Scott

I wouldn't want to disagree with the great bard himself, but I like Melrose by day. The great abbey is one of the four established or re-established by the Anglophile David I in the twelfth century. So generous was the King with his endowments that successors moaned he'd impoverished the crown. This Golden Age, the calm before three centuries of storm unleashed after 1296, witnessed a gorgeous flowering of the church-builder's art. These great, soaring masterpieces arose as a function of state policy and their modern townships grew up around them. Wars battered and scorched them, but it was the Scottish Reformation after 1560 which finally did for them.

What remains is imposing and impossibly romantic. It does seem that the abbeys, their fractured shells, embody a spirit of the borders, not just of the endless cycle of killing and destruction, but of the spirit of a Christian cradle that was around long before battle lines were drawn. Melrose has an ancient provenance. In St. Aidan's time and during Oswald's reign over Northumbria (AD 634–642), Boisil, one of the saint's followers, these were monks of the Celtic, Columban church rather than the Roman church, decided to establish a church on a bend in the Tweed, below what is now Scott's View. It's a place of astonishing beauty and calm which clearly appealed to its founder's ascetic impulse.

He founded the abbey of Old Mailros [29] and it was Boisil who saw the vast potential in the shepherd boy Cuthbert, drawn by a vision he experienced on the night that Aidan died. Cuthbert would succeed his mentor but was always more evangelist than abbot. Lindisfarne and the wind-lashed Farnes would be his home, and for a while he'd be England's patron saint [30]. By the end of the eleventh century, Boisil's abbey had fallen into near-ruin and only the chapel dedicated to St. Cuthbert was still functioning.

King David, after 1136, decided on a new site for his refreshed foundation, a Cistercian house, the first in his kingdom which was funded by wide grants of pasturage and fishing, an ecclesiastic enterprise of some magnitude. The abbey's estates would stretch from Galloway to Northumberland and would ensure its prosperity. Despite their abundant wealth, these monks were noted for the frugality and spartan austerity of their order with a famous output from their scriptorium including, of course, the great Chronica de Mailros [31].

Around the abbey the burgeoning town clustered as indeed it still does, even though King David's foundation is ravaged and bare. Canon law governed the inhabitants' lives, and it would be the fount of many, if not most, of their livelihoods. The Chronicle tells us that dedication took place on 28 July 1146, and we know that King Robert I had a serious affection for the place, much battered during the first phase of the wars, he spent £2,000.00 on the restoration [32]. It was also where his heart was buried.

More embellishment and rebuilding followed, the apogee of Scottish medieval ecclesiastical architecture. In the early fifteenth century Paris-born master-mason John Morow introduced the new wave of continental influences followed, some decades later, by a further phase under the aegis of Abbot Andrew Hunter (1441–1471) [33]. More wars brought fresh waves of destruction, like a series of terrible tsunamis and dour Reformation completed the final collapse. By the late sixteenth century, all the abbey's old privileges had passed to the laity and latterly to the Dukes of Buccleuch. There's a certain irony in that the rights and holdings of so great a religious house should pass to the descendants of Bold Buccleuch, one of the most notorious and violent ravagers.

Today the site maintains an aura of calm and dominates the town laid out around it. The church still possesses magnificence, and the surviving shell gives an impression of how glorious it must have been. The cloister, chapter house, and refectory exist only in fragments but the commendator's house [34] contains a fine, small museum. Years ago, I was there as I was reading Umberto Eco's The Name of the Rose (and yes, I struggled to understand the plot) but something of Melrose struck a chord with the book, the total dominance of the vast religious foundation and just how grand the medieval abbot of such a place must have been. An excellent in vinous lunch at Marmion's Bistro in the square set me up quite nicely and, as a total contrast there was (it no longer exists I think) a wonderfully eccentric and eclectic motor museum on the far corner.

In the aesthetic stakes Dryburgh for me has always been a close contender with Melrose. It's quite different, the adjacent dependent settlement has long vanished, and the shell is tucked away unobtrusively, set in mellow woods with the Tweed very close and a rather nice country-house hotel, just the sort of place you'd expect to find Poirot. You get there from the small, snaking road that leads you off the busy A68 and takes you up to and past Scott's View. It's remarkable, more pre-war Country Life or John Buchan and the reflection is best made over a large malt from the hotel's very well-stocked lounge bar.

Dryburgh was the first Premonstratensian house in the realm, founded by a close ally of King David, Hugh de Morville [35] in 1150. De Morville was Constable of Scotland and seems to have recruited his first contingent of canons from Alnwick; the initial phase of building extended into the early thirteenth century spurred on by an energetic abbot, Adam of Dryburgh (1144–1188). Edward II trashed the place in 1322; Richard II came back and had another go in 1385. It was damaged by fire in 1461, ravaged by war again in 1523 and yet again 21 years later during the Rough Wooing by Sir George Bowes and Brian Layton. These two, who knew a thing or two about destruction, flattened the civilian township which never recovered. This foundation had never been as wealthy as Melrose and from 1506 was run by lay commendators [36]. Come the Reformation and it was sold off.

Yet, the resonance of the place has transcended all these horrors and Scott chose to be buried here as did Field Marshal Sir Douglas Haig, whose family estate at Bemersyde abuts it. Perhaps it was Scott then who awarded the final victory. After all the ravages of English invaders, Reformation fanatics, and carpetbaggers, there is still a feeling of great piety and tranquillity here as though those generations of monks who prayed so constantly and devoutly here left their aura behind.

At Kelso it was the Tironesians who David I invited to form his monastic community. Though there'd been a Benedictine foundation in Selkirk before, the king moved his new house closer to his favoured royal burgh of Roxburgh with its dominant castle [37]. This was in 1128 and twenty-four years later he buried his eldest son Henry, Earl of Northumberland, there [38]. As with the others, it suffered badly during the long wars and, in 1544 the tower was defended to the last by both clergy and local laity in a regular Alamo [39]. Even the English were impressed, and it was thought the place could be converted into a redoubt but that never happened. After the Reformation, it was disestablished and by 1607, was in the hands of the Kerr's. Cessford, another vicious killer, was now Earl of Roxburghe. His line holds it still.

Jedburgh's different again; the old County Town of Roxburgh and the abbey ruins command the southern approach along the A68, even if today, most visitors make for the Woollen Mill outlet sheds off the northern end of the bypass. There was a foundation there centuries before King David started his building spree. Symeon of Durham tells us that in 830 Bishop Egred had founded a church on the spot [40]. No wonder, it's a superb location atop natural terraces rising from the north-west bank of the lovely Jed Water. David appointed Augustinians to run his new church which gained full abbatial status in 1154 though he'd imported his canons from France, beginning in 1138.

Reaching its zenith during the thirteenth century, its proximity to the border, only ten miles (16 kilometres), made the abbey a frequent target. It suffered like its fellow border foundations and by mid-sixteenth century was in the hands of lay commendators, in this case and not by any means surprisingly, the Humes [41]. Nonetheless, despite the absolute best efforts of iconoclastic reformers, a portion of the nave and north aisle was remodelled as a church from 1668–1671 [42]. All this great quartet of abbeys, in their day a fused triumph of church and state, are now ruined but not lost. Their stories, in peace and war, are an integral and lasting weave in the fabric of the border story. God might have despaired of the Marches, but he never quite gave up.

Native Tongues

'Keep a'haad' my grandfather used to say. He lived in Earsdon within the south-east Northumberland Coalfield and though not of mining stock, used expressions like this – literally 'keep hold', or 'hang on'. By birth he'd qualify as a Geordie, but this dialect was pitmatic – a hybrid, which was particular to the mining settlements and still at large in those areas, even though there are no more mines or miners. Geordie is more Newcastle/Tyneside and distinguished from the 'Mackem' twang of Sunderland which Geordies like to pretend not to understand.

It must be said that former mining communities in south Northumberland, such as say Ashington and Bedlington, though geographically cheek by jowl but having been previously very insular, each have a subtly different speech.

Northumbrian Old English is fast dying out, I only ever hear old people (that's older than me) speak with the rounded 'R'. It's been around for a long time and Hotspur is said either to have spoken the dialect, unlikely in a gentleman, or suffered a speech defect. John Common, a WWII veteran, aged 95 at the time of writing, once did a rendition of William Burgon's poem praising the ancient wonders of far-off Petra, 'a rose red city half as old as time'. Oddly in the dialect it sounded simply fine (John had been to Petra in 1947 while serving in the Coldstreamers – a big shift from Harbottle!).

People from my mother's hometown of Berwick upon Tweed speak with a distinctive lilt which is an idiosyncratic fusion of Border Scots and Northumbrian – well, the place did change hands 14 times, so an element of confusion is understandable. To many Northumbrians, the Berwick variant sounds very Scottish in tone; however, Scots from just up the road in Eyemouth think they sound very English! A Northumbrian Language Society was founded in 1983 to stem the rot of ages and considers the dialect to be perhaps closer to Scots than Old English. Most outsiders would find a true Northumbrian speaker largely incomprehensible but to many a strong Glaswegian accent is equally impenetrable.

Cumbria (formerly Cumberland & Westmorland) has an equally distinctive and quite different dialect. To Northumbrians it sounds flatter and harsher. While it's probably not a descendent of the ancient Cumbric language (Brythonic), now effectively extinct, some traces survive, noticeably in counting sheep: 'yan, tan, tethera' (one, two three). 'Yan' also creeps in say, 'that yan owr there' (that one over there). As with every part of the border region, there are no hard and fast boundaries for patterns of speech; there's been a fair bit of cross-fertilisation. Words like 'dyke' for wall or 'bairn' for child are common to both border English and Scots, though some like 'spuggie' for sparrow are exclusively, in this instance, Geordie. There is a viable suggestion that some Geordie derives from Norse roots, and I do note, from my Norwegian cousins, expressions like 'Gangin' hyaeme' – going home in Tyneside – are remarkably close to the Norwegian equivalent.

Southern Scots dialect is defined as that spoken in the former counties of Dumfriesshire, Roxburghshire, and Selkirkshire (modern boundaries do not respect antiquity). Berwickshire and Peeblesshire are more akin in speech to Edinburgh, a south-east Central Scottish dialect. Most of the key border towns – Jedburgh, Hawick, Kelso, Langham, Lockerbie, Newcastleton, and Selkirk – speak what's been called 'yow and mey' for 'you and my' but 'now and down' rather than 'noo' and 'doun'. Geordies struggle with both, and each would stumble with broad

Tyneside in turn. To add to the stew, several Romany words, 'barrie' for good and 'gadgie' for man, have crept in. Oddly, Gadgie crops up in Northumbrian, Pitmatic, and Geordie too.

During the twentieth century with the appearance of standardised education systems on both sides of the line plus mass travel, some population movement and now with the often unfortunate leavening of mass and social media, US TV & film imports, regional dialects both blur and diminish. Most house-buyers in southeast Northumberland are 'incomers' and have no connection to or interest in the old dialect. Mining and agriculture, the cement that used to bind communities and generations, have fractured. People are no longer tied to place by firm and ancient roots.

Back in the sixteenth century it seems not unlikely that the riding names from both countries spoke a variant that was much more homogenous and would have less difficulty understanding each other perhaps than their modern descendants. As Tough points out, evidence is pretty thin either way; one contemporary observer wrote 'but the south part of Scotland and the usual speech of the peers of the realm is like the Northern speech of England. Wherefore if any man will learn to speak some Scots – English and Scots doth follow together … In England there by sundry besides English … There is also the Northern tongue, the which is true Scottish, and the Scots tongue is the Northern tongue' [43]. So, an Elizabethan rider from Tynedale would easily understand one from Teviotdale though neither would likely understand either a gentleman from Hertfordshire or yeoman from Devon!

BRINGING BACK THE BORDER?

It would take a particular breed of pessimism to suggest that re-drawing the border line could lead to Balkan style intercnine conflict, I would not go so far as to suggest that it would, but it conceivably could. Few prophesied accurately just how bloody and murderous the collapse of the former Yugoslavia would be. The Anglo-Scottish border has a long legacy of hate and violence, enough to compete with any Bosnian Serb and the more rabid elements of extreme Scottish Nationalism tend to veer in a similar direction, certainly with keyboard warriors on social media platforms.

Secondly, this does prompt a timely re-appraisal of who these fractious borderers were. They aren't the chivalric knights' errant of Scott and Hogg. But perhaps neither are they the cynical bandits and ruthless Mafiosi that MacDonald Fraser and others, including me, have described. Looking at the contemporary, primary sources, we see time and again that the wardens, especially on the English side, though by no means exclusively, are constantly stirring the pot as a matter of policy, encouraging defectors, brewing up and fomenting feuds, hiring in reivers to do their own dirty work, and afterwards discarding them to suit.

It could be argued, and I will indeed propose that the borderers themselves were partly the victims of external intermeddling. Edward III effectively created the English riding names, uplanders and Pound-Land Samurai for an entirely political purpose. Some, the better connected after 1603, saw the light. Witness how the Bold Buccleuch, notorious killer and pillager responsible for the epic raid on Carlisle in 1596, had an epiphany moment when James VI became master of both realms. He actively pursued his old confederates, hanging any number of them, even those he'd ridden to Carlisle with!

The bulk of riding names simply didn't see it coming and whilst these were seriously dirty angels from a very rough neighbourhood, the treatment meted out to them by government after 1603 amounted to the full savagery of ethnic cleansing, veering almost towards genocide. Justice implies a man will be tried before he's hanged, not afterwards by way of postscript – Jeddart Justice. James and his gauleiters didn't set out to preach law and order by firm justice and good example; they came to obliterate.

Tying into this, a central part of my task will be an attempt to place these borderers and reivers, the Tudor equivalent of the 'Wild Colonial Boys' into a wider context, to identify how they fitted into the three-cornered conflict between England, Scotland, and France. This also affected Ireland, 1316–1318 and later during the Elizabethan Age. To an extent the riding names, though they might be undisputed masters in their own narrow glens, were nonetheless the blunt tools of successive administrations on both sides of the line. Nobody would suggest the names were witless dupes; they know when they were being used and were happy to be led if the price was right. What they didn't perhaps get was just how expendable they finally became. James, after all, had just blagged the crown of England. Some, if they dared, might say this was the greatest raid of all!

On 9 September 2013, the 500th anniversary of the Battle of Flodden in North Northumberland, I was taking a tour group up to the monument on Piper's Hill. New pathways had been laid out in anticipation of a big turnout. We trudged along to the base of the conical mound where a rather nervous young community policewoman informed us there was a few 'Scottish people' already on top and she hoped there wasn't going to be any 'bother'. The folk in the group with me were all of pensionable age, so I was able to reassure her that we could either climb the hill or start a fight but not at both once. She seemed reassured and, as it turned out, the Scots bore no grudges, and they proffered whisky.

George MacDonald Fraser pithily described Hermitage Castle in Liddesdale as shouting 'sod off in stone'. As a one-sentence summary of the Anglo-Scottish border, that's hard to beat. The men and women who inhabited this desolate threap ('wasteland') during three centuries of endemic warfare and sustained inter-tribal hatreds make ISIS seem almost cordial. They didn't just cut off your head, they hacked you into pieces sma' so whoever was left to tidy up wouldn't have much to work with. The borderers on both sides of the line were targeted by many and loved by few. When their era passed, fittingly, in a fury of Stalinist suppression, there weren't any mourners. Yet, just look in the phone book for Liddesdale, Tynedale, Redesdale or the Eden Valley and you'll still see the old 'riding' names flourishing. They're damned hard to kill off.

All my life I've studied and read about these marches with their wild inhabitants or those who were perceived as wild, traversed every inch, and studied every castle, bastle, tower, and battlefield (there's an awful lot of all those). I've taught about them, written about them, and played at being at them for the last half century. I've dug their traces and obsessed about their lives, read their ballads, collected their weapons. Good news is there's always something new to discover and the story has never actually ended, the Union of the Crowns in 1603 was a watershed but the fat lady still hasn't sung.

As an anorak I've always been keen on the armour and weapons of the Steel Bonnets. Some time ago a Geordie called Brian Moffat started up a museum of border arms and armour at Teviothead, a wonderfully eccentric ensemble of first class sixteenth-century kit, world class if on a smaller scale. He fell out with his local planning authority when they got windy about his displaying a pair of live machine-guns. I've a feeling the Armstrongs and Elliotts would have been on his side.

In my case, it's a family obsession. I toured the Marches as a boy in my father's ageing Series IIA diesel short-wheelbase Landrover, which had the speed of a rocking horse, the springs of a medieval cart, and emitted noise levels that would have shamed an asthmatic Panzer. In terms of the literature, I started off with Reverend Borland's Border Raids & Reivers plus D. L. W. Tough's seminal Last Days of a Frontier and then the late, great George MacDonald Fraser wrote Steel Bonnets and brought the reivers into a twentieth-century perspective, goodbye Walter Scott and welcome Quentin Tarantino.

Like MacDonald Fraser, Hermitage Castle pretty much sums it up for me, one of the two most instantly atmospheric sites I've ever encountered (Culloden battlefield being the other). It resonates with its very remoteness, its uncompromising and unique starkness, exuding menace, reminding us of a very dark and violent past and, at the same time, a kind of freedom. If the place had never been built then someone, perhaps Tolkien, who is said to have used the Marches as inspiration, would have had to imagine it.

NOTES:

[1] Sinclair, Sir, J., General Report on the Agricultural State and Political Circumstance of Scotland (Edinburgh: Constable & Co., 1814), p. 112.

[2] MacDonald Fraser, G., The Steel Bonnets (London: Barrie & Jenkins, 1971), p. 95 n.

[3] Ibid.

[4] Ritchie, C. I. A., 'Cumbrian Sleuth Hounds', Cumbria Lake District Life, 35.8 (November 1985), p. 474

[5] Ibid.

[6] Ibid., p. 475.

[7] Steel, Lord D. of Aikwood & J. Steel, Border Country (Edinburgh: Birlinn, 1996), p. 116.

[8] 22 June 1897.

[9] The derivation of this is somewhat obscure but may originate in the fairy-tale notion of mice deciding which of their number was brave enough to tie a bell around the cat's neck to warn of its coming, clearly a hazardous enterprise.

[10] This is wholly separate from the Reivers' Festival which tends to happen in late March.

[11] Lord Steel, op. cit., pp. 116–118.

[12] 'Souter' = shoemaker; Selkirk is an industrious town, but this was historically the most prominent trade.

[13] This has no equivalent south of the border and seems to owe more to Continental European tradition (Lord Steel, op. cit., pp. 148–149).

[14] CBP, I, p. 31.

[15] Ridpath, G., Border History (Berwick: C. Richardson, 1868), p. 394.

[16] Logan Mack, J., The Border Line (Edinburgh: Oliver & Boyd, 1924), p. 86.

[17] Ibid.

[18] Ibid., p. 87.

[19] Ridpath, op. cit., p. 394.

[20] Logan Mack, op. cit., p. 89.

[21] Ibid., p. 90.

[22] Ridpath, op. cit., p. 422.

[23] From Bishop Leslie, quoted by MacDonald Fraser, op. cit., p. 47.

[24] Ridpath, op. cit., p. 17.

[25] MacDonald Fraser, op. cit., p. 47.

[26] CBP, II, no. 627, p. 321.

[27] Introduction by Arthur Wollaston Hutton to S. R. Maitland's Essays on the Reformation (London: John Lane, 1899).

[28] 'Gilpin, George' in Dictionary of National Biography volume 21 (London: Smith Elder & Co, 1885–1900), p. 380.

[29] Nothing now remains though Boisil is commemorated by the nearby settlement of Newtown St. Boswells.

[30] Cuthbert came to Alfred in a vision inspiring him to continue the struggle against Guthrum's Great Danish Army – St. George, by comparison, is an interloper.

[31] The two sections cover the years from 735–1270 and have been found to contain the earliest independent account of the sealing of Magna Carta; removed from the precincts during the Scottish Reformation, the chronicle is now housed in the British Museum.

[32] Cruft, K., J. Dunbar & R. Fawcett, Borders, The Buildings of Scotland (London: Yale, 2006), p. 535.

[33] Ibid.

[34] A commendator is one who holds a benefice 'in commendam'; a form of lay trusteeship under canon law, many of which occur after the Reformation as ecclesiastical estates passed into lay hands.

[35] One of that cadre of Anglo-Norman adventurers who followed David back to Scotland. The date is provided by the Melrose Chronicle.

[36] Cruft, Dunbar & Fawcett, op. cit., p. 215.

[37] Scene of James II's death after one of his guns exploding during a siege in 1461 – it was slighted thereafter.

[38] Cruft, Dunbar & Fawcett, op. cit., p. 439.

[39] Ridpath, op. cit., p. 379 & note.

[40] Cruft, Dunbar & Fawcett, op. cit., p. 405.

[41] Ibid., p. 406.

[42] Ibid.

[43] Tough, D. L. W., Last Days of a Frontier (Oxford: Clarendon Press, 1928), pp. 58–59.

CHAPTER ONE: GENESIS OF A FRONTIER

> 'Blessed be the Lord who trains my hands for war and
> my fingers for battle'.
>
> *Psalm 144*

Some readers might remember a BBC TV series the Borderers with Michael Gambon and Iain Cuthbertson which was doing the rounds in the late sixties [1]. It wasn't that good, and the fight scenes were pretty awful, but it did fire my enthusiasm along with the Reverend R. E. Borland and his *Border Raids & Reivers*, so my dad and I bounced along half-hidden track-ways to discover forgotten and wonderfully romantic towers like Kirkhope and Fatlippes, Neidpath, Hollows, and Dryhope; bastles like Black Middings, Bellingham Hole, and the Combe. It's only when you start looking you realise just how extensive the traces are and most in a largely unchanged setting.

This history had soaked into the very canvas of the upland dales, the old troublesome valleys of Coquetdale, Redesdale, Tynedale, Liddesdale, and Teviotdale. Scott had given these 'roaring borderers', *boreales bobinantes*, as shocked southern chroniclers of the Wars of the Roses suddenly exposed to their more rapacious ways shuddered in fearful distaste, their first literary makeover. He created Young Lochinvar, pure Errol Flynn, dash, fire, and total bollocks but he sold an awful lot of copies. It always surprises me Hollywood has never picked up on the reivers; somebody should tell Tarantino.

DRAWING THE LINE – A FEARFUL LEGACY

Naturally it wasn't really like that at all, Errol Flynn I mean, it was very much Tarantino. The Anglo-Scottish Wars kicked off properly in 1296 and pretty much kept going, with some peaceful interregna, until 1603 when, with nice historical irony, a King of Scots, James VI also became king of England. The whole business had been about whether the King of England also ruled Scotland – the 'Great Cause'. Edward I ('Longshanks') had trashed Berwick (then Scottish) in the opening moves and that pretty much set the tone. Berwick in fact changed hands 14 times till Richard of Gloucester finally won it back in 1482, though the debate as to which side of the line the place should stand still rumbles.

National wars were punctuated with localised raids, thieving small black border cattle was the principal form of economic activity. These forays could involve anything from a handful of riders to several thousand. 'Kinmont' Will Armstrong's notoriously raided Haydon Bridge in 1587, when his many thieves cleared the place like locusts; children's clothes, shrouds, pots, pans, and even doorframes were lifted, IKEA on steroids.

If local and international wars weren't enough to sate anyone's bloodlust there was always the feud or 'feid', murderous vendettas that ploughed on for decades. It was pretty simple, one family steals from another so you have to steal twice as much back, next time they up the ante and kill a couple of your herdsmen, and so it escalates. The most notorious feud, Maxwell v Johnstone, reached its very nasty denouement in 1593 near Lockerbie in the savage battle of Dryfe Sands. The Maxwells had genocide in mind, but Johnstons got there first and at least a thousand died in the scrap, mainly Maxwells. It was still going on in 1610, more on that later.

Most of it is still there, the landscape that is; though Hawick lads exercise their brawn more on the rugby pitch than the battlefield (the two can be difficult to distinguish at times). Enjoy it though, it's your heritage. My first published book, God help me, now nearly 40 years ago, was Battle for Northumbria – a history of conflict in the county, or rather the wider county area. At that time, the idea of heritage tourism around historic battlefields was fairly new and most in the region were poorly signed and interpreted. The visitor was obliged, in many if not most instances, to turn detective, map and guide in hand. That has now changed to a considerable degree, but the region's violent past is still poorly signposted.

When King James VI of Scotland finally crossed the Tweed by a new bridge built for the occasion, he was the first Scottish ruler to do so with peaceful intentions. Two of his predecessors (Shakespeare's Malcolm and James IV) came too often and were felled [2]. William the Lion and David II were both captured. William had immolated the entire population of Warkworth inside their own parish church. Bruce's hobilers even dug up the rabbit warrens at Bamburgh to deny locals any sustenance. Nor was it at all one-sided, time and again English riders, English wardens, and English armies crossed the line to wreak havoc. All this leaves a legacy, a smear in the bloodline that doesn't go away.

It's all the Emperor's fault – Hadrian had drawn his line over the stark crags of the Great Whin Sill to mark out a boundary between 'us' and 'them'. I've encountered southerners who still think this is the current border. The early Saxon overlords of Bernicia chose the high citadel of Bamburgh for their capital (legend insists that Lancelot and, latterly, Guinevere were earlier residents). Successive periods of defensive building witnessed waves of recycling. Thirlwall Castle, near Gilsland, built to seal the strategic Irthing Gap, incorporated stones lifted from the Wall. An adjacent Victorian farmhouse robbed those same stones from the tower.

By the term 'Borders', I refer to the northern English counties of Northumberland in the east and Cumbria in the west – this latter is an amalgamation, much resented by locals, of the ancient shires of Cumberland and Westmorland. North of the border it's even worse; the Scottish counties of Berwickshire, Roxburghshire, Selkirkshire, Peeblesshire, and Dumfriesshire have been repackaged simply as Scottish Borders in the east with Dumfries & Galloway in the west. Those fine historical and cultural nuances between the ancient shires have been wiped out by a blank, dystopian flourish (see map one).

LANDSCAPES OF WAR

In geological terms this is an ancient landscape, over five hundred million years old: 'here are rocks that tell the tale of the convergence and collision of the ancient Laurentian, Avalonian, Baltican, Armorican and Gondwana tectonic plates and the compressive and extensional forces that resulted' [3]. I've no idea what any of that means but those distant seismic upheavals have formed a distinctive landscape or set of landscapes with bony ridges of high ground, the Cheviots humped in the centre of the English side, Southern Uplands over on the Scottish. Old high hills, endlessly rolling and rounded, usually still with only the wind that scours across from chilled lands north and east and that lamenting lilt of curlews haunting the emptiness (see map 1).

South of the Cheviots you find the altogether sharper edges of Simonside and south again the hard rampart of the basalt Whin Sill which carries Hadrian's Wall and much further east the great bulk of Bamburgh Castle. These uplands are slashed by the dales, North Tyne, Rede, and Coquet, which spill out onto the coastal plain and former coal measures. Old mining towns and villages like Ashington and Bedlington survive, though shorn of their original purpose. Aldi, and Lidl flourish where once the winding gear stood and the wounds left by the Miner's Strike of 1984 still fester. Borderers are good at allowing grudges to foment, we've had centuries of solid form.

Further west into England and the Eden Valley is very different. Cumberland is softer, somehow mellower. Sandstone here is a pleasing shade of red and the small villages between Brampton and Longtown look nothing like their Northumbrian counterparts. In February 2020, after monsoon like rain, the river had swelled to a mini-Amazon, its great red waters spreading over flat alluvial fields and Carlisle, badly flooded before, rightly trembled but happily was spared.

Just over the line, in the west, lies the old 'Debatable Land', synonymous with outlaws, mosstroopers,[4] and 'divers broken men [outlaws]'. As we considered above, this micro-region has been recently and brilliantly written up by Graham Robb [5] and may not necessarily have been quite the Wild West of legend. And then, over Bewcastle and Spadeadam Wastes, lies Liddesdale which definitely was wild: the epicentre of the reiver culture along with its neighbour Teviotdale. Across in the east, on the Scottish side, the Merse was frequently a target for English raids and full-scale invasions, bounded by a cold North Sea, sealed in by Lammermuir Hills to the north. No landscape in the world has seen so much systemic violence; nowhere else have so many done so much harm to so many for so long and with such gusto.

I'm going to look at the borders as a sixteenth-century March Warden might have seen them [6]. By Elizabeth's day there were three rather than two for each side of the line: divided into an East, Middle, and West March. Each one differed both from its neighbour and its counterpart while several especially unruly districts like Liddesdale and Tynedale had their own mini-wardens or 'keepers', who were inferior in status to wardens proper but pretty potent in their own fiefdoms. I'll look at each one in turn.

Great border valleys such as those of the Tweed, Teviot, Till, and Eden are deeply fertile, forming some of the best farming land in Europe. When the evil old days were put aside and the reiving habit robustly suppressed by James VI of Scotland/I of England, after the Union of 1603, the Badlands swiftly became carpetbagger lands. Up till then the Tweed marked the border as it had done since that black day of the Northumbrian clergy at Carham in 1018 (see below). Later, after Longshanks, Berwick upon Tweed became a frontier post or bastide guarding the English East March.

It used to be Scottish, in character it still is, and it was taken and retaken till 1482 when Richard of Gloucester, he of car-park fame, took it back for, up till now, the last time. Longshanks easily overcame their tatty palisade during his first blitzkrieg and the place had a series of makeovers culminating in the construction of the massive Elizabethan Walls on the 1560s, a state of the art Italian design, which are still complete though they were never actually completed. At that point the defences actually shrank, Edward's, Bruce's and Henry VIII' walls extended by a good third to the north and the castle was originally adjacent to the north gates. This was a great border fortress but now very little except a section of battered curtain wall and lower Watergate survive; the rest was thoroughly purged in the mid-nineteenth century to make room for the railway station. Still, the wondrous and elegant span of the Royal Border Bridge, which soars like a living sculpture over the river, offers significant compensation [7].

The old town has retained much of its character, complemented by splendid barrack piles built by Sir John Vanbrugh after the failure of the 1715 Jacobite rebellion and, until recently HQ for the King's Own Scottish Borderers ('KOSB'). Walking the walls with its vast bastions, topped by cavaliers, or raised earth platforms with flanking casemates ready to enfilade any attacker who got close enough to the curtain wall, is a great experience and the sheer drop exhilaratingly free of health and safety warnings. Berwick is unique and could be another York or Bath, but locals have little appetite for cultural tourism. The retail offer is as dowdy as it was in the 1950s. Like legions of besieging Scots, caravan sites ring the walls awaiting a Caledonian invasion which is now primarily limited to the school holidays.

This was the hub and anchor of the English East March: a 'forward operating base'. Its governor was a man of some standing 'one of the wisest and most approved of the nobility of England' [8]. For much of Elizabeth's reign, Sir Henry Carey, Lord Hunsdon, did the job. A tough, no-nonsense, and bluff soldier, he held the fort even when the rebellion of the Northern Earls burst into brief, doomed flames in 1569. He and the Middle March Warden, Sir John Forster, held their nerve and kept holding the line then and in the following year when 'Crookback' Leonard Dacre kicked off in the west. Carey was in fact Elizabeth's half-brother, her libidinous father's bastard by the 'other' Boleyn girl, who not only gave the king a son, but also managed to keep her head.

To the west this March was bounded by the foothills of the Cheviots, the highly evocative 'Hanging Stone' [9] and encompassed the valley of the Till while its southern edge was marked by the Aln, so whilst it was quite small in area it covered vital ground. Hunsdon declared the march was 24 miles (39 kilometres) in length and 16 miles (26 kilometres) wide [10], 'that part of Northumberland which is next to Scotland and the east side of England' [11]. The Tweed was guarded, aside from Berwick itself, by mighty Norham and (now largely vanished) Wark. The first of these, a grand northern bastion plus a fringe of land around, 'Norhamshire' with 'Islandshire', was part of the Bishopric of Durham and remained so until 1844. While there were no bridges, at least half a dozen fords allowed reasonably safe crossings between Norham and Berwick.

That long and exposed east coast with its miles of marvellous sands was dominated by Olympian Bamburgh and the equally impressive fortress of Thomas of Lancaster down the way at Dunstanburgh. Now, if on a darkening evening beneath lowering skies, you're on that stretch of coast where the blank windows of the gatehouse keep stare out at you, keep an eye open for one lonely knight, locked forever in his hopeless quest. Sir Guy was on his way home from crusade when he was locked in by perverse magic and has wandered the shore ever since. I've never seen him but I'm sure it's true.

Directly opposite the English East March lay its Scottish counterpart, that fertile belt of the Merse (from the ancient English mǣres or border) and which was made up of the old county of Berwickshire. This got its name from the town while it was part of Scotland. After Berwick upon Tweed was lost, from 1596 to 1890, the county town was Greenlaw (since then it's been Duns). Bounded by the rise of the Lammermuir's to the north, this is a rich and fertile plain; its principal misfortune is its proximity to England and so it was very handy for raiding. An English fleet could sail up the east coast to victual the armies and for a long period, the Scots lacked equivalent naval resources.

Here the powerful Humes dominated (and still do to a degree). Hume Castle once commanded a huge tract of ground from its rocky hilltop – what's left now is just a rather bland eighteenth-century folly. Another strength of the March is the thrilling Fast Castle, a borders Tintagel, standing on a high, exposed pinnacle some seven miles (11.3 kilometres) east of Cockburnspath. There is nowhere else quite like it. Originally, the tower was linked by a timber causeway, long since rotted and subsequent land spill has partially filled in the void which would have yawned like a frothing cavern, straight from Edgar Allen Poe or Game of Thrones. Indeed, the coastline here is a complete contrast, no long lordly strands but lowering cliffs, studded with such joys as the fishing settlement of Cove, a real smuggler's haven, and Eyemouth which, bolstered by the French, became a counterpart to Berwick with much scrapping and skirmishing between contesting garrisons.

Generally, a Hume occupied the role of warden. It wasn't hereditary but they considered it so. Alexander the 3rd Earl was a significant player during the reign of James IV and a very key figure at Flodden in 1513. The taint of treachery followed him like a gangrenous stink, and he was executed by the then regent in 1517. Serving Scotland at that time was the influential French knight Antoine d'Arcy, Sieur de la Bastie-sur-Meyland, who'd jousted during the marriage festivities celebrating James IV and Margaret Tudor's wedding in 1502. He was called the 'White' Knight, possibly on account of the scarf he wore as a favour from Anne of Brittany, and he returned to Scotland in the aftermath of Flodden as French ambassador. He provided much sound military and diplomatic advice before being appointed as a deputy-governor and warden of the Marches.

His patch included the Merse, and he was based at Dunbar. Now the Humes didn't take too kindly to the killing of their earl or having this Johnny Foreigner foisted on them. They showed their dislike by murdering the handiest Frenchman and defying D'Arcy. He sallied out from Dunbar on 18 September 1517 but ran into an ambush led by George Hume and Davy Hume of Wedderburn. The knight rode for it but his horse got bogged in what became known as 'Batty's Bog', in posthumous memory. George neatly lopped off the Frenchman's head, tied it by the hair to his saddle bow, Celtic style, and rode boldly into Dunbar where he fixed his trophy to a pole just to show you didn't mess with the Humes [12].

In the middle was the Middle March. On the English side this was the great heap of the Cheviot, a near impassable barrier for the movement of any large, conventional force but the territory curled around south of the Aln to take in Northumberland as far down as the Tyne. The river systems of North and South Tyne, Rede, Coquet, and Wansbeck all flow through it. The hills themselves aren't that high or even that steep. The border fence marches across the spine with little or nothing to show where one country ends, and another begins. The terrain is primeval; endless peat hags drag down feet and fill even the stoutest boots, and steep-sided burns like Trows and Usway feed through narrow hidden glens, bare of trees, into the rivers. Nothing there tells you which century or even which millennium you're in. You can easily experience all four seasons in a day, even in summer and go from ordinary bleak to near-tundra in half an hour.

In its day the Scots Middle March faced its English opposite along the high frontier of the Cheviot, from the hanging stone west to Kershopefoot with the last 8 miles (13 kilometres) abutting the English West March. It encompassed the sheriffdoms of Roxburgh, Selkirk, and Peebles with both Teviotdale and Liddesdale, those two highly tricky valleys. It was said of the Teviotdale men, not without justification, that they were 'a warlike nation which by reason of so many encounters in foregoing ages between Scottish and English was almost most ready for service and sudden invasions' [13].

Liddesdale, long a thorn in the sides of both English and Scots administrations, was the haunt of Armstrongs, Elliotts, Scottish Bells, Croziers, Nixons, and Burns – true riding names. Then it was wild, barren, and remote, a Tolkien-esque landscape devoid of roads, towns, or any visible suggestion of civilisation. Fearsome Tarras Moss, a nightmare marshland, a half world of peats hags and bog myrtle, laced with hidden part-submerged pathways, known only to the locals, a certain, sure and impenetrable refuge when vengeful English wardens came calling, and they did, pretty often. The reivers used the valley of Bowmont Water to cross the line by Cocklaw and fall upon Coquetdale, one of several reiver routes (see appendix ii).

Back into England, the great sweep of the English West March covers what was Cumberland and Westmorland, together with the Furness District of Lancashire.

While Bruce's raids after 1314 did penetrate down this far, we're more concerned with the top third from Inglewood Forest northwards. The Esk and Liddel Waters with the Kershope Burn run along the frontier with that ever-persistent thorn of the Debatable Land. The road from Newcastle pretty much traced the same line as the modern A69 though it was seriously rough and usually wet, very wet. It was so bad that Marshal Wade in 1745, struggling to move his troops west and counter the Jacobites who'd humbugged him by attacking west rather than east [14], resorted to doing what he did best in any crisis, building an all-weather highway – the Military Road, (now B6318), which now conducts us along the high part of Hadrian's Wall. Regrettably, Wade used a lot of it as hardcore.

Across the shallow, tidal reaches of the Solway lie the Scottish West March comprised of Galloway, Nithsdale, Annandale, Eskdale, Ewesdale and Wauchopedale, the Stewartries of Kirkcudbright and Annandale with the Sheriffdom of Dumfries, which generally marked the western flank of the wardenry. Like all the marches this is a very distinctive province with Dumfries as the main urban centre, and Annan perhaps as the poorer relation. Unexpectedly though, this was a hub of Britain's munitions manufacturing during the Great War, the immense and utterly astonishing spread of the Devil's Porridge (see Chapter 11)

LAWMEN

On the English side the border was a very remote frontier, far away from centres of power, difficult and expensive to police. The Scottish side is far closer to Edinburgh but no easier to control. A fairly complex means of trying to keep order was established as early as 1249, when the Scottish and English monarchies agreed that the border should be divided into 'Marches' which I referred to above. From 1297 these districts were controlled judicially and militarily by March Wardens. On the English side, officers were latterly appointed from the south of the country, to avoid the obvious possibility of bias for or against the feuding names over which they were intended to hold sway. The examples of Percy and Neville in the fifteenth century evidenced the risks attached to conferring such vice-regal powers on unruly local magnates. Both names used their licence to raise forces to build private armies and fight dynastic wars.

It was the wardens' duty to see that peace was maintained, to administer justice, and to deal with 'bills' or complaints. Backed up by a staff of deputies, captains, and troopers, they tried with varying degrees of success to administer good law, but in doing so would frequently create personal enemies (some were murdered [15]) and yet further bitterness between already bellicose riding names. In short, they frequently caused more problems than they solved and most certainly did not ensure peace and safety for the marchers.

One such Warden was the notorious Sir John Forster, not from the south, we're proud to say but a native Northumbrian: 'A regular subject of Border correspondence, he was the target of frequent accusations ranging from collusion with the Scots and neglect of duty, to using his office as a cloak for thieving and skulduggery, his accusers further adding that Sir John's catalogue of shortcomings 'would fill a large book'. Most of this was in fact true and his protestations of innocence are somewhat less than convincing' [16]. Sir John was a truly Falstaffian character whom I've played on numerous occasions. I do sincerely hope the old rogue would be flattered by these portrayals. To be fair I've offered him as choleric, addicted to strong drink, a wager or two and loose women, untrammelled by any conflict twixt duty and reward.

After a raid, with the lifting of cattle and possibly the taking of lives, the thieves would naturally set off for the relative safety of tower or sheltering moss without delay. Above all else, success would lie in the speed with which sortie and getaway were accomplished. Escaping reivers would be much hampered by the four-legged spoils – cattle are notoriously difficult to move at speed – and it was essential to be familiar with every step and inch of the landscape so that temporary lying up places and strategic sites for ambush were known.

He who was a victim of such a raid had three choices: to make complaint to the Warden, to bide his time until he could take revenge (with interest if possible), or to mount a hot trod [17]. If some time elapsed before the pursuers set out, it was known as a cold trod. Either way, the legality of the trod depended on it being within six days of the raid, and as MacDonald Fraser points out, 'a careful line was drawn, under Border law, between a trod and reprisal raid'.

If the trod was cross-Border, it was essential to make it clear that legal pursuit was underway: a lighted turf was to be clearly visible on the pursuer's lance point, 'an earnest of open and peaceful intentions'. He had a legal right to assistance from marchers across the Border and trying to hinder the trod was a punishable offence, one far more honoured in the breach than the observance. The trod could easily become a brawl; however strict the supposed rules, the chase might frequently end in a fierce skirmish during which fighters from either side stood to lose life or limb: 'The law was not likely to call a trod-follower to account if his rage got the better of him and he dispatched a reiver out of hand' [18].

It was the unenviable task of the wardens to seek to maintain law and order whilst also acting as local generals in time of war. A corpus of unique border laws, Leges Marchiarum, was drafted to cope with that vibrant brand of lawlessness which prevailed. In many instances these officials, like Sir John, who clung to his office until well into his nineties, were more of a symptom than a cure. Sir John was a leading shareholder in most disreputable ventures within his march and was far from being an exception!

'The seventh of July the smith to say/ At the Reidswire the tryst was set/ Our wardens they affixed the day/ And as they promised, so they met/ Alas that day I'll never forget! / Was sure sae feard, and then sae faire/ They came theare justice for to get/ Will never green to come again' [19]. Days of Truce had been a feature of the administration of border justice since the mid-thirteenth century when the wardenship system was formally established. In theory each March Warden was to meet with his opposite number once a month, though in practice this rarely occurred due to bad weather, hostilities between the two nations, or prevarication on the warden's part.

Protocols were exact; both parties, mounted and fully arrayed (i.e., harnessed for war) would approach the agreed meeting place. The Reidswire ("Swire" = a narrow neck of land) formed ideal ground. Before either warden met, the two parties would eye each other up then an English rider would spur forward to ask 'assurance' of the Scottish warden. Once this was given, the process was reversed then the two sides, warily, advanced.

Traditionally, meetings were held in Scotland – it was said that Scottish wardens were reluctant to enter England after one of their number Sir Robert Ker of Cessford was killed by notorious Bastard Heron at a Truce Day in 1508. We'll encounter the colourful Bastard in connection with the Flodden campaign (see Chapter 5). Whether this was a formal duel or just plain murder, the Kers were avid for revenge. Heron's two seconds or accomplices, Lilburn and Starhead, fled for their lives, but no distances could place them beyond the borderers' vengeance; both were hunted to death [20].

This assurance, or guarantee of peaceful intent, was to hold from that sunrise to next evening sunset to allow all present to reach home in one piece. The most notorious breach of this observance was the seizure of the totally reprehensible Kinmont Will Armstrong in defiance of convention in 1596 (more on that later).

Much business of the day revolved around the hearing of complaints from both sides. These indictments or bills were lodged beforehand by plaintiffs and heard on the day. Often a jury of a dozen, six from each side, was empanelled to decide the matter or a decision could be achieved on the warden's oath, or the oath 'avower' of some prominent man effectively acting as the defendant's guarantor. Trials were noisy, lively, and contentious. Most did not come with entirely clean hands and if a bill was proven or 'fyled' then the defendant had to agree compensation, if the accusation failed and the defendant found 'cleane' then no redress was due. Compensation monies could be calculated on the penal basis of 'double and sawfey' – three times the value of the goods lifted. Levels of compensation were defined at various times. In 1563 it was agreed as follows: an ox = 40s (£2.00), cow = 30s (£1.50), young ox or cow = 20s (£1.00), sheep/swine = (around) 6s (30p) [21].

These days of truce were occasions for much imbibing, betting, and gaming. Horse races were held, and everyone dressed in their finery. Hearings were held in the open and the crowd no doubt contributed vociferously. Virtually all present, from both sides of the line knew each other, they'd drunk, fought, ridden, and wagered many times before. Everyone went armed; drink was a major factor in disturbances. Frequently the wardens themselves, especially men of the cut and temperament of Sir John were far from impartial. Scott of Buccleuch ("The Bold Buccleuch"), Ker of Cessford and Lords Home and Maxwell were all active in border politics.

FORT APACHE

If you want that 'real' borderer experience and you've not got time to get to remote Hermitage in Liddesdale, try the lost village of Evistones. On the main road to Carter Bar (A696/A68), past Otterburn and around eight miles (13 kilometres) north of Bellingham, you pass a sign branching left marked 'Redesdale E.H. Farm'. This stands for Experimental Husbandry and was established by the then Ministry of Agriculture, Food and Fisheries ("MAFF"), sometime after the end of the World War Two. Its mission statement is to improve efficiencies amongst the hill farming community. One of their far-sighted innovations was to fit ageing teeth with stainless steel dentures to overcome tooth decay, which sounds like a creature Dr. Who might encounter in some parallel galaxy [22]!

Drive onto the track, pull up onto the verge and then walk downhill towards the river and Stobbs Farm on the north bank. John Dodds, in his magisterial study [23], identified this as a likely bastle in its original incarnation but there's more across the old Bailey bridge that spans the Rede. Keep on the lane which runs along the south bank heading north-west past a set of barns it turns back on itself climbing a reasonably steep incline. Halfway up look to your right and you'll see the place set some 80 yards or so above the track.

Then you'll be in Evistones and there's nowhere like it. If it was warmer and less windswept, drier, and brighter, this could be Fort Bravo or some forgotten firebase in the Mekong Delta. But it's a reiver township, a cluster of stone bastles, one of which has the vault still standing. John Dodds counts three Peles [24] but I'm prepared to hazard an assertion there's nearer a dozen; the whole compound was surrounded by a curtain wall or palisade, the footings of which can be traced on the ground. It's bare, basic, and bleak. Wuthering Heights would look like the Cotswolds by comparison. It's built for all round defence, every building planned for war, not too many parterres or peacocks.

I can't imagine there was ever anything likeable or quaint about the place; the inhabitants seem to have been Hedleys and Fletchers. A bad lot according to such scant records as exist and it seems to have been abandoned at some point in the seventeenth century. If we want to understand the reivers, this place is a real light-bulb moment, a borderer epiphany. The quickest glance will tell you the arts of peace never flourished in these surroundings and those who lived here had much to fear and lived their lives in anticipation of attack, probably by way of retribution.

ANCIENT VIBES

'Objects contain absent people'.

Julian Barnes: Metroland

On a bright Saturday in autumn 2019, one of those fleeting days of clear light and mild air, I was with a group of historians and archaeologists who trekked up to the bluffs at Yardhope, north of Elsdon on the MoD Artillery Ranges. It was a gloriously still and resonant autumn day with clear skies and light to make an artist weep for joy, crisp and precise showing the ancient shrine of the genius loci, Cocidius off to best possible effect with sweeping views of moorland landscapes scarcely changed since he was fully in vogue.

This old boy was a native North British deity worshipped by the local Celts (if I dare call them that). He was the equivalent of Roman Mars, the god of war and hunting, and also Silvanus, guardian of woods and wilderness. Rome was quite good at suborning local identities, and he was probably worshipped by auxiliaries stationed along the wall and beyond. The derivation may be from the Brythonic cocco for red and perhaps his image was originally daubed in scarlet. Cocidius might have originated in the west, by the Solway; the Roman forts of Bewcastle and Birdoswald both have inscriptions recording dedications to him.

Our border region has a rich prehistory. At Howick in Northumberland, Mesolithic hunter-gatherers built a lodge around 7,500 years ago, one of the very oldest structures in Britain. Neil Oliver memorably chronicles the transition in society from hunter-gatherers to farmers during the Neolithic and how profound a shift this was, a time when people began not only to cultivate crops and husband livestock but when they put down roots and established territories. They interred their ancestors in elaborate tombs, using, as he argues (very persuasively), their dead to fix the living to.

Iron isn't as pretty as bronze and loves rust. Happily, for archaeologists bronze doesn't and our ancestors, as part of their belief system, chucked vast quantities of precious kit into rivers or still waters to propitiate their gods. Water was seen as a portal, a gateway from this world to the next. I pretty much get that;

when you look into that mirror of shining, peat-coloured stillness, it does seem fathomless yet somehow significant, as if you could touch the surface and like Alice, disappear through the mirror. It has a wholly different heft as well. My own copy of an eighth-century BC Ewart Park (named after the archaeological find) type was lovingly crafted by Neil Burridge who uses all ancient techniques in his art. It possesses a level of fascination wholly different to the allure of say a sixteenth-century rapier.

Like bronze before it, iron was a game-changer, weapons and tools were far cheaper and easier to make, warfare no longer remained as a province of the elite, the lower orders could get stuck in too, though the sword reserved its mystique. Climate changes during the later Bronze Age [26] reduced the amount of cultivable land and put pressure on agrarian communities. Hillforts in the borders got makeovers – deeper ditches, more formidable defences, just to be ready.

The Iron Age and hillforts are inextricably linked in our understanding and these great oppida are potent survivors. Most impressive in the borders is Traprain Law [27]. It's 725 feet (221 metres) high, rising from a flat coastal plan, four miles (six kilometres) east of Haddington. It's huge, not as big as the great Gallic versions like Bibracte which even got a grudging nod from Caesar, still covering some 40 acres (16 hectares). It was certainly in use during the Bronze Age and was already fortified by the beginning of the first millennium BC. It had numerous makeovers during its long history and was lived in at the time of the Claudian Invasion, and was probably not abandoned till around the point when the Antonine Wall was being built. After that hiatus it was re-occupied until the end of the occupation with yet another and massive makeover before finally being abandoned completely.

Whilst it's far bigger than most hillforts, Traprain Law is by no means alone. There are hundreds, including Old Bewick in Northumberland, Yeavering Bell, Humbleton Hill, and through the Ingram Valley. Many of these date to, at or before the Roman Conquest and we've no evidence of any last-ditch stand like Maiden Castle, no defender's skeletons transfixed by ballistae bolts, no grave-pits like Danebury Hill. Not to say it didn't happen, just we've no evidence. Most are in fact quite small, probably high-status manorial complexes with a settlement clustered about, sort of motte & bailey style. With my dad I clambered up to and over most of them. Here were my Troy and Mycenae, with boyhood friends we fought over the ditches and ramparts with a handy arsenal of wooden weapons and just one real one, a French bandsman's sword c 1860, leaf-shaped blade, brass grip and stubby quillons, a conscious imitation of gladius hispaniensis.

THAT BLOODY GREAT WALL

> 'Just when you think you are at the world's end, you see a smoke from east
> to west as far as the eye can turn and then, under it, also as far as the eye can
> stretch, houses and temples, shops and theatres, barracks, and granaries,
> tricking along like dice behind – always behind – one long, low rising and
> falling and hiding and showing line of towers. And that is the Wall!'
>
> *Kipling: Puck of Pook's Hill [28].*

The Wall – does it for me, always has. As mentioned, I do encounter folk;
invariably from that dim region we call the 'South', who still imagine this is the
actual border between England and Scotland. Once it was far more than that; it
marked the North-West Frontier of Rome, an empire so vast its southern flank
rested on the Euphrates, on the fringes of the Sahara and, to the east on the Rhine.
Yet any soldier or merchant, who journeyed here, would instantly recognise the
distinctive and largely unvarying plan of all the forts, that playing card shape.
HQ and commandant's accommodation placed centrally with four gates feeding
through internal roadways, barrack blocks, stables, granaries, and sick bay all
where they should be.

Over there, past the Wall, was 'Indian Country', tribal lands never completely
subjugated, frequently blitzed by retaliatory sweeps, which later reivers might
have recognised as warden's raids. This wild tract beyond the limes – frontier
was occupied then abandoned. The Wall was as some of us might utter 'awesome'
and in the proper sense it was, still is. But the very act of its construction is an
admission of previous failure. Then the Emperor Hadrian, restless and always on
the move, arrived.

He devised a plan for a wall, which would run eastwards from Bowness-on-
Solway for 31 Roman miles [29], built in timber sod and turf then, for a further
49 miles, constructed in stone with a series of regular outposts or milecastles,
with towers or turrets in-between. Quite why different materials were preferred
for different sections isn't known and the plan was no sooner underway than
it was radically changed. Previously, the back-up garrisons were to be supplied
by from the Stanegate forts, but Hadrian, (it must have been him, you'd think),
decided to add a whole series of wall forts, 16 of them, on the line itself which in
places, meant demolition and rebuilding. The whole massive undertaking was
accomplished in around seven years, an astonishing feat – it normally takes that
long to get planning consent for a garage extension in the 21st century.

I spent a lot of my childhood walking the Wall, with family and various school
groups. Half a century on and the pull is every bit as strong though quite often

these days I walk as the Romans walked in full auxiliary kit. That teaches you respect. And I was very lucky to be a frequent visitor to Newcastle University's Museum of Antiquities, run in partnership with Society of Antiquaries. Located in a now demolished building, this was wonderfully intimate and for the modeller held a series of wonders – scale models (generally around 1/48th if I'm right), crafted by Billy Bulmer.

He built stone and timber milecastles (dad and I spent hours creating my own in 1/32nd scale for a school project), gateways, bath houses, smaller scale models of forts, anorak heaven and most of the time I was the only visitor – it was mine to enjoy [30]. As Dr. Lindsay Allason-Jones described the museum's role, 'in the intervening years, (it opened in 1960), the Museum has acted as the county museum for Northumberland, covering every period from the earliest prehistory to the Tudor and Stuart period. It is acknowledged as the main museum for the World Heritage Site of Hadrian's Wall and has become famous for its innovative computing and education work' [31]. At about the same time, in the early to mid-sixties Airfix started producing a range of 1/72nd scale Romans and Britons together with an excellent milecastle model. Wargamers have moved on, but I still have a great affection for those figures, they took forever to paint but you could get a fair bit of detail in. I'm afraid the Romans always won.

At Wallsend the Wall ends. Yet if you live on the east side you tend to think it begins there and ends at Bowness – no idea which way Hadrian saw it, but he probably did move east to west. We don't know what the locals thought but we could guess they weren't enthused. Why would they be, the grand new frontier project crossed tribal lands and divided communities. There's no evidence of any consultation!

I'm going to leave the summary to Dr Allason-Jones, who writes: 'Initially the Roman invasion probably didn't have much impact on the tribes-people of northern England; like the Channel Tunnel, it probably seemed to them that it would only affect the southerners. Eventually they would have learned otherwise. By the 70s AD they would have got used to seeing Roman soldiers littering the landscape, taking their food, and asking for taxes. How much fighting there was would have depended on each tribe's attitude to the invaders and whether each Roman commander behaved according to the rules or let rip'.

And as George MacDonald Fraser pithily summarises: 'And the men who built the Wall in the rain and defended it and died beneath it and begot their children to grow up beside it, and finally left it, probably looked back as it faded into the mist and thought what a waste of time it all had been; they were quite wrong' [32]. It's a great moment of writing even if it never happened that way, the Wall just fell away bit by bit, the whole massive structure too big, too long too expensive and with crumbling resources, unmanageable. But he was right, it wasn't a waste of time. It connected us here far, far to the north, plugged us into the classical mainstream and though the ideas faded, they never vanished, lying like seeds below the turf, ready for the right time to re-flower.

DIM, WEIRD, AND WEST

'That last dim weird battle in the west' – someone, I can't remember who, described the final battle between Arthur and Mordred in those terms. There were three of these 'futile' fights where Celt fought Celt instead of uniting against common enemies. One, described by William Forbes Skene (1809–1892, lawyer, antiquary, and historian), was the battle of Arfderydd, which occurred near Arthuret on the English West March. Here according to the Annales Cambriae [33]: 'The Sons of Eliffer [fought] Gwenddolau son of Ceidio; in which battle Gwenddolau fell' [34]. The date is given as 573 and we know from the Annales that these two sons, Gwrgi and Peredur, were both dead by 580 [35].

This was the clash that Skene was looking for in the nineteenth century and he relied on local oral tradition for its location, identifying Liddel Moat and the parish of Carwinley with the fallen hero. Nobody is quite sure who the combatants were, but Skene felt, and this seems plausible, that these were successors to the Novantae of Galloway and Selgovae of Dumfriesshire. This puts the dead king's ground north of Rheged, part of what might later become Strathclyde.

One of the players was the loser's bard/priest/druid, Myrddin, whom we may know better as Merlin. Whether this was Arthurian Merlin or another we don't know, date-wise he appears far too late, but the idea is appealing. Casualties were around three hundred and the dead were just dumped into marshy ground. The horror was too much for the temperamental druid who lost his wits and fled into the woods. Even with Gwenddolau killed, his war-band or at least the survivors, fought on for another six weeks which suggests a campaign consisting more of extended skirmishes and likely fought out over territory. But both factions would have done better banding together and focusing on Saxon intruders, all set to gobble up their petty realms.

Ida was a Saxon war leader who'd taken over the infant state of Bernicia in 547: 'This year Ida began his reign, from who arose the royal race of Northumbria; and he reigned twelve years and built Bamburgh …' [36]. He probably came not from the continent but an earlier settlement further down the east coast. From its inception, his new mini-kingdom embarked on an era of relentless expansion. This shouldn't imply that the Angles had it all their own way; their takeover wasn't uncontested. Largely relegated to the land of myth is that principality of Rheged whose capital may have been Carlisle and whose kings claimed descent from that late Roman governor and imperial pretender, Magnus Maximus [37]. Even the boundaries of this Celtic province remain a mystery. Nonetheless, its most celebrated ruler, Urien [38], was a favourite hero whose praises were sung by bards Taliesin and Llywarch Hen. He defeated the Angles in a series of battles and succeeded, for a while at least, in penning them up in their coastal fortresses.

Though Rheged vanished, other British kingdoms survived. Saint Patrick wrote to the Damnonii, secure in their rocky fastness at Dumbarton (future capital of Strathclyde), ruled by Coroticus or Ceredig, who was roundly lambasted by the saintly traveller for trafficking in slaves. North of the Britons lay the kingdoms of the Picts and the Scots. The former, who made up the majority, were descendants of those tribes who'd rallied to Calgacus, leading his stand against Agricola [39]. Their origins were obscure; Irish legend chronicles the Picts' first arrival as invaders from distant Scythia, an interesting if unlikely conjecture. It does appear that there were two distinct Pictish kingdoms. As early as 310, Cassius Dio refers to the Caledonii as living north of the Maeatae, who'd earlier disturbed the reign of Commodus. In 565 Columba visited the Pictish king Bridei in his fort or dun near the future site of Inverness [40].

These Anglian arrivistes were an aggressive race, sprung from Saxon stock imported as mercenaries in the service of Rome and latterly of those Romano-British chiefs they were soon to supplant. Warlords with a good track record attracted hardened warriors, household men who were expected to follow their leaders to victory or death – for one to return home when the chief had gone down was the greatest dishonour. Service wasn't determined by ethnicity; a trained and experienced warrior could always find employment. In return for absolute loyalty and good service he would expect, indeed demand, substantial rewards, silver arm rings and above all, land. A warrior could become a landowner, a thegn, while still bound to his lord. The greater success the lord enjoyed, the more men he'd stand to recruit. Of course, they'd expect to be rewarded in turn so peaceful cooperation with neighbours offered few incentives.

Ida's eventual successor Aethelfrith carved out the rising kingdom of Northumbria after a shotgun wedding with its southern neighbour Deira and went on to hammer the Goddodin, the Welsh, and anyone else who got in the way. He finally went down to his hated brother-in-law Edwin who, as thanks for his victory, converted his kingdom to Christianity before the vengeful pagan, Penda of Mercia, and Christian Cadwallon did for him in turn.

Now, if you drive westwards along General Wade's military road towards Carlisle, you'll pass a large wooden cross on the right not long before the road swoops down to Chollerford. This is Heaven's Field, in Old English Hefenfelth, where King Oswald routed the Welsh who'd occupied the land and restored the kingdom of Northumbria to its rightful owner, i.e., himself in 633/634.

He needed God's help as things were in a pretty poor state. This potent alliance between Christian Cadwallon of Gwynedd and pagan Penda of Mercia had resulted in the defeat and death of sainted king Edwin at Hatfield Chase (near Doncaster) on 12 October 633 [41]. Their victory exposed Northumbria to a hurricane of pillage. Then, the reeling kingdom was divided into two regions, old Bernicia and Deira. Eanfrith, Oswald's brother, was quickly disposed of by Cadwallon and Osric of Deira rapidly went the same way [42]. With classic showmanship and we shouldn't lose sight of the fact Bede is a superb storyteller, cometh the hour, cometh the man: 'Oswald, a man beloved by God' [43].

Oswald with a surviving brother Oswy, who'd succeed him after 642, had been in profitable exile amongst his kin, the Dalriadian Scots where he'd built up a reputation as a formidable scrapper, and was given the nickname Whiteblade [44]. King Domnall Brecc, Oswald's Scottish overlord, was happy for him to return home and try to win back his father's crown (that same gloriously Game of Thrones Aethelfrith). The Dalriadan king wouldn't technically lend military support as he was allied to Cadwallon though not to Penda, but he did provide the brothers with a strong war-band to ensure their safe passage back to Northumbria's ravaged borders [45].

Once home, Oswald rallied the Northumbrian militia or Fyrd [46] and his war-band was swelled by Scottish fighters who, even if they were disobeying their King's explicit instructions, (as he may well have anticipated, even intended), could legitimately claim they were fighting for Christ and St Columba. Abbot Segine of Iona was ranged with Oswald's affinity and this validation by the Celtic Church carried a great deal of weight. Indeed, Oswald may have brought a squad of monks with him to provide spiritual gravitas. Hopefully they were unaware of how many of their brethren his dad Aethelfrith had earlier killed at Bangor whilst chastising the Welsh.

The Exiles came down the valley of North Tyne by which time Cadwallon, still at York, became aware of the threat and immediately marched north. He came up Dere Street, then branched left along the line of the Wall at Stagshaw. Oswald had occupied a strong defensive position above Chollerford, flanked by the Vallum. During the long watches of the night before battle, Oswald received a visitation from Saint Columba (our very own Cuthbert provided similar inspiration later for Alfred at Athelney). This was most heartening as the saint promised God's strong arm would be with them; doubly helpful as Oswald was heavily outnumbered. And these portents mattered, his polyglot, ad hoc force would need all the motivation it could find. Oswald's war council was easily convinced, and his army advanced to contact.

It seems the Welsh were not expecting this. Maybe Cadwallon was lulled by too many easy victories but this time the clash of shield walls was decisive. After a short sharp shock, the invaders broke, their front hemmed in by Vallum and Wall, far too narrow for their greater numbers to tell. The broken army was chased back down the length of the Denise Burn in a running fight. They'd made no friends in Northumbria and probably plenty locals were willing to lend a hand now their enemy was beaten. Cadwallon was amongst the dead and Northumbria was reunited under a new king, one who would soon be recognised as Bretwalda – king of kings. As Bede exulted: 'The place is shown to this day and held in much veneration where Oswald, being about to engage, erected the sign of the holy cross and on his knees prayed to God that he would assist his worshippers in their great distress' [47].

Oswald's reign and supremacy were relatively short lived as Penda saw him off as well, leaving Oswy to salvage what was left. He did that and more, ending the remarkable career of the ageing pagan king of Mercia and bringing Northumbria to the very zenith of its power. Oswy it was who facilitated the great Synod of Whitby in 664 where procedural breaches with Rome were papered over in Rome's favour and Bishop Wilfrid clearly got the upper hand. Celticism was marginalised but didn't disappear; Cuthbert was a mightily important political figure, much favoured by Oswy's son and successor Ecgfrith. This last of Northumbria's heroic line seems to have been bold and aggressive to the point of rashness. He first bashed up the Irish 'sending Beort, his general, with an army into Ireland, miserably wasted that harmless nation ... in their hostile rage [they] spared not even the churches or monasteries' [48].

The disaster which a confederation of Picts and Scots and Britons from Strathclyde inflicted on the hitherto almost invincible Northumbrian army possibly at Dunnichen Moss (Nechtansmere) in the Sidlaw hills in the spring of 685 was a momentous victory for them and proof of Ecgfrith's gung-ho folly, a regular local Little Big Horn [49]. This Anglian Gotterdammerung put an end to systematic inroads onto Scottish soil which had threatened to turn the Pictish kingdom into a Northumbrian client. On the 1300th anniversary of the fight in 1985 it was hailed as the most decisive battle in Scottish history [50]. Bridei mac Bile, who beat Ecgfrith, brought all the Picts under his own colours and moved against the Scots on the western seaboard, attacking Dunadd. His descendant Oengus Mac Fergus (752–761) finally defeated the Scots and established Pictish hegemony [51]. For Northumbria, this was bad news.

Ecgfrith had had nothing but contempt for the Picts, born out of earlier easy victories. Apparently, quite early in his reign, a Pictish confederation had rebelled against the Northumbrian yoke, only to be cut up when the Angles stormed their base. Ecgfrith's cavalry, possibly aided by disaffected Pictish allies, slaughtered their lightly armed opposition in a lightning attack, 'filling two rivers with the corpses', according to the Anglian Chronicler Eddi [52].

A classic case of familiarity breeds contempt: 'that same king, rashly leading an army to ravage the province of the Picts, much against the advice of his friends … was drawn into the straits of inaccessible mountains and slain' [53]. Bede's making a further point here; if you don't listen to your bishop, in this case Cuthbert, you're headed for the rocks! Though Ecgfrith was succeeded by his half-brother Aldfrith, the long decline of Aethelfrith's grand empire had begun. The earlier 'heroic' age was succeeded by the culturally heightened 'golden' age. This was an astonishing outpouring of artistic achievement, due unexpectedly, to be cut short by the explosive arrival of unwelcome visitors from across the cold northern sea.

Nasty Norsemen

'A furore Nordmannorum, libera nos, domine - 'From the fury of the Northmen O Lord, deliver us' was a litany without need of vellum. It was graven on the hearts of men whenever and for as long as that fury fell' [54].

In 2013, throughout July, August, and September, the Lindisfarne Gospels were on display in Durham, quite literally a once in a lifetime chance to see this astonishing work of art, one of the most important survivors of the early Middle Ages and yes, it was written here in Northumbria. Eadfrith, latterly Bishop of Lindisfarne, may have spent as long as a decade copying and illuminating the Gospels. This was around the year 700 and the work was bound in its original unpretentious leather bindings. The current, blinged up version is a Victorian gothic fantasy.

This was just as well. The Anglo-Saxon Chronicle records that the portents for the year 793 were unfavourable: 'these were excessive whirlwinds and lightning, and fiery dragons were seen flying in the air' [55]. If so, then for the inhabitants of Northumbria at least, this dire forecast was pretty much spot on. In that year the community of Lindisfarne was the first to taste the fury of the Northmen. They came out of a bright clear sky, sunlight chasing the movement of the oars, three long, sleek ships of a kind not before seen in these coastal waters. They were elegant and graceful, seeming to skim across a placid sea, but the great square sail snarled pagan imagery and a dragon's head reared from the curved prow. They 'lamentably destroyed God's Church on Lindisfarne through rapine and slaughter' [56].

Those men who swept ashore were tall and well proportioned, clad in gleaming ring mail, their weapons, spears, Danish axes, and double-edged blades sang of death. The monks were killed or abused without pity or comment. Anything of value was methodically looted and piled; any likely girl or boy was seized as trade. In the brief fury of the sack, lay people and clergy were pillaged, the settlement and monastery given to the flames, the place stripped and emptied. The Vikings had arrived. That the Gospels escaped the Vikings' attentions verges on the miraculous – the great work was probably saved by its unostentatious binding, no bling and it wasn't worth nicking.

Such scenes were to be enacted and re-enacted along the coasts of England, Scotland, and Ireland as the sea-rovers made their presence felt. This sudden and terrible swiftness – the emerging of these pagan warriors in their rapier craft, springing from the very vastness of the oceans is a powerful one but probably misleading. The Norse raiders were, of course, good sailors but long voyages over open water were risky, island or coast-hopping was preferable. After 865, coastal raiding gave way to conquest and the ancient, tottering kingdom of Northumbria was the first of the Saxon Homelands to fall. Happily, despite many adventures, the Gospels survived.

Though these Norsemen first blitzed Northumbria in 793 and for several seasons following, these were hit and run raids with slaves and booty as main prizes. But it was a long while, not quite a full century before the Vikings came back to stay, led by the sons of the legendary Ragnar Lodbrok ('hairy breeches'), revived recently for TV's Vikings. He may or may not have existed but Ivar the Boneless [57] certainly did and his ambitions extended far beyond mere banditry. He came to conquer.

Between those times Northumbrians and Scots still found plenty to fight over. Just on the northern fringe of the Border Marches, in the Lothians is the pleasant village of Athelstaneford. It stands on a short east/west ridge and covers a route over the (Scottish) River Tyne; it's not too far from mighty Traprain Law. Since Aethelfrith's day Northumbria had maintained influence over this region, stronger at some times than others, probably not any direct form of vassalage but some if its rulers might have been Northumbrian clients.

King Oengus (Angus) II, ruler of Pictland, led a raid during 832, a savage spoiling which prompted instant reprisal. King Athelstan of Northumbria hurried north with a sizeable war-band and caught the Picts just north of Athelstaneford, surrounding their camp with superior numbers. Fervent prayer seemed an appealing tactic and Oengus vowed to honour God and everyone else, especially St. Andrew if they'd just spare a moment to extricate him from this particular pickle. Happily, the saint came through for the Scots and the Northumbrians got seriously duffed up.

Successful resistance to the Norsemen came from the 'Last Kingdom' Wessex which gradually extended its sway over most of what is now England, Northumbria was relegated to a mere earldom while a succession of petty kings grabbed York. It was Alfred's grandson Athelstan who completed the process by extending his rule northwards and ensuring all there bent their knee, however grudgingly.

With the north-east of England apparently secure Athelstan, in 934, conducted a chevauchee through Scotland, an enthusiastic show of strength that witnessed an English fleet sailing as far as Caithness [58]. Constantine, thoroughly alarmed, clearly decided that a buffer state in northern England was needed to insulate Scotland from the West Saxons. In 937 he formed an alliance with Olaf and the Strathclyde British; Scots, Norse and Britons driven by fear of Wessex. Olaf, with a fleet said to number six hundred keels, sailed boldly up the Humber to reclaim his lost kingdom. His ranks swelled by Norse and Britons from the west and by Scots from the north, he posed a substantial threat to Athelstan.

This Saxon king was not so easily deterred and raising his substantial own forces, confronted the allies possibly somewhere on Humberside [59]. A fearsome battle ensued: the combat began at dawn and raged till dusk. Mercians against Norse, Saxons pitted against Scots. Constantine's son was amongst the many dead and this catastrophic defeat seems to have broken the king's spirit; 'This year King Athelstan and Edmund his brother led a force to Brumby and there fought against Anlaf and, Christ helping, had the victory and they there slew five kings and seven earls' [60]. Any hope of Scotland creating a 'buffer zone' or of even annexing Bernicia outright perished on that field and in 943 King Constantine withdrew to monastic life.

Sometime later however, there was a resurgence of Danish power centred on York, and Malcolm I of Scotland (943–964) was able to conclude a treaty with Edmund of Wessex, whereby the Scots effectively 'leased' Cumbria, hopefully in Edmund's view, closing the 'back door' from Ireland. Nonetheless, English influence steadily increased. In 973 King Edgar steered his ceremonial barge down the River Dee; at the oars were six client kings, including Kenneth II of Scotland (971–995). The unhappy reign of Ethelred the Unraed ('ill-advised' rather than just 'Unready', though he was both) provided an opportunity for the Scots to reassert themselves and warlike Malcolm II was quick to profit.

He annexed Strathclyde and in 1006 swept through Northumbria, terrorising the ineffectual Earl Waltheof. Dismayed by the older man's apparent faint-heartedness, his son Uhtred fought back. He raised the siege of Durham, and then pushed Malcolm's forces back across the Tweed. Newly created earl in his father's stead, Uhtred went over to the offensive, driving Malcolm north almost to the Tay and re-asserting Northumbria's ancient grip on Lothian. In 1016 the earl's career was cut short by assassins and his less aggressive brother Edwulf, who succeeded to the title, withdrew. Malcolm gained both a respite and an opportunity.

Loss of substantial revenue from estates in Lothian outraged the Northumbri-an clergy who in 1018 swore to protect their income by force of arms. A great levy of warriors was raised, amply blessed, and commanded by prelates, which clashed with a Scots army led by Malcolm at Carham on the Tweed, probably at a location, quarter of a mile or so north-west of the Norman motte at Wark.

After a savage fight the Scots emerged victorious and many English went down, including a fair score of Northumbrian nobility and no fewer than 18 leading churchmen. The fight proved – with time – decisive, for the line of the Tweed finally became the accepted border and English claims to Lothian lapsed. King Malcolm's victory at Carham raised the question of the annexation of Bernicia once again to create a buffer zone between the Scots and English but a late resurgence, last gasp you could say, of Northumbrian power under Siward the Dane forestalled any such attempt.

Siward, who features so aggressively in Macbeth, was a Norse warlord who King Cnut hired in to keep the north in order, which involved fighting against the Bard's Macbeth: '1054; [Siward] led a great army into Scotland and made much slaughter of the Scots and put them to flight … And many fell on his side, as well Danish-men as English and also his own son' [61]. He did a good job, rather better than King Harold II's brother Tostig who was kicked out by the fractious Northumbrians [62] but returned with a vengeance in the company of fearsome old Harald Hardrada. He defeated local forces under the brother earls Edwin and Morcar at Gate Fulford adjacent to York then, with his sponsor, was killed at Stamford Bridge by his brother [63], who was then killed by Duke William at Hastings. Game over for Anglo-Saxon England and hi to the Middle Ages with, of course, feudalism.

King William wasn't necessarily that bothered with Northumbria or the border region. Edwin and Morcar submitted but, having then transgressed, he handed the earldom to Copsig, of Tostig's old affinity. A poor choice he soon went down in another intercnine brawl, replaced by Cospatric who defected during another abortive rebellion led by the two brothers. This soon fizzled out but William's attempt to install a garrison in Durham under Robert Comines ended in a flaming Norman Alamo, locals: 'slew him and 900 others' [64]. This sparked yet another Northern uprising and William was obliged to lead an army north to restore his grip.

A fresh garrison under William Fitz Osbern was left in York but resurgent rebels, aided by opportunistic Norse reinforcements wiped them out; 'and so they went to York, demolished the castle … they also slew many hundred Frenchmen' [65]. This was too much for William who then decided upon a final solution to his northern problem, very final indeed, the ruthless 'Harrying of the North', pacification by wholesale destruction. Northumberland north of the Wear escaped the worst, probably too poor to be worth wasting.

Now it was (another) Earl Waltheof's turn, Siward's surviving son and outwardly a safe bet. Yet he too raised a rebel flag in 1075 and ended up in gaol. The King now turned to Bishop Walcher of Lorraine who was installed at Durham. Another local dispute sparked yet another fracas and the Bishop, together with his Norman household knights, was immolated at Gateshead. William sent his capable and avaricious half-brother Bishop Odo of Bayeux to give Northumbrians a taste of his brand of final solution and to restore order.

Sometime earlier, in 1072, the King had dealt with Scottish raids instigated by Malcolm III; 'led an army and a fleet against Scotland … King Malcolm came and treated with king William and delivered hostages and became his liege-man'. But, after the conqueror's death, Shakespeare's Canmore came back with more fire and sword, firstly in 1079, when he 'laid waste Northumberland as far as the Tyne' [66]. He should have stayed away after that as he came fatally to grief at Alnwick in 1093 [67]. He wouldn't be the last Scottish monarch to lose out in Northumberland; William the Lion was also defeated and captured at Alnwick in 1174, David II likewise at Neville's Cross in 1346, and most famously, James IV died at Flodden in September 1513. The line of the border might be settled geographically but it would remain an impenetrable frontier and warring armies would march both ways for the next six centuries.

THE FRONTIER LINE

David I of Scotland spent many years as a pensioner of the English court; his chances of reigning seemed distant but matured unexpectedly when both his older brothers died childless. He was the last of Malcolm III's (Canmore) sons, a man of great ability and something of an Anglophile. Having spent so long at the English court, it was thought 'he had rubbed off all the tarnish of Scottish barbarity' [68]. It was he who introduced Norman feudalism into Scotland more by infiltration than invasion; the de Brus were significant beneficiaries as, more tangentially, were those rising stars the Percies. King David had first pounced in 1136 but Stephen had obliged him to back down. Two years later and Matilda was ahead on points – time for a second try. This was a well planned and executed two-pronged invasion, a thrust, (extraordinarily successful), into Cumbria and a major blow in the east aimed at asserting his rights in Northumberland. The new marcher lords said no.

On 22 August 1138 English knights and men-at-arms deployed a couple of miles (3.2 kilometres) north of Northallerton in North Yorkshire, looking uphill at a dazzling array of Scottish lords, banners blazing and backed by a tough looking crew of Gallowegians from the south-west. A wild downhill charge from the Scots was met with an archery barrage which decimated King David's unarmoured Gallowegians, their bodies so studded with arrows they seemed 'like hedgehogs with quills' [69].

While the wily King of Scots might have lost the war, he did win the peace. Stephen was too weak to open a second front on his northern border, so granted Northumbria's earldom to David who installed his son Henry as proxy, thus achieving his goal of a border hegemony, his writ running down to the Tees. William Percy, a significant player from this burgeoning dynasty, who held lands in Craven, meanwhile had to adjust to Scots' supremacy in the west where David's deputy and winner of another, if smaller, fight at Clitheroe, William Fitz Duncan, enjoyed quasi vice-regal status. In fact, and this is a tribute to William's charm and acumen, the two men rubbed along very well and established a lasting amity.

King Stephen, hopeless and worn out was probably happy to hand over the reins to Matilda's son by Geoffrey of Anjou, the charismatic and able Henry II. By now King David of Scotland was dead too, as was his son Henry, leaving a boy, Malcolm IV on the throne. Henry II intended to fully reclaim the north and browbeat young Malcolm into agreeing a deal whereby he was bought off with the Earldom of Huntingdon and Regality of Tynedale. The well-named William the Lion, having fallen out with those powerful de Umfravilles, invaded Northumberland in 1174 in a tsunami of violence which culminated in his defeat and capture at Alnwick. The Lion was tamed and obliged to bend his knees to Henry II, admitting the English king was his feudal superior, thereby confirming an ancient song with a very long finish.

NOTES:

[1] The Borderers ran for 26 episodes on BBC from December 1968 to March 1970.
[2] 'Malcolm's Cross' still stands just east of Alnwick Castle Park, close to the line of the present A1, see note 67 below.
[3] https://www.geologynorth.uk/southern-uplands/ accessed 9 March 2022.
[4] 'Mosstroopers' can mean just bandits, but the name was applied to Scottish light cavalry during Cromwell's Dunbar campaign in 1650.
[5] Robb, G., The Debatable Land (London: Picador, 2018); traditionally this stretch of ground was ten miles (16 kilometres) from north to south four and a half miles (6.4 kilometres) in width, bounded by the Liddel and Esk in the east and Sark in the west.
[6] A March was supposedly the distance a man could cover in a day's march, more likely a day's ride and even then, rather a long haul.
[7] A magnificent span, built between 1847 and 1850, opened by Queen Victoria.
[8] Tough, op. cit., p. 7.
[9] NT8919; a suitably gruesome legends tells that the name was given after a pack-man slipped and the rope got caught around the stone and throttled him.
[10] Tough, op. cit., p. 3.
[11] Ibid.

[12] Lindsay of Pitscottie, Chronicles of Scotland, vol. 2 (Edinburgh: n. pub., 1814), p. 307.

[13] Tough, op. cit., p. 19.

[14] Wade had his very own verse added to the National Anthem.

[15] Sir John Carmichael, Keeper of Liddesdale, Forster's nemesis at the Reidswire was murdered by Armstrongs 14 June 1600.

[16] Watson, G., The Border Reivers (Newcastle upon Tyne: Sandhill, 1974), p. 9.

[17] MacDonald Fraser, op. cit., pp. 114–115.

[18] Ibid., p. 116.

[19] Raid of the Reidswire, Border Ballad, see Marsden, J., The Illustrated Border Ballads (London: Macmillan, 1990), pp. 46–56.

[20] MacDonald Fraser, op. cit., p. 173.

[21] Ibid., p. 162.

[22] Dodds, J. F., Bastles & Belligerents (London: Blackwell, 1999), p. 336.

[23] Ibid.

[24] Ibid.

[25] Oliver, N., A History of Ancient Britain (London: Weidenfeld & Nicolson, 2010), p. 29.

[26] Ibid., p. 213.

[27] The name dates only from the eighteenth century, whereas older maps refer to it by the name 'Dunpendyrlaw'.

[28] http://www.writersmugs.com/books/books.php?book=236&name=Rudyard_Kipling&title=Puck_of_Pook_s_Hill, accessed 15 March 2022.

[29] As described in my trusty copy of Collingwood Bruce, published in 1957 by Andrew Reid.

[30] The late Professor Brian Shefton, who died in 2012, had amassed a fabulous collection of Classical Greek artefacts, including some wondrous Corinthian helmets and these were displayed in a secret little museum hidden in the depths of Armstrong Building at Newcastle University, which he'd set up in 1956 with a grant of £20.00 from the rector!

[31] https://www.ncl.ac.uk/events/public-lectures/archive/item/themuseumofantiquitiesaretrospective.html, accessed 15 March 2022.

[32] MacDonald Fraser, op. cit., p. 15.

[33] Welsh triads and genealogies, http://maryjones.us/ctexts/triads1.html, accessed 18 January 2022.

[34] Higham, N. J., The Kingdom of Northumbria 350–1100 (Gloucester: Alan Sutton, 1993), p. 82.

[35] This battle isn't mentioned by Bede or in the Anglo-Saxon Chronicle.

[36] Anglo-Saxon Chronicle ["ASC"] (London: George Bell & Sons, 1880), Anno 525–560, p. 312.

[37] Magnus Maximus also feature in the Welsh sources as Prince Macsen; Ammianus Marcellinus, The Later Roman Empire (London: Penguin, 1986), p. 417.

[38] Possibly born towards the end of the fifth century, Thornton, David E., 'Urien of Rheged', in Oxford Dictionary of National Biography (online edition; Oxford University Press doi:10.1093/ref:odnb/28016); his memory survives in a rather strange retail centre outside Penrith, not sure he'd feel in any way flattered!

[39] Calgacus – 'The Swordsman'; leader of the Caledonian confederacy defeated by Agricola at Mons Graupius in AD 84.

[40] Venerable Bede's, Ecclesiastical History of England (London: George Bell & Sons, 1880), Book I, chapter 1, pp. 5–6.

[41] Ibid., Book II, chapter 20, p. 106/ASC Anno 627–635, p. 318.

[42] Ibid., Book II, chapter 1, p. 108.

[43] Ibid., Book III, chapter 1, p. 109.

[44] Another unfinished epic was the independent film Whiteblade filmed near Bishop Auckland in 2015/2016 but never made it onto the screen.

[45] ASC Anno 627–635, p. 318.

[46] The 'Fyrd' comprised both a general levy and a 'select' element that were better trained and equipped.

[47] Bede, Book III, chapter 2, p. 110.

[48] Ibid., Book IV, chapter 25, p. 223.

[49] ASC Anno 677–685, p. 329.

[50] Lynch, M., Scotland a New History (London: Pimlico, 1992), p. 14.

[51] Ibid., p. 19.

[52] Vita Sancta Wilfrithi – he was Wilfrid's chanter and latterly biographer, (Cambridge: Cambridge University Press, 1985).

[53] Bede, Book IV, chapter 23, p. 223.

[54] https://www.tandfonline.com/doi/abs/10.1080/0458063X.1994.10392215, accessed 1 March 2022.

[55] ASC Anno 783–794, p. 342.

[56] Ibid.

[57] Ivar the Boneless – it's not certain what his name implies, possibly he may have been disabled, or he may have been impotent or simply this refers to his cunning, slippery as a snake

[58] ASC Anno 924–937, p. 375.

[59] https://www.historyextra.com/period/anglo-saxon/where-did-brunanburh-battle-take-place-location-england-michael-wood/, accessed 17 January 2022.

[60] ASC Anno 937–941, p. 377.

[61] Ibid., Anno 1054–1055, p. 432.

[62] Ibid., Anno 1063–1065, p. 437.

[63] Ibid., Anno 1068–1069, p. 446.

[64] Ibid.

[65] Ibid., Anno 1071–1074, p. 453.

[66] Ibid., Anno 1077–1080, p. 456.

[67] A stone memorial still stands on the east side of the town, legend asserts that the Scottish king was pierced through the eye by a Norman knight pretending to offer him the keys to the citadel and earned himself the name 'Pierce-Eye' – Percy in due course, a complete myth but an alluring one.

[68] Lynch, op. cit., p. 53.

[69] Kinross, J., Walking and Exploring the Battlefields of Britain (London: David & Charles, 1988), p. 48.

CHAPTER TWO: FALL OF THE HAMMER

'When Alexander our king was dead
That Scotland led in love and security
Departed was abundance of aloe and bread
Of wine and wax, of games and glee'.

Andrew Wyntoun

Just around the time of lockdown, 2020 was the seven hundredth anniversary of the signing of the Declaration of Arbroath, seismic in its day and a banner for Scottish nationalists ever since. In the sometimes-clouded view of Scottish writers, this period has two great heroes, Wallace and Robert Bruce, and a classic baddie, Edward I of England, 'a villain to hand, ready at the wings' [1]. Both Wallace and Bruce are viewed rather differently in Northumberland, as murderous, ruthless terrorists but I'd never dare say that in Scotland. Despite the gap of those seven centuries, the weight of history hangs heavy and is used, not necessary with impartiality, to inform the current nationalist debate.

A GREAT CAUSE

The 44-year-old Alexander III of Scotland was, according to certain of his contemporaries, a man of healthy appetites, especially where the opposite sex was concerned: 'Neither storm nor floods nor rocky cliffs would prevent him from visiting matrons and nuns, virgins and widows, by day or by night as the fancy seized him' [2]. In November 1285, he had married his second wife, Yolande, daughter of the Count of Dreux. On 18 March 1286, the king, having presided over his council at Edinburgh, decided to return to his new wife at Kinghorn in Fife.

His adult sons had predeceased him, and he was in desperate need of a male heir; his dynastic duty was an imperative. Though the day was blustery and inclement, and it was getting late, Alexander chose to brush aside the cautious warnings of his courtiers and delay his trip, dynastic duty is dynastic duty and the weel of his kingdom depended on it. Yolande was also beautiful and 30 odd years her husband's junior. It was snowing heavily; a cold wind whipped the leaden waters of the Forth as the king reached the crossing at Queensferry.

Ignoring further warnings, this time from the boatman, a perilous crossing brought the royal party to Inverkeithing. Here, the road passed along the foreshore and in the bleak, smothering darkness the king became separated from his guides and some time on that fateful night, he met his death, a fall that plunged his country into a deeper abyss than any who discovered his mangled body on the foreshore next day could have possibly imagined.

England was ruled by Edward I ('Longshanks'): 'Like Alexander, he would speedily subdue the whole world, if fortune's moving wheel would stand still forever' [3] whom later spin was to christen Malleus Scottorum, 'Hammer of the Scots' [4]. Longshanks, 'a great and terrible King', had earlier crushed the English barons led by de Montfort on the bloody field of Evesham, thunder and lightning adding background music to what was a very nasty and distinctly unchivalrous butchery, realpolitik with sharp edges. Though he later became a staunch and trusted ally, the de Vesci Earl of Northumberland was one of those Montfortian remnants who'd needed a tap on the shoulder to remind them of their due obeisance [5].

Edward had systematically conquered those hitherto independent Welsh principalities and now, possibly seeking new horizons, cast his eyes northward. A peerless knight and accomplished commander, Edward was a force of almost elemental power, single-minded to the point of obsession, austere, and utterly ruthless. When Alexander took his fatal tumble, his only direct heir was a child, his granddaughter, the Maid of Norway. Edward was quick to propose a marriage alliance with his own young son, the first Prince of Wales. Unhappily the little girl died in Orkney on her way to Scotland, leaving an empty throne. In fairness, Longshanks had enjoyed cordial relations with his brother-in-law Alexander III and had shown no interest in adding Scotland to his portfolio, at least not yet.

However, as opportunity came knocking, he wasn't one to let it pass and though his early attempts to overawe the Scottish regency council or 'Guardians' fell flat, and he failed to intimidate them as he expected and indeed usually did [6]. The Guardians, naively perhaps with hindsight, assumed Edward would just choose between John Balliol and Robert Bruce, 'The Competitor' (grandfather of the future king). But baulked in his efforts to coerce the council into accepting the fact of England's feudal superiority, Edward took a sideways step, outflanked the Guardians, and demanded fealty from all candidates and just to muddy the waters a bit more opened the field to any who thought he had a claim [7].

Of enthusiastic hopefuls, there was no shortage. Bruce and Balliol, the latter of whom was backed by the powerful Comyns, were already at each other's throats in Galloway. Longshanks also wanted control, strictly temporary of course, of all key Scottish castles. Edward and the tribunal's final judgement favoured Balliol, whose claim in law was undoubtedly the strongest [8]. Longshanks went home well pleased, having by forcefulness and diplomacy effectively added Scotland to his titles without striking a blow. Eventually, however, King John reached the limit of malleability and rebelled, dragged along by a wave of anti-English sentiment. From Edward's point of view, the war that followed was no chivalric contest but a squalid revolt to be put down swiftly, effectively, and without mercy. That pretty much set the tone for the next three centuries. King Alexander's fatal tumble set in motion rivers of blood.

John Balliol was scarcely cast in a heroic mould. Though the Scots drew first blood by raiding south, Edward was swift to retaliate and stormed northward; on 30 March 1296 he overran Berwick upon Tweed in a day, brushing aside the timber palisade and ditch. Bower tells us [9] that Longshanks used captured Scottish banners, a ruse which he'd employed at Evesham over 30 years earlier, to confuse the enemy and therefore allow him to get up close [10]. This heraldic Trojan horse worked only too well, and Berwick opened its gates, 'as soon as the deception was revealed and the truth learnt, they endeavoured to resist' [11]. Much good it did them, the sack was terrible. Berwick was then a major port, one of Scotland's largest towns, which far outshone its Northumbrian rival Newcastle. As an intimation of the carnage to come, Berwick was systematically pillaged, and its merchants ruthlessly slaughtered. Thereafter the town would be rebuilt as a fortified outpost in a hostile land like a bastide [12] in Gascony or the castles of Wales.

Whilst Berwick burned, the Scots army was still north of Dunbar and on 23 April Edward dispatched John de Warenne, Earl of Surrey, with a mounted contingent to secure the castle. In theory this shouldn't have been difficult. Patrick, Earl of Dunbar, had remained loyal to the English crown but his wife, a patriot, duped her husband's household knights and opened the gates of the fortress to King John's forces. De Warenne wasn't dismayed and leaving a skeletal force to man the works and counter a sally, drew up in battle array to face the Scots as they came over the brow of Spottismuir. The English commander didn't intend to stand just on the defensive and pushed his men downhill towards the crossing of the Spott Burn, which flowed across the front of both armies. The

Scots, assuming that the English were about to flee, abandoned their vantage to launch a precipitate charge. Counter-attacking in good order, de Warenne drove the Scots back. Amongst the infantry, hundreds were cut down and many knights captured [13].

This debacle demonstrated with chilling clarity the weaknesses of the unprepared Scottish host, hopelessly outfought by the English. Edward's campaign became a triumphal march; the king simply overawed the Scottish nobles with these terrible lessons of Berwick and Dunbar still fresh. He confronted his abject puppet at Montrose where Balliol was ritually humiliated, his coat of arms torn from him and flung to the ground. On Balliol's surrender, '[Edward] having entered Scotland with his strength, had conquered and seized it as a lord might in justice do with his fee upon the vassal's renouncing his homage and behaving as Baliol had done' [14].

That sacred Stone of Destiny was amongst the haul, pillaged from Scone, along with the most treasured relic in Scotland, the Black Rood of St Margaret. Tired of local surrogates, Edward chose to ignore the claims of Bruce, or any other, and appointed an English viceroy to govern. Scotland was a kingdom no more. As Edward recrossed the border into England, he is said to have summed up his feelings towards Scotland in a simple, pithy sentence: 'A man does good business when he rids himself of a turd' [15].

BRAVEHEARTS

Though her army had been shattered, her pride broken, her nobles enfeebled, the guttering flame of liberty was not extinguished, and one man at least would never surrender Scotland's freedom while he lived. The origins and antecedents of William Wallace are uncertain. He belonged to the minor gentry, a younger son of a tenant of the Steward, Sir Malcolm Wallace of Elderslie. 'Wallace stature of greatness and of height/was judged thus by discretion of sight/that saw him both on Cheval and in Weed' [16].

Bower was equally swift to eulogise, '… The famous William Wallace, the hammer of the English … was a tall man with the body of a giant, cheerful in appearance with agreeable features, broad shouldered and big-boned … pleasing in appearance but with a wild look' [17]. He certainly appears to have been outlawed and hid out in the forest of Selkirk, a northerly Sherwood infested with broken men and desperadoes. Legend relates that his mistress and her family perished, burnt out by an English patrol after a skirmish with the hero and his merry men. Wallace is said to have sought out the perpetrators and dispatched them all [18].

William Wallace was not alone in fomenting resistance. In Moray, Andrew Murray, son of Sir Andrew Murray of Petty, who'd been caught in the debacle at Dunbar, raised the flag of rebellion. As scattered patriots gathered support, their example rekindled defiance, prompting the former governor of Berwick, Sir William Douglas, and James Stewart, a leading landowner, to throw off the English yoke. The Scots nobility, tied by their oaths to Edward and fearful for their estates, vacillated. The king even sent Robert Bruce to lay siege to Douglas's castle, so confident was he of loyalty – overly confident as it turned out as his protégé experienced a change of heart and threw his lot in with the patriots.

Northumberland quickly felt Wallace's sting. Early on in 1296 he raided Redesdale. By the summer of 1297 he was becoming more than an irritant. In August, his partisans fought a running battle with the English garrison of Glasgow led by Anthony Bek, the fighting Bishop of Durham, who was driven from the streets and obliged to seek refuge in Bothwell Castle. De Warenne, victor of Dunbar, commanded English forces in Scotland, though this responsibility appears to have been shared with Hugh Cressingham, Edward's chief tax collector and one for whom the patriots reserved a particular hate.

In the first week of September Surrey's forces had reached Stirling to find Wallace, now joined by Murray and the men of the northern shires, strongly posted on the far side of the River Forth. What followed was a masterpiece of expanded guerrilla tactics, exploiting English complacency and tactical folly to win a key battle. With his and Murray's victory at Stirling Bridge [19], Wallace's prestige soared. At a stroke the shame of Dunbar had been wiped away and the myth of English invincibility punctured. In the autumn Wallace raided Northumberland, again based in Forest of Rothbury. His guerrillas 'took up' Tynedale, even robbing Hexham Abbey for which their commander had to apologise to the monks; '... they killed many and collected great spoils ... priests and monks of all orders flying for their lives' [20]. In the forest of Selkirk, in the spring of 1298, Wallace was entrusted with sole Guardianship of the Realm [21].

Edward had meantime become entangled in his difficult relations with France and in more wrangling with his own barons but matters in the north couldn't be avoided and by the following spring he'd planted his royal standard at York and was preparing to deal with Wallace once and for all. Longshank's army was formidable: 2,500 cavalry, as many as 12,000 foot soldiers, a heterogeneous force with archers from Wales, and crossbowmen from Gascony. By July this leviathan was plodding northward advancing up the east coast, an English fleet in close support. Energetic Bishop Bek took Dirleton and a brace of other garrisons but the logistical difficulties in feeding such a large army were massive and supplies soon dwindled. Wallace and his power seemed to have disappeared and Edward was seriously thinking of withdrawing when Gilbert de Umfraville and Patrick, Earl of Dunbar, brought vital intelligence – the Scots were a bare 15 miles (24 kilometres) away bivouacked in Callander Wood, Falkirk. Edward proceeded to win an impressive all-arms victory using heavy cavalry, infantry, and bowmen to utterly defeat Wallace whose army was destroyed. The day of the great Welsh/English warbow was on hand.

THE BRUCE

The Road to Bannockburn – Wallace's star plummeted after Falkirk, there was no coming back from so great a defeat. He spent the miserable years till his capture and execution in 1305 as a hunted outlaw, rejected by the Scottish polity but never giving up. Like any decent martyr he accomplished in death what he'd failed to do in life. He did have to wait till 1995 for Mel Gibson, a rabid Anglophobe, to revive him in the movies. Braveheart, despite only a passing resemblance to history, became an instant cult favourite and its fantasy became reality for a generation of Scottish nationalists.

With Wallace gone, the mantle of leadership passed to Robert Bruce. Though, in the early years, the future king lived – as had his predecessor – the life of an outlaw. Bruce, however, had the inestimable advantage of noble birth and a legitimate claim to the throne. On 10 February 1306 he met with his arch-rival John Comyn in the sacrosanct cloisters of Greyfriars' Church in Dumfries. Harsh words passed between the two men, neither noted for his patience, and Bruce or his affinity settled the argument with daggers [22]. Within five weeks, he was enthroned at Scone.

Experience had tempered the hot-blooded passion of the Scottish king's youth. He was dogged, single-minded, courageous, a superb warrior, and natural leader who had the rare gift of being able to combine generalship with statesmanship; he'd need both. Bruce could be both violent and ruthless whilst capable of compassion; his conviction and charisma won over old enemies and promoted fierce loyalty [23]. He chose his subordinates well. The names of Edward Bruce, Douglas, and Randolph became synonymous with dash and daring. Longshanks, though ageing, had not forgotten Scotland and he chose as his lieutenant his half-cousin Aymer de Valence, who also happened to be brother-in-law to the murdered Comyn.

De Valence was given a free hand in his treatment of the Scottish rebels and set to work with a will. By June he'd secured Perth and left a trail of victims swinging in the breeze. Bruce rashly decided to take the offensive and on 18 June came on but was roundly defeated at Methven Wood. The king's fortunes were now at their lowest, a fugitive, hunted; his family dead or in chains, his wife and sister held, like captive birds, in iron cages hung suspended over the battlements of Berwick and Roxburgh. Longshanks wasn't the temperate sort and rebels deserve no better.

Such savagery just fed the patriot cause and in the following year, the old warrior king died almost literally in the saddle at Burgh on Sands as he prepared for yet another campaign. Though dead, his spirit seemed destined to live on – he left instructions for his son, now crowned Edward II, to continue the offensive and that the king's coffin, like some malevolent talisman, be carried before the army [24]. But Edward II was not the man his father had been. He was indolent, pleasure-seeking, and surrounded by favoured catamites. War did not hold the same allure. Scotland got a respite. Bruce did not – he had to begin with a nasty civil war, stamping his will on Balliol's old partisans and his enemies Comyns and MacDougalls. Fratricidal it certainly was but Bruce was learning and honing his art of war, training the nucleus of what would prove to be a battle winning army. Castle after castle, town after town fell; the pro-English faction was harried to death or despair, their increasingly desperate begging for aid from England ignored.

Edward made no effort to stem the rot until 1310 when he came north in force. Declining battle, King Robert pursued a Fabian course until the English withdrew leaving Northumberland to bear the fury of Scottish vengeance. By 1314 Stirling Castle was the only major fortress that remained in English hands, her only significant claim to dominion. Soon Stirling itself was besieged and, according to custom, the castellan undertook to strike his colours if not relieved by 25 June next year. Reluctantly stung into action by this threat to his last remaining bastion, King Edward summoned a vast army including the flower of chivalry. This force, which mustered at Wark on 10 June might have numbered as many as 17,000 including a substantial Scots contingent: the Comyns, still unreconciled, the MacDougalls, and the Macnabs. A train of two hundred wagons was needed to equip and feed such a behemoth. Though Edward himself commanded in name, he relied heavily on the advice of a council of war made up of such seasoned campaigners as the Earls of Hereford and Gloucester [25].

Though King Robert was anxious to prevent the relief of Stirling, he could not hope to match the English numbers, relying, at best, on perhaps five thousand seasoned infantry and barely five hundred light cavalry. Edward commanded bowmen drawn from the breadth of his dominions, from Wales, Ireland, and the northern shires. On 17 June the English army marched from Wark, a dazzling array of the hot spring sun glancing from burnished plate and mail, a forest of pennons proclaiming the pride of English knighthood, the greatest army ever to cross the border. Edinburgh was reached without opposition and a halt was called to await resupply by sea.

On the 22nd the army marched on to Falkirk. The next morning the old Roman road echoed to the tramp of marching feet and the ring of hoof-beats as the English set out for Stirling. They had two days left before the deadline expired. A contemporary chronicler has left us an image of the English army on the march during the Scottish campaign of 1300: 'There were many rich caparisons embroidered on silks and satins; many a beautiful pennon fixed to a lance; many a banner displayed. The neighing of horses was heard from afar; the mountains and valleys were covered with pack-horses, tents, and pavilions' [26].

Such a colourful vision, which could come directly from the pen of Scott or Tennyson, is highly idealised. The reality would be rather more mundane. Knights would ride light horses, palfreys, on the line of march, saving their precious destriers for combat. The armies would proceed in a cacophony of noise and dust, mounted arm to the front and as rearguard, mainly with harness stowed, horses throwing up vast clouds of muck; the foot tramping in long, straggling columns, ill-fed, ill-accoutred, and swallowing the laden dust of their betters. A vast caravanserai of livestock, for the army took its provisions along on the hoof, wagons laden with small beer, tents, cordage, baggage, and provisions.

Battle was joined south of Stirling Castle on 23 June 1314 and continued the next day. Edward's lumbering army was broken and scattered, Stirling fell, and Scotland was free. It was a real game-changer. I've been to Bannockburn many times; the old visitor centre had a wonderful clunky charm to it even though the main battle site, whilst not fully agreed upon, has long been obscured by modern housing estates.

From then on, this memory of Bannockburn would haunt any king of England who dared to venture north of the border and never again would England reduce her northern neighbour to mere dominion. But this phase of the very long wars left a bitter legacy. Scotland was now a nation in arms and her success meant the full fury would fall on Northumberland and the other northern shires. King Edward had recovered his nerve sufficiently by 1322 to come north again, sacking Holyrood and Melrose and leaving Dryburgh in flames, but this aggression was brief. In 1318 Bruce recovered Berwick, and in the following year the Scots won a victory at Mytton. Three years later Bruce chased Edward from the field at Byland. 'Robert Bruce, as King Robert I of Scotland, was to inflict upon Northumberland the darkest and most miserable conditions it has ever had to endure' [27].

John Barbour in his epic the Bruce recounts the many deeds of his hero king and of Douglas, perhaps King Robert's chief and most enthusiastic enforcer, gleefully celebrating Black Jamie's many triumphs including successful combats with leading English knights including Lord Neville: 'Qwhen Nevell thus was brought to ground … the dred of the Lord Douglas and his renown awa scalit ['armoured' – consolidated] was throughout the marches of England, that all that was thar-in duelland dred him as the devil of Hell' [28].

Edward II's feeble efforts, rare as they were, swiftly came unstuck, as Bower gloats: 'On 1st October [1322] King Robert entered England with hostile intent and laid it utterly waste as far as York, after despoiling monasteries and putting very many towns and villages to the torch …' Edward's ad hoc forces were scattered at Byland, 'not without great slaughter' [29]. Durham set up a regular mechanism for paying off the Scots, almost a direct debit. In 1327 the monastery of Blanchland claimed it had lost 40 acres of wheat and rye, a hundred acres each of oats and hay; five hundred sheep with an additional 20 marks worth of food sent from Newcastle. The canons didn't just blame the Scots; they accused government purveyors of requisitioning goods on account without payment [30].

Many other claims came from ecclesiastical institutions hit by the Scots. Durham Cathedral had a large South Tweedside estate including Norham and Holy Island, entitled to a steady income stream from over 30 settlements and various other rents. The Bursar's accounts show that a normal income of say £400.00 – £420.00 declined in 1314/1315 to £280.00; then fell steadily, down to just £9.00 by 1318/1319. Temporary truces brokered in December 1319 and June 1323 had little reviving effect [31]. Evidence from elsewhere in the county is equally depressing: rents collapsed, and lands were wasted [32].

This was economic warfare, 'frightfulness' as it was called – now we'd call it terrorism and it was very effective. Northumbrian gentry weren't just losing revenue; they ran the risk of death or capture, and the loss of armour, weapons, and horses. The crown was distinctly laggard in paying any monies due. Some, out of sheer desperation, 'defected' to the Scots or just took to banditry. I live in the village of Belsay held since just after the Conquest by the Middletons. Sir Gilbert de Middleton was one of those who went 'bad'.

He and Sir Walter Selby of Seghill ambushed Bishop of Durham elect Louis de Beaumont and his brother Henry at Rushyford about ten miles (17 kilometres) north of Darlington, on their way to Durham for the bishop's enthronement. The haul of victims included two cardinals, Gaucelin D'Eauze and Luca Fieschi, who were travelling to Scotland as international mediators. The cardinals were released but not before they'd been robbed of everything they had. Middleton and Selby dragged the Beaumont brothers to Sir Gilbert's lair at Mitford Castle to be held until ransomed. In December, Middleton and his brother John were both captured there by Sir William de Felton, sent in chains down to London, and executed on 26 January 1318 [33]. Selby got away with it for the moment, holed up at Horton near Blyth. He held out for two years before giving himself up in the hope of a pardon. He didn't swing but had a long wait, 'banged up' until 1327 [34].

Frustrations with Edward's seeming mix of indifference and incompetence drove Sir Andrew de Harcla from the English West March, who'd saved the king's bacon by defeating the Earl of Lancaster's rebels at Boroughbridge in 1322, to mediate a separate peace with Bruce. Lancaster had, as early as 1313, been in treasonous communication with the Scottish king and Harcla's efforts, undoubtedly genuine, still cost him his head. Virtue did not bring rewards: John de Fawdon had participated in the apprehension of the Middletons and was promised an annuity of 20 marks – he never got it but was captured twice by the Scots for ransom and burnt out on no less than three occasions [35]! Men such as Harcla and de Fawdon found just how thin the gratitude of princes can be, especially one like Edward II.

On the dire consequences of these raids, Ridpath writes: 'These desolations of war increased the scarcity and dearth which had arisen from a succession of destructive seasons so that a quarter of wheat was sold in the north of England for 40 shillings (£2.00) and the Northumbrians were driven to the necessity of eating the flesh of dogs and horses and other unclean things' [36]. This was echoed by later accounts including Cadwallader Bates in the late nineteenth century: 'The condition of Northumberland was terrible in the extreme. For 15 years after 1316 the whole county remained waste, no one daring to live in it except under the shadow of a castle or walled town. If having the Scots on your back wasn't bad enough, English royal officials were just as happy to profiteer from the troubles; The poor people of Bamburgh Ward were not allowed by the Constable of the castle to purchase a truce from the Scots unless they gave him a similar amount of blackmail ...' [37]

LANDSCAPES OF WAR

King Robert, for these lightning campaigns, a Scottish Blitzkrieg, had created a new class of soldier, a breed of light cavalry that defied every chivalric contention. These were the hobilers, the genesis of what or who would devolve into the Steel Bonnets. Lightly armoured riders on sturdy ponies – the hobbys that gave them their name. They rode fast and they struck hard, tactical equivalent of 'float like a butterfly, sting like a bee'. They could outride what they couldn't outfight and outfight what they couldn't outride.

They were not slowed down by baggage trains or towing legions of camp-followers. They were what much, much later, the Boers of the Transvaal would call 'commandos'. Subsequent generations of British commanders would find out how successful such will o' the wisp riders could be; essential Boer tactics were speed in concentration and attack with a readiness to withdraw. And they led vastly superior forces on a merry dance over the veldt.

These hobilers then were very effective and perfectly suited to the ground over which they ranged. Conventional forces couldn't catch them, and locals couldn't match them. Archbishop Melton of York tried to challenge a Scottish commando at Mytton, seven miles (11 kilometres) east of Boroughbridge. The Scots dismounted and formed up as a schlitron, fighting as infantry, and firing haystacks to give smoke cover. This was not an unusual Scottish gambit; the smoke would obscure the infantry advancing to contact, shielding them from arrows). They routed the Yorkshiremen leaving many dead, using their lances as spears. The idea worked and went on working [38]. Ridpath picks up the description: '... the rest of their provision consisted of oatmeal which they were wont to carry in bags behind them and of which made a thin paste that they baked into cakes by the help of iron plates trussed in their saddle; their drink was from the nearest fountain, stream or lake' [39]. That was the hobiler commissariat. England had no immediate answer to these long-riders but soon got the concept.

Andrew de Harcla used hobilers in the English West March as did his contemporary and rival Anthony de Lucy. As early as 1316, just two years after Bannockburn, he had 40 such riders with only 15 men-at-arms stationed at his outpost of Staward Pele in South Tynedale [40]. This adoption of such indigenous light cavalry marked a sea change in the history of the Marches; border warfare now took on a distinct character of its own. It proved very easy to adopt and adapt, but shrugging off the habit would be far trickier.

In 1323 the English king agreed to a formal truce to last 13 years, and three years later, with the treaty of Corbeil, Bruce and Charles IV of France renewed the 'auld alliance'. In 1328 Bruce's excommunication, which Edward had secured, was withdrawn, while Edward himself was deposed in a coup d'état engineered by his estranged wife and her paramour Roger Mortimer. Imprisoned, the king may have suffered a hideous death (or perhaps not) whilst his son, a temporary puppet of Mortimer and the Queen, was crowned Edward III. In March the following year a draft treaty was agreed by Queen Isabella at Edinburgh and ratified, most unwillingly, by Edward at Northampton.

Within two years he had taken Mortimer's head, packed his mum off, and assumed full authority. Before that Edward, who was far more his grandfather than father, campaigned on the border in the dank summer of 1327. The Weardale Campaign was a bit of a fiasco, hugely expensive and left the young king weeping tears of rage and frustration. You could see why, those nimble Scottish hobilers ran rings around his knights but this prince, unlike his supine father, was a quick learner. His expedition comprised of a conventional force of barded [41] knights and men-at-arms, expensively hired and provisioned. He commanded a detachment from his wife's duchy of Hainault and chronicler John le Bel accompanied the column.

First blood was self-inflicted. The Hainaulters fell out with Lincolnshire bowmen at York over dice and it descended into violence. A bad beginning and that was just the start. Leaving York on 1 July, Edward reached Durham on the 19th. Both Douglas and Randolph were ahead of the game, two flying columns were beating up the West March and North Tynedale. There was no viable opposition and the western pincer barrelled down as far as Appleby and Kirby Stephen. De Lucy was fearful for Carlisle but it's more likely the two arms would link up in Weardale. It's possible even probable this was a calculated pre-emptive strike [42].

Edward's lumbering knights, heavy men on heavy horses with no local knowledge, were fully equipped and straining for a great cavalry charge that would brush this irritating enemy aside, a finale that never played. Chasing shadows was enervating and exhausting, supplies were gobbled up at an alarming rate and no enemy had yet even been sighted, just the distant smudges of smoke, darker grey on grey skies, from burning byres and shocked, bereaved peasantry. It was cold and it was wet; destriers stumbled in the endless morasses and got lost in dense thickets of bog oak and myrtle. It would be like taking today's Blues & Royals in full ceremonial kit and dumping them among Afghanistan's mountains. It was all very ungentlemanly.

Jean le Bel had a degree of admiration for these invaders: 'In just such a fashion they'd now invaded the country and were burning and laying waste the land and finding more livestock than they knew what do to with. They numbered three thousand heavy cavalry, knights, and squires … and fully twenty thousand other men, fierce and bold, armed in the fashion of their country and riding the smaller hackneys … And I tell you, they had two very fine captains … a most noble and worthy prince the Earl of Moray … and James, Lord Douglas who was considered the boldest and most daring knight in either kingdom' [43].

At last, on 31 July, a scout spotted the Scots. Edward marched out after them next day, a nine-mile dash towards the Wear but Douglas and Randolph didn't want to play. They just dug in on high ground forming an ad hoc redoubt, too well entrenched to attack. It appeared to be stalemate, but it was just a tactic. No sooner had the English sat down than the Scots slipped out from their camp and mounted a brilliant night attack on Edward's. Nobody on the English side had seen this one coming and the King, at one point, was in imminent risk of capture.

The Scots were seen off but only after casualties had been sustained. Fully on alert now, the young king waited for more, but none came. The enemy had gone but stayed well ahead on points [44]. Ridpath describes the scene that greeted Edward's men as they recce'd the deserted enemy base: 'The English who passed over to view the deserted camp, saw in it proofs of that simplicity and hardiness of living which gave their enemies, when under proper direction, a superiority to forces far more numerous and regular but at the same time more luxurious than themselves. The skins of the beasts they had slain for food being in the form of a bag suspended loosely on stakes were hanging over the remains of their fires; these hides serving as kettles for boiling the flesh; a great number of spits had meat roasting on them with many carcasses of black cattle' [45].

No sooner had Edward withdrawn, out of cash and out of luck than King Robert, just to underscore the point, conducted a major raid through North Northumberland which the King of England was powerless to prevent. It was pretty much game, set, and match to the Scots. The Weardale Campaign was a costly joke, but Edward learnt the lessons, and these wouldn't be forgotten in a hurry. Nonetheless, the Treaty of Northampton was the crowning moment of Bruce's highly eventful career; he was recognised by his inveterate enemies as a free prince and, as his health failed, he bequeathed an orderly realm to his successor.

After his death, his heart was taken by the faithful Douglas, now also ageing, on a journey to the Holy Land, an adventure the doughty Scot did not live to complete, dying a quixotic death in an insignificant Spanish skirmish. Randolph, the last of the paladins, died at Musselburgh in 1332, thus bringing a magnificent era to an end. With the death of Bruce, Scotland was left with two harbingers of dissent: a boy king and a caste of exiles; Scottish nobles who had thrown in their lot with England and as a direct consequence, had suffered the forfeiture of their estates [46].

The 'Disinherited'

Despite having given his name to the Treaty of Northampton, Edward III was determined to avenge the humiliation of Bannockburn and to recover Berwick, upon which so much English treasure had been lavished and which remained, as always, the key to the eastern marches. Bower warned the Scots: 'An Englishman is an angel who no one can believe; when he greets you, beware of him as an enemy' [47]. He may, of course have been prone to bias! This class of redundant Scottish nobles led by Edward Balliol, son of the unlamented King John, provided a ready-made insurgency and the English king was happy to provide a fleet of eighty-odd ships, in which the adventurers set sail from the Humber in the summer of 1332. The Disinherited made an unopposed landing at Kinghorn and boldly marched inland to Dunfermline, aiming for Perth. This manoeuvre was interrupted when they found their advance blocked by a superior force under the regent Donald, Earl of Mar. What followed was a stunning warbow victory as lumbering Scottish spears in dense schlitrons were shot to pieces.

Mar, the earls of Menteith and Moray; Robert Bruce, lord of Liddesdale; Alexander Fraser, the High Chamberlain, 18 lesser nobles, three-score knights and

perhaps two thousand rank and file were killed [48]. The Disinherited reported
losses of only thirty-odd knights and men-at-arms, a victory cheaply bought. Not
one archer is said to have died. Balliol had won himself a kingdom and Dupplin
Moor, as the battle is known, became a model for later English victories at Halidon
Hill and Neville's Cross (Balliol fought again at both). The lesson of Dupplin Moor
was plain: lumbering spearmen would always be vulnerable to archery and should
not seek to engage unsupported – a lesson that went largely unheeded.

Balliol's flimsy grip on the throne proved as insecure as his father's and
though he was crowned at Scone, he failed to command any serious following. In
December of that same year the new regent, Andrew Moray of Bothwell, passed
the baton of command to Randolph's son, the Earl of Moray, who surprised and
scattered the Disinherited at Annan, driving Balliol 'half-naked' from the realm.
Short-lived as it had been, Baliol's incumbency had given him a taste for power,
and he remained game for another try. He sought, successfully, to solicit English
support by promising to cede Berwick. Next summer, Edward marched north and
laid siege to the town. The king conducted his campaign with a professionalism
and ruthlessness of which his grandfather would have been proud. Two young
sons of the castellan, handed over as hostages, were hanged without compunction.

Archibald Douglas, the new Scottish regent, kick-started the forthcoming
campaign by raiding into the English West March and 'took up' Gilsland below
Spadeadam Waste, striking at Dacre's Lordship. Anthony Lucy from Cockermouth
retaliated, beating up the Scottish west and winning a skirmish at Lochmaben
despite sustaining severe wounds [49]. By 15 July, the garrison at Berwick was
in desperate straits and the grieving governor conceded that he would strike his
colours if not relieved by the 20th. A relief army, hastily assembled, was on its way
led by Douglas – unfortunately a poor successor to his legendary predecessor.
Having feinted unsuccessfully against Bamburgh, seeking to divert Edward and
failing, the Scots prepared to march directly to the aid of the beleaguered town
and provoke contact.

Leaving only sufficient men to deter a sally by hungry defenders, the English
withdrew from the siege lines to deploy on the south-facing slope of Halidon
Hill which rises some six hundred feet (183 metres) above sea-level, now neatly
bisected by the A6105, an ideal defensive site whose summit was crowned by
trees, with a bog at its base (see map two). Edward formed his knights and men-
at-arms into three divisions, or battles, drawn up in line with each battle flanked
by a contingent of archers; the right was commanded by Thomas, Earl of Norfolk,
the king led the centre, and Balliol took the left [50]. Douglas blundered onto the
field with the more numerous army, 1200 knights and men-at-arms with perhaps
13,500 spearmen, who were formed into four dense schlitrons.

His first brigade was commanded by John, Earl of Moray; the second nominally under David, the boy king, but in reality commanded by Sir James Stewart; the third by Douglas with the Earl of Carrick; and the last by Hugh, Earl of Ross. Attacking, apparently without pause for any tactical considerations, the Scots advanced down a gentle slope but lost all momentum, stumbling and thrashing through the mire, barely having time to dress ranks and begin lumbering up the slope towards the English when their archers began to shoot.

The English bowmen, those men 'of the grey goose feather', had practised since childhood to build their fearful skill and stamina. They were unique, world class, and properly deployed nigh on unbeatable. King Edward knew his trade. Calmly, methodically, volley after volley was loosed into the packed files, men dropping by the score, tussocks soon slippery with blood. We have no idea how terrible the arrow storm was. It didn't kill like a machine gun kills, no numbing shock of the bullet. Men were transfixed writhing, stuck with repeated shafts, shuddering, and screaming. After the dreadful toil of that fatal climb, the Scots never really came to grips. As the schlitrons wavered, Edward gave the order to mount, and the English knights swooped like falcons. The rout continued for five corpse-strewn miles.

Douglas paid for his blundering with his life, as did the Earls of Ross, Sutherland, and Carrick, hundreds of men-at-arms and thousands of spearmen. King Edward had proved to be a master tactician, combining lance and bow to near perfection and keeping his cavalry in reserve, to follow and capitalise upon success. No more balaklavering charges – this was very much an all-arms war machine. Berwick surrendered and English balladeers finally had reason to be cheerful: 'Scottes out of Berwick and out of Aberdeen/At the Burn of Bannock ye were far too keen/King Edward has avenged it now, and fully too I ween' [51]. Now Balliol enjoyed a second brief spree in charge, no more popular than the first. The Scots, though beaten, were not cowed and young King David was sent to safety in France. The puppet king danced to the same tune as his father, doing homage and ceding his acres on demand.

Resistance continued and Edward was forced to administer some more of the same medicine three years after Halidon Hill, laying waste as far as Lochindorb in Moray. In time the English king began to lose interest since his attention was focused more on his ambitions in France, where he would lead his armies to further legendary victories. The patriot cause received a significant boost with the defeat of the Balliol faction and the death of David of Strathbogie at the Battle of Culbean on 30 November 1335 [52].

NEVILLE'S CROSS

In 1341 King David returned from France, a young man of 17 but apparently deemed fit to rule in his own right. His reign was destined to be long yet far from happy. Any promise of his youth was dissipated by middle age and the 11 years (1346–1357) he'd be held captive in England. King Edward's obsession with France seemed to have spared Scotland but David, unwisely, responded to a plea from the hard-pressed King Philip to intervene on his behalf: 'A thousand and three hundred year/and six and forty thereto clear/the King of France set him to raise/the siege lying about Calais/and wrote in Scotland to our king/and made him right special praying/that he would make war on England ... Then King David/that was young stout and well-made/and yearned for to see fighting/agreed to fulfil his yearning/and gathered his host speedily' [53].

In the autumn of 1346, at the head of his army, David descended on Northumberland. Hexham and Lanercost were burnt and by 16 October the Scots had advanced as far south as Bearpark near Durham. King Philip naturally hoped that this harrying by the Scots would divert the King of England from his ambitions in France, but Edward was fortunate in his northern barons, Neville, and Percy, who were not intimidated. This would be the first major test for Edward's scheme of homeland defence and the northerners weren't about to let him down. Jean le Bel recounts how the Queen responded: 'As soon as the Queen of England heard the news, she went to Newcastle upon Tyne to give heart to her people there, and summoned the bishops, archbishops, and all the able-bodied men left in England to muster between the city of Durham and Northumberland, each of them with all the troops, archers and foot soldiers he could muster and as well armed and provisioned as he could manage' [54].

Obeying the Queen and under the aegis of the archbishop of York, the northern magnates were soon mustering at Bishop Auckland; by the morning of 17 October, they were on the march and intercepted a foraging party under Sir William Douglas some three miles north-west of the town. The Scots, wholly unprepared, departed with indecent haste. King David, whose scouting was clearly lax, only learnt they English were marching towards him when Douglas' survivors barged back into camp.

By this time the English, perhaps 15,000 strong, were deploying within sight of the Scots camp at Bearpark, along a low ridge running north to south, near to one of a series of ancient crosses that ringed the city of Durham, which was soon to be renamed Neville's Cross in honour of their commander, Ralph Neville. The ground fell quite gently towards the Scots position about two hundred feet (61 metres) below. Drawn up in their customary three battles with a body of archers in front, Henry Percy took the right; Neville the centre; and Sir Thomas Rokeby, aided by the spiritual guidance of the archbishop, commanded the left. Cannily, Neville deployed a mounted reserve under the irrepressible Balliol, concealed by a fold in the ground behind his line (see map three).

King David had the larger army, as many as 20,000, who advanced to contact, brigaded in three strong columns; Sir William Douglas, recovered from his unpleasant surprise, commanded the right, David led the centre, and Robert, the High Steward, took the left [55]. The ground wasn't suited to such cumbersome formations: Crossgate Moor, which the Scots were obliged to traverse, was split by a natural defile, and bisected by a deeper cut which deflected Douglas from his line of march towards the English left, echeloning his men into the king's division, the whole concentrated mass presenting a superb target for English longbows. Jean le Bel continues: 'The Battle was fought on a Tuesday around the hour of terce [around 09.00] and was as fierce and as mighty as any ever seen, with as many fine feats of prowess and bold ventures and valiant rescues as ever were made by Roland and Oliver... '[56].

English arrows sped death and confusion. Already the Scots were in trouble and made little headway on the right. Their left, under the Steward, fared better, driving hard against the English right, pushing back the screen of archers, and crashing into the infantry. The fight hung in the balance. On the embattled right of the English line sheer pressure of numbers began to tell. Edward Balliol, a seasoned fighter whatever else, chose his moment and with superb tactical skill launched his horsemen in a flank attack on the Steward's division, neatly tipping the scales and driving the Scots back in near rout.

With his left flank gone and his right a shambles the Scottish king's brigade was horribly isolated and the English, like wolves closing upon a wounded bear, hacked at his exposed spearmen. David, whose courage outweighed his judgement, fought superbly, rallying his faltering ranks, now almost encircled but bravery alone wasn't sufficient; the battle was soon lost and with 'lamentable slaughter' [57]. Tired, wounded, and dispirited, the king, now alone, was captured as he hid beneath the span of Aldin Grange Bridge: 'There John of Coupland took the king/by force, not yielding in the taking/the king two teeth out of his head/ with a blow of his knife him robbed' [58].

The loss of the king was a disaster for his country, and he remained a prisoner in the Tower for those 11 years whilst both sides haggled over his ransom. Edward Balliol enjoyed a final tenure as a vassal of England before King Edward finally pensioned him off [59]. The Scots were neither cowed nor passive and won a skirmish at Nesbit Hill, briefly recovering the town of Berwick though the castle remained in English hands. King Edward retaliated with vigour, laying waste Haddington and Edinburgh. By the Treaty of Berwick, signed on 3 October 1357, the captive king of the Scots was returned to his throne, at a cost of a hundred thousand marks, payable over ten years.

At last King David resumed his interrupted rule and reigned until his death 14 years later. His realm was in a relatively prosperous state, despite being wasted by near-continuous war and after 1348, by the horrors of the Black Death. The king's popularity waned; he never enjoyed an easy relationship with his magnates. In 1363, whilst visiting London and with the payments of his ransom hopelessly in arrears, he promised that should he die childless, his crown would pass to England. The Scottish Estates refused to ratify so unpalatable an undertaking, preferring to seek yet a further rescheduling. David died in February 1371 and was succeeded by the Steward as Robert II. The Stewart dynasty had begun.

CASTING THE MOULD

It could be said and indeed I and others would say that it was in this conflagration that the border character was forged. A generation of endemic warfare and the creation of a specialised breed of fighter, the hobiler, helped to create a class of uplanders on both sides of the line who were distinct and unique. In part this was due to circumstances and the seemingly endless round of devastation meted out by both polities but equally arose from a deliberate policy of plantation devised by Edward III.

After Halidon Hill and the creation of an English Pale in the Scottish borderland, Edward had no real interest in conquering Scotland as his grandfather had attempted. Like Agricola's 'suits' back in Rome, he probably realised that it couldn't be done and even if it could, the game, in accounting terms, just wasn't worth the candle. Besides, he had another throne in mind and this one was very much to play for. From his mother, the formidable 'She-Wolf', he'd inherited a claim to the throne of France. This would be disallowed by the French, but he'd be ready to take what was his by force of arms. This kicked off the Hundred Years War, broadening out Anglo-Scottish enmity into a wider conflict. Edward knew if he was to siphon off the cream of England's fighting men, he couldn't leave the back door open.

The border with Scotland must be secured and he wasn't about to adopt his father's blithe indifference to the fate of his northern subjects. They would be got ready but must also be ready to see to their own homeland defence. He wouldn't be disappointed. Times were bad anyway even without the Scots. There'd been famine in 1315 and for the next two years, perhaps 15 per cent of the local population had died [60]. The climate was changing; the medieval warm period (c. 800 – c. 1250) was ending, and the climate was becoming colder and wetter. Just drive through Upper Coquetdale and you'll see high medieval terracing sculpting the hills. That was farmed land before the shift, but you couldn't hope to plant there today.

There was worse, in 1348–1349 bubonic/pneumonic plague, the Black Death, reached Britain and spread from south to north. Nationally, mortality rates were between 40 to 50 percent. That was in more populous regions, it seems likely the borderlands, proportionately suffered less; how much less cannot be ascertained [61]. Such had been the nihilistic fury of Bruce's raiding campaign after Bannockburn that the upland dales had become virtually uninhabitable and there had clearly been a diaspora of kinds.

Re-stocking was needed, a breed of Pound-Land Samurai who would keep that back door closed. These would be hobilers and Edward was keen both to sustain those who'd clung on through the storm and to fill the many gaps with newcomers. These may have been, in Tynedale, the Charltons, Millburns and Dodds, though these families will always tell you they go back far further and wouldn't be seen off by any gang of rampaging Scotsmen [62]! Halls and Redes filtered back into Redesdale and these survivors might well be augmented by new recruits Hunter, Stamper, Wilkinson, and Yarrow appear in Tynedale, Potts, Forster and Fletcher in Redesdale [63].

At the same time existing feudal tenures were being converted into military holdings and offered at discounts, a form of plantation. Agriculture wasn't the lure; these lands would be held by the sword. The earlier depopulation was being countered by an increasing tempo of militarisation. Edward was, from the earlier chaos, forming a new kind of frontier society [64]. This was where the reivers sprang from, not by accident but policy. War did bring some dividends; a heap of beasts and booty went north during Bruce's hegemony along with blackmail and ransoms. Scottish borderers would have had their share. Armies for all the harm they did could bring dividends in terms of a market for supply, income generated by garrisons and building work on new or better fortifications [65]. Overall, the effects on both sides were negative; death, destruction and degradation were the real spoils of these wars [66].

Some writers have likened the border to a kind of frontier society – a British Wild West, where the circumstances of the rugged marchlands produced a strong degree of alienation from national government – 'we do things differently here'. There's widespread resentment at any level of government intermeddling and rampant criminality [67]. I think this is a false analogy. The frontiersman comes into a wilderness, generally not previously settled, except by indigenous peoples who tend not to count in his thinking. That was never the case here. The border had been settled since prehistory with, by the thirteenth century, a long tradition of settled Christian worship and monastic culture. It wasn't a frontier but had become a war zone and it was that violent dislocation and subsequent re-structuring that produced this wild borderland. Degradation of the key feudal component of good lordship when neither monarch nor magnate could shield their tenants led to a partial reconstruction based wholly on a concept of militarisation.

What was the key message in all this – very simple, you're on your own, get on with it and they did. A new society emerged, which was self-dependent, geared for raiding and war where what others might term criminality became the new norm, the default survival mode. New affinities based on family and blood with wider alliances of networking names and powerful marcher lords – the Percies, the Nevilles, the Umfravilles, and the Douglases – whose notions of lordship were counted in broadswords. It was a new world, not a nice one but it was all that could hope to maintain survival. The landscape of these wars was never going to be pretty.

Fiona Watson in her masterful study suggests, most persuasively, that Scots came to look on the era before Edward I's invasion as a 'supposed thirteenth century Scottish Golden Age ... the justification for the anti-English feeling which so often characterises public expressions of Scottish nationalism' [68]. Relying on a shared heritage of hatred for ancient enemies is not confined to Scotland and focusing internal dissent outwards towards a perceived national threat is a well-honed political tool. This year in which I'm writing marks the 40th anniversary of the Falklands War where a murderous military junta in Argentina tried to galvanise public support and defuse mounting opposition by attacking Britain. History shows that such actions, expedient at the time, can often backfire! Dr Watson does also issue a wise caveat by pointing out the overall paucity of records especially on the Scottish side [69]. She further and trenchantly points out that Robert Bruce was as adept at 'hybrid' warfare as he was effective on the battlefield, thoroughly trashing his limp predecessor and arch enemies the Comyns [70].

NOTES:

[1] Fisher, A., William Wallace (Edinburgh: John Donald, 1986), p. 19.

[2] Sir Herbert Maxwell of Monteith, Chronicles of Lanercost 1272-1346 (Glasgow: James MacLehose & Sons, 1913), pp. 115–118, it could be the chronicler may have exercised a degree of bias as the King seems generally not to have been noted for his alleged licentiousness, see Reid, N. H., 'Alexander III; the Historiography of a Myth', in Scotland in the Reign of Alexander III 1249 – 1286 (Edinburgh: John Donald, 1990), p. 218.

[3] Kingsford, C. L., ed., The Song of Lewes (Oxford: Clarendon Press, 1890).

[4] This was a much later addition to Longshank's CV.

[5] Morris, M., Edward I – a Great and Terrible King (London: Random House, 2008), p. 78.

[6] Ibid., p. 241.

[7] Ibid.

[8] The entire panel of jurors totalled over a hundred with lengthy delays to allow aspirants to work up their claims – such delays also helped Edward consolidate his grip.

[9] Bower, W., Scotichronicon, ed. D. E. R. Watt (Edinburgh: John Donald, 2012), Book XI, p. 183.

[10] In that battle, he carried captured banners taken from the Montfortians during his earlier raid on Kenilworth.

[11] Scotichronicon, Book XI, p. 183.

[12] These were new 'model' towns set out in a regular grid pattern. The best surviving example is Monpazier.

[13] Scotichronicon, Book XI, p. 184.

[14] Ridpath, op. cit., p. 129.

[15] Bon besoigne fait qui de merde se delivrer.

[16] Blind Harry, The Wallace, ed. A. McKim (Michigan: Medieval Institute Publications, 2003), Book II, p. 281 & Ridpath, op. cit., p. 142.

[17] Scotichronicon, Book XI, p. 186.

[18] Mackay, J., Braveheart (Edinburgh: Mainstream, 1995), pp. 105–113; the unlucky woman was Marian Braidfute, daughter of Hugh Braidfute of Lamington.

[19] Murray succumbed to injuries received at Stirling.

[20] Ridpath, op. cit., p. 144.

[21] Fisher, op. cit., p. 55.

[22] Barrow, G. W. S., Robert Bruce (Los Angeles: University of California Press, 1965), pp. 206–208.

[23] Ibid., pp. 275–276.

[24] Ibid., p. 245.

[25] Ibid., pp. 290–296.

[26] Prestwich, M., Armies and Warfare in the Middle Ages (London: Yale University Press, 1996), p. 58.

[27] Lomas, R., County of Conflict: Northumberland from Conquest to Civil War (East Lothian: Tuckwell Press, 1996), p. 58.

[28] Barbour, J., The Bruce (Edinburgh: Canongate, 2007), p. 94.

[29] Scotichronicon, Book XIII, p. 211.

[30] Lomas, op. cit., p. 41.

[31] Ibid.

[32] Ibid., p. 42.

[33] Ibid., p. 43.

[34] Ibid., p. 43.

[35] Ibid., p. 44.

[36] Ridpath, op. cit., p. 148.

[37] Bates, C. J., History of Northumberland (London: Elliott Stock, 1895), p. 156.

[38] Sadler, D. J., Border Fury (Harlow: Longmans/Pearson, 2004), p. 148.

[39] Ridpath, op. cit., p. 197.

[40] Robson, R., The Rise and Fall of the English Highland Clans (Edinburgh: John Donald, 1989), p. 34.

[41] 'Barded' = caparisoned.

[42] Sadler, op. cit., pp. 169–170.

[43] The True Chronicles of Jean le Bel, translated by N. Bryant (Woodbridge: the Boydell Press, 2011), Chapter X, p. 40.

[44] Ibid.

[45] Ridpath, op. cit., p. 197.

[46] Lynch, op. cit., pp. 128–131.

[47] Scotichronicon, Book XIII, p. 217.

[48] Oman, Sir, C., A History of the Art of War in the Middle Ages, vol. 2 (London: Greenhill, 1924), p. 103.

[49] Ridpath, op. cit., p. 209.

[50] Oman, op. cit., p. 106.

[51] Ibid.

[52] David III Strathbogie, titular earl of Atholl, was one of Edward Balliol's most important adherents, his defeat and death is regarded as the last significant event in the 2nd Scottish War of Independence.

[53] Jean le Bel, Chapter LXXVI, p. 189.

[54] Ibid., Chapter LXXVI, p. 189.

[55] Scotichronicon, Book XIV, p. 229.

[56] Jean le Bel, Chapter LXXVI, p. 189.

[57] Scotichronicon, Book XIV, p. 230.

[58] Wyntoun, p. 187.

[59] Balliol finally gave up in 1356 and assigned his right to Edward III who, by then, had clearly decided a captive David II was the better bet.

[60] Lomas, op. cit., p. 69

[61] Ibid., pp. 70–71.

[62] Robson, op. cit., p. 34.

[63] Ibid.

[64] Lomas, op. cit., p. 35.

[65] Aydon Castle rising entrancingly above the Cor Burn near Corbridge is a fine example of successive waves of building up-grading the defences.

[66] Macdonald, A. J., Border Bloodshed – Scotland and England at War 1369–1403 (East Linton: Tuckwell Press, 2000), pp. 197–198.

[67] Ibid., p. 200.

[68], Watson, F., Under the Hammer (East Linton: Tuckwell Press 1998), p. 1.

[69] Ibid., p. 4.

[70] Ibid.

CHAPTER THREE: CHEVY CHASE

'For deer to hunt and slay/ and see them bleed/ any hardship adds to his courage/ and In his mind he takes heed/ imagining taking them by surprise/ aged sixteen years to wage war/ to joust and ride with castles to assail/ to skirmish and to scourge/ and setting watches for nightly perils'.

John Hardyng

Young Harry Percy, who the Scots were to christen 'Hotspur', has a mixed reputation. In his day he was the ideal beau sabreur though Shakespeare paints him as hot-headed and reckless. He probably wasn't [1] but he could be capricious, arrogant, and cruel. He would be catapulted from the training ground to the battlefield at a frighteningly early age, as severe a testing as can be imagined and whatever is said of Hotspur, he passed the test and kept on passing. To achieve this, he had to be bred to it, the sum of all his ancestors' parts. Harry Percy lived in an age harsher than our worst imagining, for gentleman and commoner alike. Death was a constant companion, an everyday occurrence, even without endemic warfare.

ROARING NORTHERNERS

Richard of Bordeaux, on his accession at a dangerously young age, appeared to inherit a measure of stability, though this soon proved a chimera. Edward III had consolidated his northern border with a string of brilliant successes, topped by that resounding triumph of the Northern English at Neville's Cross in October

1346 which netted King David II of Scotland amongst the spoils. The subsequent establishment of a buffer zone throughout southern Scotland, the 'Pale', shielded the north from raids and indeed the years immediately after Neville's Cross marked an era of relative prosperity.

Border violence never went away. It simply oscillated, from all out relentless interstate war to magnatial quarrels and low-level endemic thievery from the riding names. In many cases lords behaved no better than common reivers but aristocratic thuggery was wont to be enacted on a larger scale and had a consequentially more de-stabilising effect. The later Percy/Neville feud of the mid-fifteenth century is a good example; this not only affected the region but had national implications. Hotspur's father married a Neville, but the rivalry remained, though not yet marred by violence.

Hostilities along the line were intricately linked to events in France. The English performance across the Channel formed a barometer for events in the north. France's recovery was Scotland's opportunity. A lull or truce in France implied a backing off along the border. Subtle strategists like George Dunbar (see below) saw the value in stealth while maximising the shield offered by England's difficulties abroad. By 1369, this English grip, the 'Pale' was largely confined to three bulging salients. In the west, like a fat finger pointing north from the Solway and taking in Annandale, the Pale here had Lochmaben very nearly at its apex. Teviotdale, in the centre, was mainly under English influence with important centres and castles such as Hawick, Kelso, Roxburgh, and Jedforest holding garrisons. It was the same with most of the Merse, from Berwick to the rise of the Lammermuirs, with gaunt and lonely Fast Castle in the north-east and prosperous Coldingham just to the south [2].

These tracts weren't delineated on any map, instead they were zones of influence rather than hard occupation. Castles were manned and held but control was limited according to who was in the ascendancy at any one time. Locals were compliant only if they were intimidated or bribed, and powerful Scottish lords who'd been alienated, such as the Douglases, hovered on the edges awaiting their chance. Weakness was corrosive. As the old king of England slid into the abyss of enfeebling senility, his strong hand and that of his equally enfeebled eldest son, the Black Prince, slackened their collective grip. The Pale began to contract, shrinking by bite-sized chunks. A handy reference is the Berwick Chamberlain's accounts which detail rents received from lands under control. The entry for 1369–1370 refers to nine manors no longer held, and the next year's returns speak of another two which have just been lost [3].

Despite his humiliation on the battlefield and years of incarceration, David II remained something of an Anglophile. He shared Edward III's obsession with chivalry and bore no grudge against his captors, staying on cordial terms with England until his death, at a relatively early age, in 1371 [4]. This doesn't imply he was blind to opportunities and if he did not overtly support the hawks, neither did he hinder them from flying. His successor Robert II, not a direct heir as David died childless, has often had a poor press; he has been seen as rather weak and ineffective, with his royal power undermined by aggressive magnates. He had plenty of these, but a revisionist view suggests the king was adept in channelling their ardour while appearing to keep a safe distance. Allowing George Dunbar to maintain an active front against the Pale worked well for both and avoided provoking large-scale English retaliation.

It got worse. In 1372, the unthinkable occurred, England was defeated at sea. A Castilian squadron beat the earl of Pembroke's ships at La Rochelle, and he was captured. King Robert then moved to renew the old Franco-Scottish alliance and his policy began to harden; there were reservations over the payment of the outstanding balance of King David's ransom. By now Scots were aware that their powerful friend used them as allies of convenience, a handy distraction against England, one that had led them to disaster at Neville's Cross. Though they might want to damage England, Scots were increasingly aware French aid could carry a hefty price tag. This would rather come to a head during the invasion of 1385 when the two found out not only that they had quite different tactical objectives, but a vastly different cultural outlook.

One of the prime players who'd play a major role as presiding genius during this Risorgimento, was George Dunbar 10th Earl of Dunbar and March 12th Lord of Annandale, titular Lord of the Isle of Man. Machiavelli would have loved George Dunbar, a brilliant general of marvellous fluidity. He understood that meeting the English head on was a path to catastrophe. His predecessors' failures at Dupplin Moor, Halidon Hill, and Neville's Cross, not to mention the many reverses of their French allies, had shown that all too clearly, all too many times. He too would adopt a subtle, Fabian strategy, clawing back, piece by piece, the whole of the English Pale, mirroring Robert Bruce's successful campaigns in the lead up to Bannockburn. Attrition, something the French when in Scotland during the 1385 campaign signally failed to appreciate, was a far surer policy than confrontation. Staying below the radar conferred pain-free dividends.

Dunbar would be partnered with James Douglas, 2nd Earl Douglas, the son of William, 1st Earl Douglas, who in 1371 (or 1373) married Isabel, daughter of King Robert. There is a mirror reflecting on Douglas and Percy; 'Two households, both alike in dignity/ From ancient grudge break to new mutiny ...' On the Scottish side the rise of the House of Douglas seemed equally inexorable. Jamie 'Black' Douglas had been the Achilles of Bruce's wars – formidable, clever, bold, and ruthless; a dark hero for a dark time. Still, his family's rivalry with Percy wasn't any chivalric contest but a more mundane matter of real property, dear to any magnate's heart.

It concerned lawful possession of Jedburgh and Jedforest, a grand swathe of territory stretching from Teviot Water to Carter Bar. King Robert had granted this to Jamie Douglas, but a year after his major win at Halidon Hill in 1333, Edward III handed the whole lot to Henry Lord Percy II and the family had enjoyed possession since Neville's Cross. Continuing English hegemony had ensured Percies remained in occupation, but Douglas didn't have to like it. Honour and flying pennons may be the stuff of romantic legend, but control of profitable acres was what counted. It is certainly possible there was some periodic sparring on the ground between Douglas and Percy retainers.

On 16 February 1373, an English commission was appointed to investigate; the Scots were requested to do the same and this commission renewed its brief the following year [5]. As ever on the marches, national policy was inextricably linked to local interest to the extent the tail frequently appears to have been wagging the dog. Edward III, even if he was past his prime, saw this and appointed non-marchers to his commission [6]. For the Douglases, clawing back Jedforest was both a personal and national cause. They wanted to recover what they believed to be theirs which had, as a bonus, the effect of further shaking the English grip. Meanwhile, Henry Percy had no intention of letting go.

Just to set the tone of relations, Lord Percy, Hotspur's father, had had a bruising encounter with Dunbar in the summer of 1370. He'd been appointed Governor of both Berwick and Roxburgh on attaining his majority, so was in charge when a fracas erupted at the annual fair. Drink was usually a factor and both sides tanked up liberally. In the ensuing scrap, the Scots were bested and several of Dunbar's retainers lay among the dead when the smoke cleared. The Scottish earl appealed to Percy as castellan for redress but got none. A bad man to disappoint, he led a big raid against the English West March, dragging back livestock and hostages. Percy retaliated and took a large force over the border to even the score. He got as far as Duns. Hector Boece says he commanded seven thousand mainly mounted fighters. Dunbar, canny as ever, appears to have resorted to what would now be classed as psychological warfare ('psy-ops') by creating such a nocturnal racket that the English horses broke free and bolted in fear, shortly followed by their owners [7]!

Marchers, on both sides of the border, had finely attuned antennae, essential for continued survival. While there had been some element of stability during the couple of decades before 1369, a sense that the mood was shifting and that the bad old days were firmly on their way back quickly surfaced. If this English

Pale was finally and fully eliminated, then the northern frontier was once again a frontline. Those terrible years after Bannockburn would not have been forgotten. This new paradigm ushered in a spate of frantic building and rebuilding. John of Gaunt undertook a phase of further construction at his great northern fortress of Dunstanburgh, a key coastal redoubt. Lochmaben, Berwick, and Bamburgh received extensive makeovers, as did a slew of manorial castles and towers.

For a short time, mid-decade, hostilities cooled as a putative ceasefire between England and France appeared possible. The Scots took heed, all too aware that France wouldn't hesitate to sacrifice their interest if expediency dictated. In fact, there was no rapprochement likely, the French were just buying time to restock their arsenals and allow their able and energetic admiral John de Vienne to construct a fleet of galleys copying the specifications that had worked so well for Castile. It was still very much game on and this game, from the borderers' perspective, would continue for 30 years. It would be Hotspur's inheritance, his proving ground and it would be he who, in 1402, brought this Scottish renaissance crashing down.

That was a long way off in 1377; the future paladin was only 13, though he'd soon be playing his part. But that year saw a significant shift in the scale of activity along the border and it was the Scots, orchestrated by Dunbar, who were making the running [8]. Historians debate whether this upsurge reflected crown policy or just George Dunbar forcing the pace, perhaps a shaded combination of both, with the Scottish earl in the driving seat.

It's surely no coincidence that this offensive was timed to capitalise on a further deterioration in Anglo-French relations. Sir John Gordon, Scotland's new Achilles, got the better of an English contingent at Carham and captured its captain, Sir John Lilburn. Gaunt came north again with a significant array and again achieved remarkably little. As Froissart perhaps flippantly but correctly comments, 'Scotland was the place in the world whereby England might be most annoyed' [9]. To add further injury Thomas Musgrave, keeper of Berwick, was captured along with his grandson by the hyper-active Gordon that same summer [10].

As Alistair Macdonald points out, this was a palpable shift away from a previously almost unbroken line of English successes [11]. Lands were wasted and renders declined, and consequently a revival of that dark spectre of Bruce's hegemony loomed. This time it would be different. Edward III's forward policy and his canny re-stocking of Northumberland's upland dales with good fighting stock had forged a new race, those hobilers. There'd be no easy pickings this time around.

Just as his father had been mentored by Henry of Grosmont [12], the 9-year-old Hotspur followed his parent to France. Part of a knight's education was to witness war at first hand. He would have been learning all about the theory but there's no school like harsh reality. Imbued as he clearly was by notions of chivalry, what he saw in France would have been hugely different. This brand of campaigning proceeded by frightfulness, terrorism as we'd call it today, pillage and destruction on a grand scale trying to impress or at least cow the French. This was, on a grander scale, like his future apprenticeship in border warfare, where brutal reality was the name of the game.

Knighthood wasn't just about skill at arms and derring-do, it was a practical military induction. On campaign in France, the boy would learn to comprehend the necessities of war rather than the frills; logistics and concentration, the real sinews of conflict, mastery of which mattered as much as tactical skill or strategic purpose. Command of subordinates, liaison with allies, control of supply, the politics of leadership, who to trust, who to advance, who to be wary of, who to listen to and ponder, who to hear out but ignore. It was unfortunate that the commander-in-chief – John of Gaunt came into the latter category.

Young Henry's mother was a Neville, a marriage alliance was about as close as you can keep your enemies and while there was no sign of any real feud between these two magnatial families emerging, they both wanted to be cocks of their particular midden. As a taste of things to come, the future Hotspur's introduction to Continental warfare was none too inspiring. He arrived at the fag-end of English hegemony, which was crumbling at an alarming rate, exposing fully Gaunt's weaknesses as generalissimo. There'd be no return to the glory days, with all those lovely ransoms and juicy fiefdoms, England was now in full retreat.

De Fonblanque tells us that Percy crossed over to France early in the new year after the debacle at Duns but was soon back on the Anglo-Scottish border and just as soon back in the saddle. In his absence the Scots had taken another crack at Roxburgh and smashed the town up. Percy retaliated against the lands of firebrand Sir John Gordon which prompted yet more tit for tat [13]. Younger Henry was getting a balanced and fruitful introduction to the realities of cross-border violence twinned with the liberal application of 'frightfulness' by both sides. This would be his arena, and on this terrain his legend would take root.

All the chroniclers agree that this was war without pity or, for that matter, much in the way of honour. For those in the south this was just an uncouth, largely forgotten frontier. This present bout wasn't just low-level cross-border raiding, but activity openly encouraged and led by the leading magnates, unrestrained by royal authority on either side. This was war with hate, short-term gain, and revenge as the principal motivations, though, from the Scottish side, Dunbar was steadily nibbling away at the Pale and whittling down those vestiges of English hegemony.

Meanwhile, the inexorable waning of Gaunt's star rebounded on Percy. Military failure abroad, coupled by high taxation to fund it, fuelled a swelling public discontent which focused on Lancaster. Some suspected that as the old King weakened and as his son was visibly dying, Gaunt might hope to supplant his nephew Richard of Bordeaux. When, in April 1376, the 'Good Parliament' met, more than a whiff of reform was in the air. Despite his closeness to the now generally despised John of Gaunt, Henry Percy was appointed as a commissioner to promote and facilitate this reforming process which naturally now stood him in the opposite corner to his former comrade-in-arms.

It was the ailing Black Prince who did his younger sibling an inestimable service of dying, thus creating a void that Gaunt alone could fill. By this timely demise, the Duke of Lancaster regained his seat at the head of the constitutional table and Parliament, which assembled in January 1377, proved far more pliant. Percy, by this point, had earned his marshal's baton and succeeded in hanging on to it. By now, he was firmly back in Gaunt's camp and looking forward to becoming an earl, the next step up the baronial ladder, far higher than any his ancestors, however diligent and illustrious, had attained.

Then Percy blundered. He espoused the cause of the heretic John Wyclif [14]. This was strong stuff, but he was just echoing Gaunt's own stance, so we can safely assume clerical reform wasn't necessarily a cause dear to his heart. Percy's brand of magnatial thuggery didn't suit theological debate, however heated, and he snarled at the bishops in full street-fighting mode. Walsingham, no friend of Gaunt's and therefore by association not one of Northumberland's partisans, was outraged. Both Henry Percy and John of Gaunt had misread the general mood which their high-handedness had merely stoked. Percy's town house on Aldersgate was sacked, an unlucky priest, mistaken for him in disguise was murdered [15], followed by more larceny at Gaunt's sumptuous Savoy Palace. The time for braggadocio had passed and both had to run for their lives. Happily, the Princess of Wales, with whom they'd sought refuge, interceded on her uncle's behalf and the danger subsided. Still, Percy had seriously damaged his standing.

If his father's star had slipped from its stellar orbit, that of his son, young Harry Percy, was about to rise. At age 13 he was knighted by the ageing king at Windsor that April. Kneeling with him were Richard of Bordeaux, soon to be King Richard II, and Gaunt's own son Henry Bolingbroke. The lives of these three youths were to be inextricably entwined thereafter. Two would be kings, one a kingmaker and one the death of both the others. Harry's younger siblings, Thomas, and Ralph, were also dubbed, yet within two months Edward III would be dead and Richard of Bordeaux the new sovereign.

John of Gaunt now came into his own, neatly sweeping his past failures under the carpet and ensuring his loyal pal Henry Percy profited from steadfast loyalty. On 15 July 1377, Lord Percy was elevated to his long-coveted earldom. He had finally arrived. This time round he bathed himself in humility, no more swaggering, well not that much anyway. The new earl continued to fill the office of Marshal of England, though not strictly his to perform much to the vociferous annoyance of the earl of Norfolk's eldest daughter Margaret. This was embarrassing; it ill-behoved Percy to assume offices that weren't his and he was glad to depart rapidly for less troubled waters on the borders. Less troubled politically, but George Dunbar had drunk the young king's health in the flames of Roxburgh.

BLOODING AT BERWICK

Inadvertently, the wily Scot had helped dig his adversary out of the hole and Percy returned the compliment with interest, spurring over the line for a three-day spree of arson. Ridpath tells us he 'entered Scotland at the head of 10,000 men and during the space of three days ravaged the lands of the earl of March' [16]. His service didn't go unnoticed and before the year was out, he'd been appointed warden of both East and West Marches. He and Lord Neville, a formidable partnership when working in harmony, attempted to broker some form of lasting truce. Despite their best efforts the frontier stayed ticklish; in November 1378 Berwick was targeted.

Great border valleys such as those of the Tweed, Teviot, Till, and Eden are deeply fertile, some of the best farming land in Europe. The Tweed marked the border as it had done since that black day of the Northumbrian clergy at Carham in 1018. Later, after Longshanks, Berwick upon Tweed became a frontier post or bastide guarding the English East March. It used to be Scottish in character (to this day it still is and I'm part native), taken and retaken till 1482 when Richard of Gloucester, (he of car-park fame), took it back for, up till now, the last time.

Originally, the castle stood beyond the medieval enceinte on the far bank of the river, where it was very exposed to attack. Though held by the English, the Scots constantly desired to repossess the place. The mere sight of the Cross of St. George fluttering over battlements was an insult and a goad. It had been English again since Halidon Hill but as the Scots began to gobble up the various enclaves making up the English Pale, Berwick became increasingly vulnerable. Despite the place's signal importance, the walls were sadly neglected and in disrepair. France had taken priority in the old king's time and England's treasury echoed bare.

'About this time, in fact on the Thursday next before the feast of St. Andrew the Apostle [30 November], some brigands from the March of the Scottish King [probably led by John Hogg and Alexander Ramsay] secretly entered the castle of

Berwick by night, making use of a door in one of the towers, and coming upon Sir Robert Boynton, the constable of the castle, unawares, they killed that brave soldier on the spot. They did allow his wife and sons and some of their household to leave the castle on condition that they either paid them three thousand marks within three weeks or otherwise gave themselves up to captivity. Then the next day these robbers went out and ravaged the neighbouring countryside …' [17].

Fordun asserts the original commando was only seven strong, 'desperate fellows' – Leighert, Artwood, Grey, Hog, Hempsede, a Jack de Fordun and led, inevitably, by Sir John Gordon. Once they'd taken the place, they opened the doors to a larger reinforcement and command devolved to Alexander Ramsay [26]. While this might seem like a classic case of private enterprise, the prevailing sentiment locally was that the Scottish nobility were behind it, and certainly this kind of caper was just up Dunbar's street. Percy may well have thought so too as he wasted no time in pulling together a posse 400 strong [18] and laying siege to his pilfered castle.

The earl brought up an array of timber-framed siege engines and pelted the walls without respite. Ridpath tells us the siege lasted eight days and the earl deployed 7,000 archers backed by 3,000 hobilers (a suspiciously large number, we should probably move the decimal point on both). He was supported by lords Neville, Lucy, and Stafford [19]. Hotspur was only 14 but already a knight and we can assume he was more than ready to prove himself worthy. Young Harry raised his banner in front of the main gate, while Sir Alan Heron, Sir Thomas Ilderton, and the Heron retinue covered the other flanks, ready for a general assault.

Despite the fury of the bombardment, these hardy Scots weren't in the least cowed, since they probably realised their chances of obtaining mercy were limited. For two hours they held their attackers at bay, doggedly defending broken walls. Resistance finally collapsed as Walsingham records; English assault parties all broke through at the same moment. According to the chronicler, the Northumbrians got off very lightly with only two killed and few wounded. Four dozen Scots were accounted for, 'trampled on and finished off with the sword' [20]. Three survivors were spared for 'interrogation' then probably dealt with afterwards. Walsingham waxes quite lyrical over the destruction of these intruders but the fight was clearly a dangerous beginning for Hotspur, crowned with victory and, if the chronicler is credible, one quite cheaply bought.

Harry Percy had had his baptism of fire; he was no longer a trainee but had graduated to fully fledged practitioner in the art of war. It was a good beginning, and the start of a reputation that would swell into legend on a frontier where standards were harsh and accolades awfully hard to come by. For his father the earl, this was a good job well done. He'd left any embarrassments in London behind him and smitten the young king's enemies with a flaming rod of iron. From now on though, this was to be a family concern, father and son, open for business, as we'd say now 24/7.

Northumberland had written to George Dunbar accusing him of being party to this seizure which the slippery Scot promptly denied. He even appeared before the besieged walls as honest broker demanding the defenders hand the place back. Nobody was surprised when they refused [21]. Later, when Walsingham is writing of a cross-Channel expedition in 1386, he mentions the younger Percy's nickname 'Hotspur' – not as one given to him by his own people but rather from his Scottish opponents: '… a young man who was a shining example of all goodness and military prowess … And indeed, previously as governor of the town of Berwick, he had compelled that completely restless race, the Scots to take a rest and had often worn them out by his own eager restlessness. So, in their own language they called this Henry "Hotspur"' [22]. Catchy, and it would stick, Hotspur would blazon as the very embodiment of chivalry.

His youthful triumph in storming Berwick Castle was followed just over a year later, 10 December 1379 by his marriage to Elizabeth Mortimer. This was an advantageous union, even by expansionist Percy standards, as the nine-year-old girl was the daughter of Edmund Mortimer, English Earl of March. These were great marcher lords from the frontier of Wales, and she was related, on her mother's side, to Edward III's second son Lionel Duke of Clarence. It was a promising match but ultimately the Mortimer connection would, at least in part, be Hotspur's undoing [23].

As the new decade of the 1380s opened, the earl of Northumberland devolved increasing responsibilities onto his eldest son which Hotspur embraced at the gallop. In 1381 young Harry was the judge in a trial by combat between the Scot John Chattowe and his English opponent William de Badby, which was held at Liliot's Cross (a regular location for days of Truce in Teviotdale). This was serious business for a 17-year-old [24]. But his father, the earl, was about to fall out with his old mucker John of Gaunt as well as with his Neville in laws. That infamous Percy temper would get him into serious hot water, again.

Just before the great boil of popular discontent in England burst, Lancaster had again come north with an army to deal with the Scots. At Berwick late that autumn he met the bishops of Glasgow and Dunkeld, together with the earls of Douglas and Dunbar. It was provided that the Duke, as befitting his rank, would meet with the heir to the Scottish throne, the earl of Carrick (the future Robert III). It rather seems, or so his contemporaries thought, that the wily Scots, surely orchestrated by the very wily Dunbar, ran rings round Gaunt, 'no advantage was gained from this formidable expedition … which is said to have cost the public

11,000 marks' [25]. Gaunt's attention had already turned to his proposed Spanish adventure (see below). The talks with Carrick at Ayton in fact produced nothing more substantial than a series of phased extensions to the truce [26]. This was very soon to be the least of John of Gaunt's worries and he'd shortly be seeing the earl of Carrick again but in vastly different circumstances.

REVOLTING PEASANTS

Walter Bower took a dim view of rebellious commoners: '... nothing is crueller than a poor man when he rises high. And for that reason, as soon as they have risen in revolt, they must be subdued lest they get the upper hand. As Jerome says: Kill your enemy while he is young, so that his villainy is crushed as a seed' [27]. When the explosion occurred, the mob's main fury was directed at Gaunt, 'there was no person among those more hateful to the rabble than the duke of Lancaster whom they regarded as the chief author of their oppression' [28].

Lancaster and Percy had sheltered together during the backlash following Wyclif's inquisition and the duke was again in everybody's sights. Earl Percy was safe in Northumberland but denied old Gaunt sanctuary when he begged for it. No doubt he feared being dragged into the mire, but this does seem both petty and spiteful and his refusal would have consequences. At the time that disturbances broke out in the south and Gaunt's opulent Savoy Palace was torched, the duke himself was also in the north where he'd been negotiating with Dunbar at Berwick, irritating Percy, who was not used to playing second fiddle.

Shunned by his old friend, he craved asylum across the border and wrote, presumably in desperation, to the earl of Carrick. Sensing a fortuitous opportunity to win friends, the Scot agreed, 'and sent Sir William earl of Douglas and Archibald de Douglas lord of Galloway with an honourable following to accompany him on his journey from the borders to Scotland ...' [29]. The duke was safely and comfortably housed in Edinburgh till the storm abated. For the Scots, this generous hospitality was a sound investment, Gaunt would now be in their debt. Cannily, Dunbar refrained from seeking any military advantage from the confusion in southern England, Gaunt's goodwill was a greater prize. Both Carrick and Dunbar showed far more finesse than Northumberland whose silly hubris would massively alienate Lancaster and lead Percy back into dangerous waters.

Just to pile on the insults when he tried to return to England through the bastide at Berwick, Gaunt found to his redoubled fury that Percy had one last spiteful trick to play. Northumberland had instructed his castellan, Matthew Redmayne, to deny access to any coming in from Scotland and the governor interpreted this to the letter. Gaunt was shut out [30]! This was foolish, petty, schoolyard stuff, a silly gaffe Percy's subtle brother would never have made. And like Percy, Gaunt knew how to bear a grudge. He didn't have long to wait. When matters had calmed and he was back in control, the king, at his suggestion, invited Northumberland to a grand feast at Berkhamsted where the duke wasted no time in flinging accusations, accusing Northumberland of overreaching himself in denying him, Lancaster, entry to England.

No doubt Percy's smoother brother Thomas could have found some oil to pour on these troubled waters, but Henry Percy rose to the bait. More harsh words followed and there was nearly a brawl. Percy had to be restrained and was briefly arrested. The feud festered [31]. Unhappily for Northumberland, Lancaster had the perfect ally to hand in John Neville. Percy's rise had been Neville's eclipse, but he stayed loyal to Lancaster and indeed would remain so right up to and including the Shrewsbury campaign 20 odd years later. This spark of enmity would reach its apogee in the 1450s and climax in the fracas on St. Albans' blood-slicked cobbles in April 1455.

Gaunt now began to favour Neville and their testing ground became a contest for the march wardenry. As we saw, this means of trying to keep order on the borders had been established as early as 1249, when both monarchies agreed that the border should be divided into districts or marches [32] (two a side at this point). From 1297 these territories were controlled judicially and militarily by the march wardens. It was their duty to see that peace was maintained, to administer justice and to deal with 'bills' or complaints. Backed up by a staff of deputies, captains, and troopers, they tried with varying degrees of success to administer good law, but in doing so would frequently create personal enemies (some were murdered [33]) and further bitterness between already bellicose riding names. In short, they frequently caused more problems than they solved and most certainly did not implement peace and safety for the marchers. For magnates such as Percy or Neville, these roles were the principal building blocks for their regional affinities.

In 1381 the existing truce with Scotland still had three years to run but during the previous year Percy, used to having a free hand, was raising a posse of 120 men-at-arms with 200 archers to take revenge for a Scottish raid, pretty much business as usual, the truce notwithstanding. Enter Gaunt once again, who had himself nominated as King's Lieutenant on the marches. This put him directly in charge of Percy who didn't much enjoy having his wings so publicly clipped. The prickly earl saw this as a sneering tap on the shoulder by his former comrade, a personal affront. Hence, the knee-jerk reaction when Gaunt, in desperation, came banging on his door. The rebuff might have felt good, but it was a political blunder of seismic magnitude.

After the quarrel at Berkhamsted Percy found himself briefly confined while Neville, as the smiling assassin scooped a major prize, sole wardenship of the east march. The earl still had friends while Gaunt had few and Percy avoided gaol. His reinstatement hadn't made Lancaster any more effective as a politician, nor had the chastening experience of the Peasant's Revolt produced any miraculous conversion to humility. Percy did pick up a consolation prize, wardenry of the emerging middle march. This brief wasn't yet fully defined; the three-march system wouldn't properly emerge till the next century, but it was better than nothing. In the spring of 1382, Percy and Neville were jointly appointed as wardens for both East and West Marches.

Gaunt might have done best to let the vendetta he was stoking fizzle out, but he wasn't through yet and next year Neville netted both posts endowed with a handsome annuity. Percy was relegated to subordinate and Gaunt kept up his interference in border affairs. As he'd previously undertaken with Carrick, Gaunt met the Scottish prince at Liliot's Cross during the early days of July 1383. It was a cordial meeting, Lancaster had cause to remember his opposite number's kindness and the truce was extended. It was even hoped that a more lasting accord between the kings of both realms could be brokered but again Gaunt was being led. Robert II was already in correspondence with Charles VI of France to launch a second front on the border. There were no free lunches where cross-border politics were concerned.

When the existing truce expired in February 1384, it all kicked off again with the Scots successfully seizing Lochmaben Castle and hi-jacking a fat supply convoy en route to Roxburgh. Naturally, it was Lancaster who insisted on leading the charge. His new chevauchee lasted a fortnight and achieved no more than any of the others. In fairness, he was in a delicate position, he could hardly torch Edinburgh, the city which had earlier offered him such much needed respite: 'About Easter the duke of Lancaster invaded Scotland and embraced the opportunity he had given him of showing his gratitude for the hospitable reception he had met with at Edinburgh three years before by sparing that city when he had it in his power to destroy it' [34].

Now, Gaunt was back in his saviours' realm with fire and sword. Nonetheless, Bower deals charitably with him at this point, insisting the Duke minimised the damage his countrymen inflicted out of respect for the kindness and courtesy shown to him when he was on the run four years before, 'he imposed as little harm as he could' [35]. More, we might suspect, by good luck than kindness Bower's own Abbey of St. Columba of Inchcolm, in the Firth of Forth, was spared immolation, even though the place was thoroughly looted [36].

While the duke sojourned in the Scottish capital, Douglas stuck back, grabbing most of Teviotdale. As Andrew Boardman points out, once Gaunt had played at being a general, now it was left to the wardens to plug the gaps. The pendulum swung back, with Lancaster's farce becoming Northumberland's overture. He recovered the governorship of both Berwick and Carlisle, netted £4,000 to charge his war chest, neatly trumped Neville for control of Roxburgh, the surviving key bastion of the shrinking English Pale. Just to cap it all, Percy managed to recover the wardenship of both marches [37]. Neville was again on the back foot. In May 1385 Hotspur took over from his father. This was very much the family business, and he was deemed responsible enough to look after the silver.

Meanwhile, Berwick was back in the news as the Scots pulled off a second coup. This time they relied on corruption rather than brute force, but it was equally embarrassing for Northumberland. Lancaster couldn't believe his luck, here was a mighty big stick to beat Percy with. And he did. The earl was accused of treason, arraigned, and convicted in absentia, his lands and probably his neck forfeit. Luckily for the House of Percy, Northumberland was quick on his feet, swiftly bought off the Scots and recovered the castle. He was immediately pardoned, despite Lancaster's shrill cries of protest [38]. It had to be that the young king was beginning to find his overbearing uncle's intermeddling tiresome.

One tricky matter still outstanding was the residue of King David II's ransom. After he'd been negligent enough to get captured at Neville's Cross, Scotland was burdened with the huge debt due to England's coffers. Hotspur, together with both his father and Lord Neville, was dispatched to settle the thorny matter of arrears. In 1385, the younger Percy was appointed governor of Berwick, a more peaceful arrangement than his previous visit! Neville, ever resilient and this time with Roger Clifford [39], was soon reappointed as joint warden of both marches. The crown was rightfully wary of concentrating too many plums in too few hands. Fighting the Scots needed northern satraps but these, as the Percies would so clearly show, could prove a double-edged sword. On 20 May 1385 Hotspur garnered the position of sole East March Warden. His star, uncontaminated by his father's spats with Lancaster and boosted by his own restless energy, continued to rise.

Next season, 1385, Richard II led another chevauchee over the border, accompanied by young Percy and inevitably John of Gaunt. Also, in his retinue rode a Welsh knight named Owain Glyndŵr – nobody had heard of him, though many soon would, not least Henry Hotspur: 'indenture, whereby the earl of Northumberland, John, Sire de Neville, Sire de Clifford, Henry Percy warden of Berwick upon Tweed … agree to attend the king for 29 days … Sir Henry Percy with 100 men at arms and 200 archers beyond his garrison' [40]. In part the expedition was defensive; 2,000 French men-at-arms, commanded by the formidable John de Vienne, Admiral of France had been shipped in along with a fat war chest containing 50,000 livres [41] in gold. That was a lot of money yet in fact it didn't buy that much and relations between these two allies soon cooled, and then froze over.

This raid was, as usual, a costly waste. Scots were masters of guerrilla warfare and under Dunbar's sage counsel had come to appreciate that Fabian tactics produced dividends whereas head on produced only high body counts. The earls of Fife, Douglas, and Dunbar countered by beating up the English West March, doing a fair amount of profitable damage, yet the French were disappointed that Dunbar avoided confrontation. This wasn't what they'd come for, but the Scots weren't too keen on being used as expendable allies of easy convenience.

Certainly, Bower wasn't impressed, or cowed by Richard's grand army: '… About the feast of St. Laurance [10 August] Richard … sick at heart that the Scots and French were plundering his land so cruelly and were attacking his fortresses and razing them to the ground, assembled a large army and entered Scotland at the age of 19. He advanced in the midst of an arrogant host, destroying everything on all sides and saving nothing. He burned to ashes with consuming flames churches devoted to God and monastic sanctuaries (namely the monasteries of Dryburgh, Melrose and Newbattle), and the noble royal town of Edinburgh with its church of St. Giles' [42]. Despite this orgy of iconoclasm, Gaunt persuaded the king to spare Holyrood (then an abbey) [43].

Richard was able to pretend it was job done when he occupied Edinburgh but was savvy enough to ignore Gaunt's suggestion the expedition should press on, kind remembrance only stretched so far. It was a modest PR success, and the King was wisely content. The war lasted a fortnight, harvested some meagre loot but consumed treasure at a far greater rate. Dunbar's next riposte was laying siege to Roxburgh, judging the time ripe to recover this great jewel. The French were keen to help but only on the basis that the castle, once taken, should become property of the king of France as compensation for his outlay.

This proved to be a demand too far and the end of a once beautiful friendship. The siege was abandoned, and the French stomped off home [44]. Soon after Hotspur, probably, or his father possibly, was engaged in inspecting Carlisle's defences, his report didn't make comforting reading: 'Petition to the King and Council by the Mayor and citizens of Carlisle that he would take note of the report of the lords Percy and Clifford, marchers, and others who were lately there on a March [truce] day, as to the state of their city. Their walls are in part fallen, and great part on the point of falling from weakness …' [45].

In March 1386 Ralph Neville and Thomas Clifford replaced their fathers as joint wardens with handsome retainers. Both northern magnatial families were pursuing their ambitions via sons while their fathers, apparently at least, took a back seat. As neither the earl of Northumberland nor Lord Neville were any longer in the flower of youth, this made sense. This business of policing the line was a young man's game. It was physically taxing, frequently demoralising, and always dangerous. These appointments might be coveted but were never sinecures. The warden always earned his stipend and was frequently out of pocket for his troubles. At best, the crown was parsimonious and very often forgetful. Richard II, if not his uncle, had realised that campaigning on the borders was both hugely expensive and totally ineffective, so he was happy to leave matters in the north in the hands of surrogates. Hotspur like his fellow officers' sallying out from Berwick with a flying column of a hundred men-at-arms and twice as many archers was happy to oblige. This was his natural element.

In 1386, John of Gaunt was 46 but his restless ambition, not blessed with any significant abilities, remained undiminished. He'd got used to being the power behind a young king's throne, but Richard was growing weary of his uncle's constant and damaging dominance. Gaunt probably wasn't bright enough, and his self-absorption was so total that he failed, as in so many other things, to appreciate his nephew's febrile and often mercurial temperament. Richard too was imbued with a sense of his own importance; of the semi-divine, absolutist nature of his sovereignty.

He lacked the streetwise savviness of his predecessors who, though they wanted their own way and meant to have it, perceived there were rules to this game and whilst English monarchs might be anointed with holy oil, they could never be despots. Richard, had he been less blinkered, could have studied the unfortunate example of his great-grandfather Edward II and learned from his forebears' mistakes. He chose not to, preferring smooth sycophants to robust advisors.

In 1387, the king was 20 and had ruled for a decade. By medieval standards he was easily old enough to rule but also to be accountable. A powerful triumvirate of magnates – the duke of Gloucester, (his younger uncle), with the earls of Warwick and Arundel, together labelled 'The lords Appellant' – 'appealed' to Richard to seek wiser guidance, ideally theirs. Their offer was not appreciated and matters quickly escalated till swords were drawn and the king humiliated in a fracas at Radcot Bridge on the Thames. These Lords Appellant had ample support; Gaunt's son Bolingbroke was with them as well as possibly Hotspur, though not at the forefront. Richard's exalted ideas of monarchy were deeply outraged. He forgot nothing and learnt nothing. Those who'd conspired against him were now marked men.

Gaunt, more by accident than design, escaped the fallout. He had found a new project to occupy his ambition and no doubt his nephew encouraged him in this.

Thomas Percy accompanied the Duke on his expedition to Spain where in right of his second wife, Constance he had a claim to rule Castile and Leon. Ultimately, like all his other grand schemes this one would end in expensive failure but at least it kept him out of the firing line while his own younger sibling Gloucester took the king in hand.

It was a harsh process. These Lords Appellant, through the medium of the 'Merciless' Parliament, ruthlessly cleared out all advisors they deemed unsuitable, and they didn't spare the axe. Robert de Vere, Duke of Ireland, was a prime target. De Vere's loss was Hotspur's gain. In fact, 1388 opened quite well for the Percies. John Neville had died which neatly removed the main competition and Hotspur had been reappointed both as East March Warden and governor of Berwick with a handsome wage of £3,000 per annum in peacetime, quadrupled in war (over £3 million today) [46]. An indenture dated 3rd April reads: 'Henry Percy eldest son of the earl of Northumberland, undertakes the keeping of the east march of Scotland [i.e., adjoining Scotland] and the town of Berwick upon Tweed for three years from 19th June at £12,000 per annum, reduced to £3,000 during a truce or peace' [47].

OTTERBURN

> 'Of all the battles and encounterings that I have made mention of heretofore in all this history, great or small, this battle that I treat of now was one of the sorest and best foughten without cowardice or faint hearts'.
>
> *Froissart*

'History is but a fable agreed upon', a casual throwaway remark attributed to Napoleon (and presumably before Waterloo) could easily be applied to the Battle of Otterburn except that historians generally cannot agree. George Ridpath, a comprehensive and redoubtable early complier (1787), gives extraordinarily little detail and relies on Percy's Reliques [48]. He affirms the fighting began at evening, continued under moonlight and lists casualties on both sides. Irritatingly, he says nothing about the ground [49]. White (1857) gives a far fuller account of the terrain. He describes the Scottish force as passing the 'tower' (Otterburn Castle, now the Towers Hotel) and taking up position on 'The eminence north-west of Hott-Wood above Greenchesters – this forms a kind of promontory, jutting out to the south-west from the high land behind'. He goes on to suggest that 'Hott' comes from 'Holt' indicated the rise was previously wooded [50].

I see no compelling reason to argue with this and the 1:25,000 OS Map clearly supports him – the high ground is still called the Holt and Greenchesters Camp crowns the crest (see map four). He gives the distance from the Tower as a 1 ½ miles (2.4 kilometres) and this is also correct. He goes on to say the Scots made camp here on this commanding rise which gave them the necessary 'long view' to warn of any approach by English forces. Based on 'inherent military probability' ("IMP") this makes sound sense. The Scots wouldn't establish their main position on the low-lying, wet ground directly below them towards the Rede. They would see that as a natural trap if they were attacked (as indeed it became for those stuck there). White does confirm that pilfered beasts with the bouches inutiles were sent into the wet bottom [51].

Redoubtable Colonel A. H. Burne (1952) [52] was the first since White to have a serious look. He points out that the present road, the turnpike (A696), follows the line of the old medieval way. He rightly notes that the Scots defensive position covers the 'pass' between the river and rising ground north. He identifies two key problems (1) location of the Scottish camp and (2) flank marches by both armies. Burne argues that the English flank attack struck out northwards from the right of Hotspur's army in a wide flanking movement which today would take Umfraville past Otterburn Hall as far as Hopefoot (the way they'd just come) westwards, skirting Blakeman's Law to attack along a north/south axis, hitting the north flank of the higher camp. Burne projects the line of Douglas's own flank attack as an inside track, west to east around Greenchesters, parallel with Otterburn Hall.

The colonel had walked the ground and is confident Douglas was able to strike, initially undetected, against the right flank of Hotspur's main brigade at a point close to the current marker. Burne admits he struggled to work out what then happened to Umfraville, or how these two flanking manoeuvres failed to collide [53]. He rejects any notion that Umfraville attacked on the left and not on the right – he feels the river prevents this. This is a touch of dues ex machine, and we may suspect Burne was adapting the possibilities to suit his own hypothesis.

He rejects Greenchesters as any site for a 2nd camp on the basis it's too ancient; so what we might cry. It pains me to disagree with so respected an authority, one I grew up revering, but Burne's vision is wrong. The idea of two large bodies of armoured men passing each other without noticing, even allowing for poor light and scrub/tree cover just doesn't add up. If Umfraville had to march back up the Davyshiels Road then strike out cross country, that's over three miles (4.8 kilometres) in distance. Yet if he'd tried a tighter angle, he'd have smacked into Douglas.

Andrew Boardman considers the battle in considerable detail and carefully analyses both ground and sources; he gives the date as 19 August. He points out that the area generally agreed upon was known, on early maps as Battle Riggs

[54]. He further observes that the line of the river is an important constraint and narrows the area available to the combatants. Now he says, quite rightly of course, that Froissart asserts the Castle 'stood in the Marsh' [55]. This is a different marsh to that at Greenchesters or, more likely at the time, a continuous belt of low-lying alluvial bog. Boardman asserts, and Colonel Burne would have approved, that it was this very marsh which had partly frustrated Douglas's attempts to take the Tower which is after all built close to the confluence of the Otter Burn and Rede and I can't criticise any of that. He confidently accepts the idea of two Scottish encampments –one on higher, and another on lower ground – and that the defence of one could be supported by reserves from the other.

Boardman cites Oman and his analysis of Scottish fourteenth-century tactics, based on King Robert's Manual [56]. This is important because it strongly implies, as the accounts seem to support, that the Scots were not relying just on defence. This was a clever diversion to pin the English while Douglas circled their flank. Boardman is adamant that Redmayne and Ogle attacked the lower camp by the river. He goes on to suggest that light from cooking fires would have alerted Hotspur to the reality of two enemy camps and he intended to strike at the upper base with the bulk of his forces, having divined that the lower camp was not his prime objective.

THE BATTLE

Dunbar was the clever architect of Scottish strategy in 1388, a cleverly orchestrated pincer movement, feinting down through Northumberland with an inferior but fast-moving force whilst the main blow was directed in the west. In the event and very far from what the earl intended; Northumberland would become the main show with a battle the Scots had neither planned nor even wanted.

Though not a major fight, the very intensity of the battle and the balladry this inspired guaranteed its lasting fame. And though he lost, Hotspur's legend began to flourish. Froissart lets us know that while Harry might have been beaten, his ransom (7,000 marks) was soon raised and paid over. Hotspur suffered no fallout from the defeat. How then do we summarise the facts as they appear to us and reconcile the various anomalies? We can accept the facts of the Scottish invasion as the sources broadly agree and that here was some skirmishing outside the walls of Newcastle near the extended timber outer barbican or barrier; whether knightly pennons changed hands, as Froissart tells us, and that Percy having come off second best was lusting for another crack; we can choose if we go for this or not. What we can accept is that Percy, realising he was facing far fewer numbers than he anticipated, decided to seize the initiative, which the Scots had so far monopolised, and go after them.

That his force at say 6,000–7,000 was substantively larger seems reasonable. On that afternoon, to cover 32 miles (51 kilometres) given that most would be mounted on hobbies, and at say seven to eight mph probably means they could have covered the distance in perhaps five to six hours. If they marched at noon that means they could be approaching Otterburn by late afternoon/early evening, the hour of Vespers, plenty of time to deliver a knockout blow in daylight given you'd expect dusk by say 21.00 hours. To risk an immediate assault and avoid leaguering for the night made tactical sense. The Scots, being outnumbered, would, in all probability, have used the cover of darkness to clear off, content with keeping their loot intact. Given how far the beasts had been driven and at a rapid pace, they had probably needed to rest before going on to make that long climb to the border, so hanging on at Otterburn and bashing away at the Tower as Dunbar had elected to do, didn't appear to entail much risk as the speed of Hotspur's reaction was partly unanticipated.

Let's also assume Douglas and Dunbar were, in part surprised to find themselves under attack, their dispositions were still sound. The livestock was guarded by the ad hoc defences of the lower camp and the watchers could be relied upon to give a decent account of themselves; holding out long enough to be reinforced. Douglas had clearly trained his men-at-arms in the flanking manoeuvre they'd execute if attacked frontally. Walking the ground confirms the feasibility of this and we know the scrub and tree cover was denser at the time. Hotspur was relying on speed and dash rather than careful reconnaissance and he'd be aware of the risk that entailed.

His plan to divide his forces does make sense if we accept that he knew the location of the Scots lower camp but not that of their main fighting base. What developed were almost two separate battles. Redmayne and Ogle performed their allotted task admirably and beat up the Scots guarding the camp; even reinforcements of men-at-arms couldn't finally stem the rot. Fatally, however, the flank attack developed into a wild pursuit, and they were unable to come to Hotspur's aid. As Percy hesitated and this would be necessary to marshal his men for the second prong of his assault, Douglas gained the respite he needed. If, as we've suggested, Hotspur commanded up to 7,000 men and that these were mounted, his column in line of march would have stretched back for up to 8 miles (13 kilometres) and taken a deal of time and sweat to deploy for the attack. We are ready to surmise that a large part of his strength never in fact engaged.

As the column came north from Elsdon, they'd know the enemy was close, both sides would. Much has been said of the Scots being surprised but both sides would have had their prickers ranging. What the English would notice would be the absence of livestock and only the mournful dirge of curlews punctuating summer's evening. The Scots would have lifted whatever they could and whatever locals had failed to spirit away or conceal and that creates a feeling of unnatural calm.

We know, we experienced this here in Northumberland again as recently as 2001 when Foot & Mouth disease resulted in mass culling and emptied fields. A rural landscape suddenly cleared of livestock is uncanny; we don't realise how much so till it happens. It feels like a harbinger. At what point did the fighters dismount? We think Hotspur dismounted his men as he prepared to deploy. This would take time. We don't think Douglas mounted for his flank attack; the Scots tradition was to fight on foot in dense packed spear phalanxes – the schlitron. That short distance over difficult ground must imply the Scots came down on foot, already marshalled into battalions so they could deliver their own counterattack while maintaining an element of surprise and with it, tactical initiative.

At first the English were caught off guard but soon rallied and were able to hold their ground. The fight degenerated into stalemate, a materielschlacht in which the English possibly still had an advantage in numbers, though they'd be knackered after their exhausting tab while Douglas' men were fit and rested. Both sides had reason to feel confident in their officers and neither at this stage could claim any morale advantage. Now, if the Earl of Douglas had, like a good student, been reading up on old King Bob's testament, he'd have done what the great man did at Bannockburn and keep one battalion in reserve to deal a decisive blow.

We're thinking that is what Douglas did in fact do; his attack was no berserker rush but a sound and well executed strike against Percy's extreme right flank which was effectively in the air. Clearly, the Earl led from the front, and it cost him his life, but he died unrecognised, so his men didn't lose heart. This whole tactic was a well-rehearsed manoeuvre and his charge the signal for a renewed effort along the line with serial bruisers like Swinton showing the way. It worked.

We look at plans of troop deployments and moves on maps, but we must always bear in mind that while careful cartography and writer's hindsight appear to make sense of the whole thing, it was never like that on the day. Medieval commanders had no means of controlling a fight once it began other than by flags or messenger. 'No plan ever survives contact with the enemy' is a sound military maxim and the face of battle changes everything. It's also very ugly and confused. Finally, after much hard fighting, Percy's line faltered and then broke, knots of fighters spilling untidily in the gathering dusk. If we assume the English reached the battlefield at say 18.00 hours and were attacking on their left by 18.30 with Douglas' counter punch ramming home at say 19.00–1930 hours that's over an hour of decent daylight to win the day. We don't think the battle was, at any salient point, fought by moonlight but the pursuit would have been.

So, on the English left, Redmayne and Ogle pelted after their beaten opponents, losing all contact with Hotspur on their right and playing no further significant role in the overall decision. They cheered after the fleeing Scots, jubilantly relieving them of anything that was worth nicking or perhaps re-nicking. On Hotspur's right I'm going to offer the heroic assumption there was no rout and that while many men were captured, a large part of Percy's 'tail' would have got off in good order and retreated towards Elsdon, harried all the way but still in fighting trim.

An even more famous loser, Robert E. Lee noted that: 'there is always hazard in military movements, but we must decide between the positive loss of inaction and the risk of action'. James Wolfe, a posthumous winner, said very much the same: 'In war something must be left to chance and fortune, seeing that it is in its nature hazardous and an option of difficulties'.

NOTES:

[1] My new biography of Hotspur which will aim to challenge many current assumptions was published by Pen & Sword in Spring 2022.

[2] See map in Macdonald, A. J., Border Bloodshed (East Linton: Tuckwell Press, 2000), p. 12.

[3] PRO, SC6/951/5 & see Macdonald, p. 17.

[4] Macdonald, op. cit., p. 22.

[5] Rot. Scot., 1, 985 & Foedera, iii, ii, 971.

[6] See Bean, J. M. W., 'The Percies and their Estates in Scotland', Archaeologia Aeliana, 4th Series, 35 (1957), pp. 91–99, they in fact clung on to Jedforest till 1404 and the fallout from Shrewsbury.

[7] Hector Boece, The Buik of Croniclis of Scotland, trans. W. Stewart, ed. W. B. Turnbull, vol. 3 (Cambridge: Cambridge Library Collection, 2012), p. 396 & note De Fonblanque, E. B., Annals of the House of Percy: From the Conquest to the opening of the nineteenth century, vol. 1 (London: R. Clay & Sons, 1887), p. 110.

[8] Campbell, J., 'England, Scotland and the Hundred Years War', in J. R. Hale et al (eds.), Europe in the Later Middle Ages (London: Faber & Faber, 1965), pp. 184–216 & Macdonald, op. cit., p. 45 et seq.

[9] Froissart, p. 213.

[10] Wyntoun, iii, 13.

[11] Macdonald, op. cit., p. 49.

[12] Henry of Grosmont, 1st Duke of Lancaster (1310–1361).

[13] De Fonblanque, op. cit., p. 111.

[14] John Wycliff (d. 1384) was a religious reformer, philosopher, and academic.

[15] De Fonblanque, op. cit., p. 120.

[16] Ridpath, op. cit., p. 241.

[17] Walsingham, p. 77.

[18] Walsingham, p. 77.

[19] Ridpath, op. cit., p. 242.

[20] Walsingham, p. 78.

[21] Ibid.

[22] Ibid., p. 239.

[23] Mortimer was a Norman name, probably from Mortemer in the Seine Maritime, active in the service of William I as early as 1054. After the Conquest they became powerful marcher lords on the troublesome Welsh border and highly active in the 2nd Barons' War. Roger Mortimer, 1st Earl of March, led an unsuccessful rising, the Despenser War, against Edward II but then became Queen

Isabella's lover and accomplice in a successful coup. He may or may not have arranged the gruesome murder of the deposed king in Berkeley Castle and ruled, effectively as military dictator, for three years before young Edward III carried out a countercoup at Nottingham in 1330 and removed his head.

[24] Rymer, T., ed., Foedera, Conventiones, Litterae … 1704 – 1735, vol. 7, p. 353. See also Hamer, E., Anglo-Scottish relations in the reigns of Robert II & Robert III, (unpublished thesis, University of Glasgow 1971 http://theses.gla.ac.uk/72755/1/10647029.pdf), p. 158, accessed 20 April 2021.

[25] Ridpath, op. cit., p. 242: a mark = 13s 4d or say £0.67p or say £4.5 million in today's money.

[26] Ridpath, op. cit., p. 243.

[27] Scotichronicon, Book XIV, p. 249.

[28] Ridpath, op. cit., p. 243.

[29] Scotichronicon, Book XIV, p. 248 & Wyntoun, chapter 5, p. 283.

[30] Ridpath, op. cit., p. 243.

[31] De Fonblanque, op. cit., pp. 134–135.

[32] In theory each district was measured by the span of a day's 'march' though more probably on horseback.

[33] These incidents occurred mainly in the sixteenth century, Sir Walter Kerr of Cessford and Sir John Carmichael were two examples and Queen Mary's Bothwell came close.

[34] Ridpath, op. cit., p. 244.

[35] Scotichronicon, Book XIV, p. 250.

[36] Ibid., Book XIV, p. 251.

[37] Ridpath, op. cit., p. 245.

[38] Ridpath, op. cit., p. 245.

[39] Baron de Clifford, the title was created in 1299 and the family, Anglo-Normans active in border affairs, the 1st Baron fell at Bannockburn.

[40] CDS, 340, p. 77.

[41] A livre was a form of currency, first established by Charlemagne and equal in value to a pound of silver (0.45 kg), divided into 20 sous.

[42] Scotichronicon, Book XIV, p. 253.

[43] Ibid., Book XIV, p. 254.

[44] Ridpath, op. cit., p. 246.

[45] CDS, 347, p. 78.

[46] An indenture was a document where the terms were repeated and then it was cut erratically across the divide so that the two halves would indent or fit together to prove authenticity.

[47] CDS, 377, p. 83.

[48] Percy, Thomas, Reliques of Ancient English Poetry, edited by J. V. Pritchard, Book One: I 'Chevy Chase' (London: J. Dodsley, 1775).

[49] Ridpath, op. cit., p. 247.

[50] White, R., History of the Battle of Otterburn fought in 1388 etc (Newcastle upon Tyne: Emerson Charnley, 1857), p. 30.

[51] White, op. cit., p. 31.

[52] Burne, Lt.-Colonel A. H., More Battlefields of England (London: Methuen & Co, 1952), pp. 127–140.

[53] Ibid., p. 136.

[54] Boardman, op. cit., p. 63.

[55] Froissart, p. 371.

[56] King Robert's Testament was the Seven Pillars of Wisdom of its day.

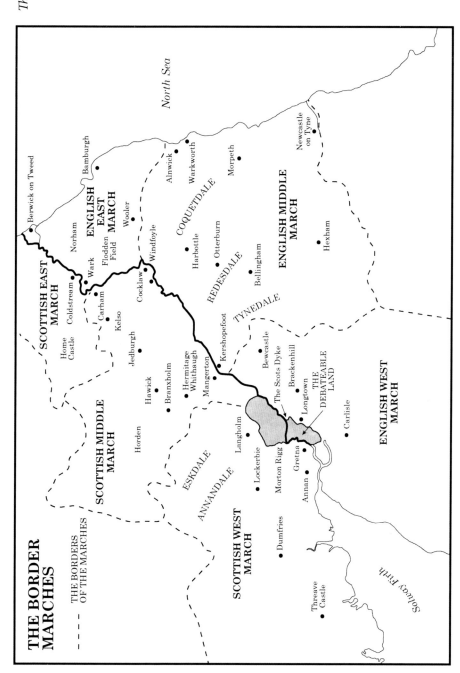

THE BORDER
MARCHES

- - - - THE BORDERS
OF THE MARCHES

North Sea

Solway Firth

Berwick on Tweed

Bamburgh

Norham

**SCOTTISH EAST
MARCH**

**ENGLISH
EAST
MARCH**

Alnwick

Warkworth

Morpeth

Newcastle
on Tyne

Coldstream

Wark

Flodden
Field

Wooler

Windfoyle

COQUETDALE

Carham

Home
Castle

Kelso

Cocklaw

Harbottle

Otterburn

**ENGLISH MIDDLE
MARCH**

Jedburgh

Kershopefoot

REDESDALE

Bellingham

Hexham

Hawick

Hermitage
Whithaugh

Mangerton

TYNEDALE

**SCOTTISH MIDDLE
MARCH**

Branxholm

Bewcastle

Brackenhill

Horden

Langholm

The Scots Dyke

Longtown

**THE
DEBATEABLE
LAND**

Carlisle

ESKDALE

Lockerbie

Morton Rigg

Gretna

**ENGLISH WEST
MARCH**

ANNANDALE

Annan

**SCOTTISH WEST
MARCH**

Dumfries

Threave
Castle

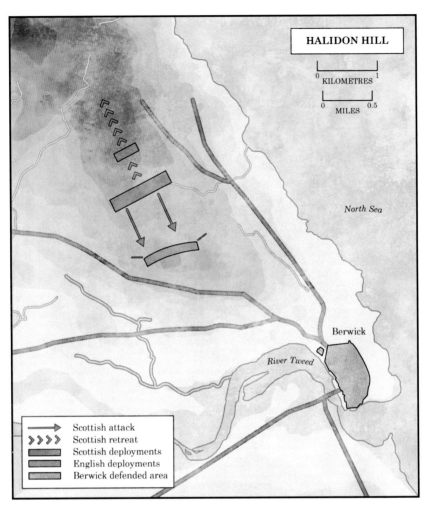

Battle of Halidon Hill 1333

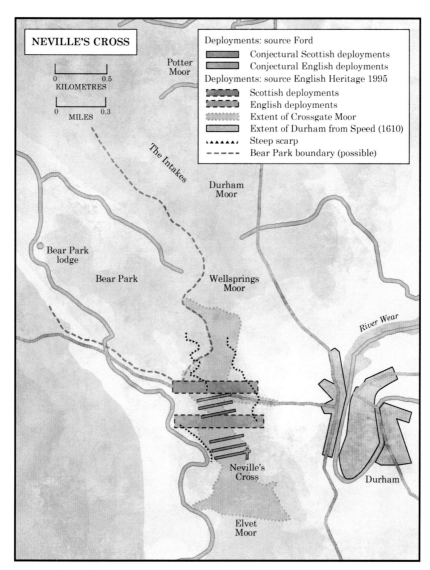

Battle of Neville's Cross 1346

Battle of Otterburn 1388

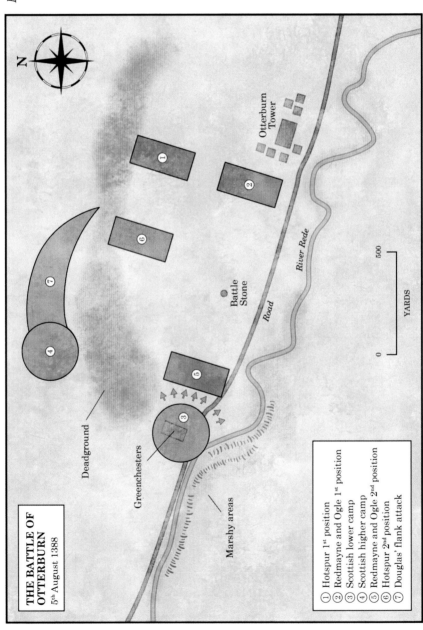

THE BATTLE OF
OTTERBURN
5th August 1388

① Hotspur 1st position
② Redmayne and Ogle 1st position
③ Scottish lower camp
④ Scottish higher camp
⑤ Redmayne and Ogle 2nd position
⑥ Hotspur 2nd position
⑦ Douglas' flank attack

Deadground

Greenchesters

Marshy areas

Battle
Stone

Otterburn
Tower

River Rede

Road

YARDS

0   500

N

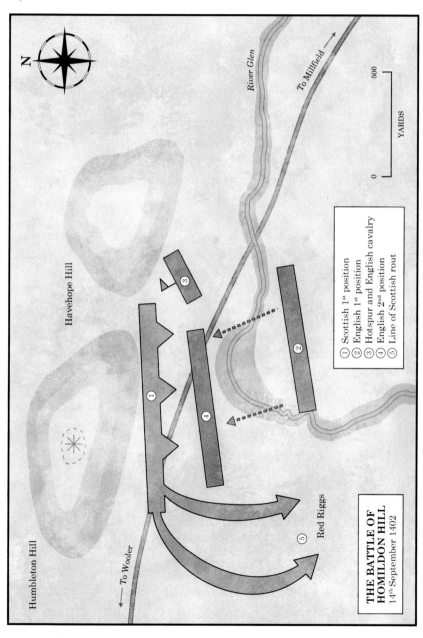

N

Humbleton Hill

Havehope Hill

To Wooler

River Glen

To Millfield

Red Riggs

① Scottish 1st position
② English 1st position
③ Hotspur and English cavalry
④ English 2nd position
⑤ Line of Scottish rout

THE BATTLE OF HOMILDON HILL
14th September 1402

YARDS

0   500

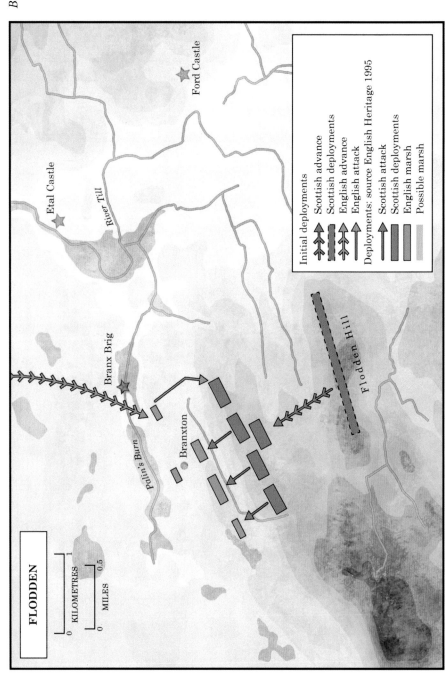

Battle of Flodden 1513

Battle of Pinkie 1547

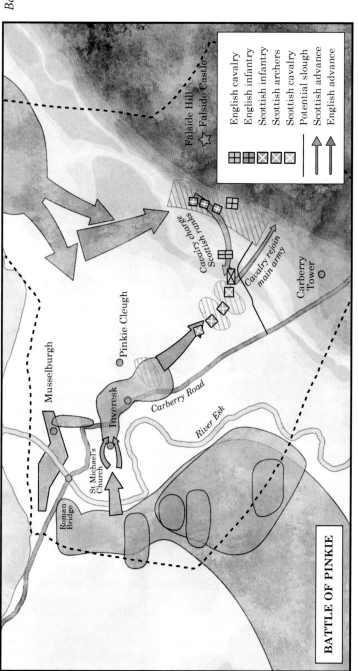

Falside Hill
✩ Falside Castle

English cavalry
English infantry
Scottish infantry
Scottish archers
Scottish cavalry
Potential slough
Scottish advance
English advance

Cavalry charge
Scottish ranks

Cavalry rejoin
main army

Carberry
Tower

Pinkie Cleugh

Musselburgh

Inveresk

St Michael's
Church

Carberry Road

River Esk

Roman
Bridge

BATTLE OF PINKIE

Newcastle Keep (Adam Barr); built on the site of the principia of the old Roman fort, the bulk of the keep dates from the reign of Henry II, a magnificent Norman donjon, having features in common with Dover, it wasn't really tested till the great siege of 1644 but had held (and sometimes failed to hold) numerous notorious border ruffians.

The Walls of Newcastle (Adam Barr); this surviving stretch facing towards the northwest would have been standing at the time of the Great Siege in 1644, the suburbs standing outside were burnt down by Mayor Marley to deny cover to the Scots besiegers. Inevitably, the ancient medieval walls could not stem the tide once the assaults went in.

Left: Hexham Gaol (Wikimedia 8641587448); believed to be the oldest purpose built prison in England and many a border ruffian languished in the grim undercroft. Henry Beaufort Duke of Somerset spent his last night here in 1464, prior to his execution in the marketplace, it now houses a border history museum with an ingenious lift down into the bowels.

Top Left: Bamburgh Castle (Adam Barr); the grandest of grand coastal fortresses, possibly Lancelot's castle but certainly the capital of the emerging Anglian state of Northumbria, scene of the siege of 1464 and finally restored in the late nineteenth century by William Lord Armstrong, a medieval gem preserved by the father of mass industrial warfare!

Top right: Dunstanburgh Castle (Adam Barr); The fortress of Earl Thomas of Lancaster, haunt it is said of forlorn Sir Guy wandering on his ceaseless quest. Another castle which featured heavily during the turbulence of the War in the North 1461 – 1464. It enjoys a spectacular location a bracing walk north from the picturesque village of Craster.

Above: The Horse Statue, Hawick (Scotland Starts Here); a fine equestrian statue, known as 'The Horse', completed by Hawick born sculptor William F. Beattie in 1914, intended to commemorate a local victory over the English at Hornshole four centuries before. Hawick now hosts the annual reiver gathering.

Left: Hotspur Statue by Keith Maddison (Gerry Tomlinson); At fourteen feet high and brandishing a sword, this dramatic new statue of legendary Northumbrian knight, Sir Henry Percy ('Hotspur'), was hoisted into place at the Duke's Memorial Garden on Pottergate in Alnwick, just yards from the castle which was his home more than six centuries ago.

Right: Otterburn Memorial (UK Battlefield Trust); taken on 26 August 2021, he Dukes of Buccleuch and Northumberland – Douglas & Percy meet for the first time on the battlefield of Otterburn since their respective ancestors clashed there in 1388. They are in fact first cousins and the day passed without further bloodshed!

Left: The Fletcher Statue, Selkirk (Trip Advisor); created by Thomas Clapperton in 1913, Fletcher does look more like a Prussian cuirassier than border horse, but legend asserts he was the only survivor of the 80 strong company from the town which marched out to follow King James IV to Flodden and returned with the banner of the Accrington contingent of Surrey's army.

Right: The Silloans Sword replica (Defence Photography); crafted by Haltwhistle armourer Ulfric, this fine replica of the battered original found at Silloans on the MoD ranges in 1986 will shortly be on show full time in St. Cuthbert's Church Elsdon. It may also be that the mass grave for the English dead from the battle now lies in the churchyard.

Far left: Swords of the reiver era (Adam Barr); two facsimile backswords, created by Ulfric and closely based on surviving examples previously seen in the wonderful Johnnie Armstrong Museum of Arms & Armour at Teviothead.

Left: Polearm (Adam Barr); a Jeddart Staff weapon, essentially a cleaver like axe blade on an ash shaft, terrible in close contact, and responsible for those fearsome cuts or 'Lockerbie Licks' dealt out by the Johnstons against their Maxwell would-be oppressors at Dryfe Sands in 1593.

The Matchlock musket (Adam Barr); close-up of the mechanism of a working facsimile of a matchlock musket of the late 16th/early 17th centuries. The jaws hold the lighted cord which is lowered by the trigger onto the exposed pan to fire the incendiary charge of fine powder which flashes through to the breech to ignite (hopefully) the primary charge.

Winter's Gibbet, Elsdon (Bev Palin); This grim reminder recalls the fate of William Winter who was hanged for the murder of Margaret Crozier and gibbeted within sight of the crime scene, caught by the testimony of an eagle-eyed shepherd lad who'd noticed the distinctive pattern of hobnails on the murderer's boots.

Left: Hexham Market Place (Britain's Best Market Towns); scene of the executions after Lancaster's defeat south of the town in 1464 and later the location of the infamous massacre enacted by North Yorks Militia there in 1761, Northumberland's own and far bloodier Peterloo. The colonnaded arcade, or Shambles were built some years later.

Middle: Hermitage Castle (Wikimedia Commons); 'Sod off in stone' as the late and great George Macdonald Fraser dubbed this gaunt and forbidding hold, key to wild Liddesdale. Its history abounds in dark legend including the salutary tale of 'wicked' Lord Soulis, a supposed necromancer who was rolled alive in lead and boiled up at the Ninestanerig stone circle. He never re-offended!

Lower: Smailholm Tower (Visitors Guide to Scotland); a seat of the Pringles, west of Kelso and perched on its rocky crag, the very epitome of the perfect Scottish tower house. It was his stay here recovering from illness, living with relatives in the farm below, that gave a youthful Walter Scott his romantic inspiration.

Cessford Castle (Castle Finders); seat of Ker of Cessford, a name very often associated equally with wardenry and villainy. It looks like a blockhouse and so it was, it would slot quite easily into the Atlantic Wall, and it proved, on several occasions, a very tough nut to crack. Simon Hawkins, Fabulous North.

Caerlaverock Castle (Wikimedia Commons 2016); a remarkable and beautiful Scottish West March castle with an earlier foundation close by. The mellow red stone and distinctive triangular shape, set in perfect country rather belie its very active history as a seat of the Maxwells and bastion of the west, all too often the object of English intentions including a spectacular siege by Longshanks in 1300.

Carlisle Castle Gateway (Historic UK); the great red sandstone bastion of the west, which saw off several Scottish sieges until taken by the Jacobites after a largely token resistance in 1745. It was soon recovered by the Duke of Cumberland as Prince Charles Edward's army withdrew from Derby and crossed back into Scotland, no mercy for the doomed garrison.

Tantallon Castle (Conde Nast); a very fitting stage for High Dunsinane, set against a wild coastal backdrop. Built by the Douglases in the mid fourteenth century, its still formidable ramparts dominate the landward side while formidable cliffs seal off the seaward approaches. It saw a fair bit of action throughout, up to and including the Civil Wars.

The Walls of Berwick upon Tweed (Bev Palin); The great bastion of the English East March, though originally a Scottish town. The medieval castle fell victim to industrial progress when the railways were being built, but all of the great circuit of magnificent Elizabethan Walls remains intact and fully accessible.

Above: The Reidswire Stone (Colin Green Photography), on its bleak eminence this stone commemorated the Raid of the Reidswire fought in July 1575 when a day of Truce turned into a brawl, not for the first or final time. Another fracas erupted a decade later, the common denominator, probably to nobody's surprise, was Sir John Forster, the English Warden. Walter Baxter, Geograph NT6907.

Left: The Battle of Flodden Memorial on Piper's Hill, Branxton (Ford & Etal Estates); erected by the Berwickshire Naturalists in 1910, this stands on ground occupied by Howard's Division during the battle with the English gun line on the forward slope lying past the cross.

Chapter Four: 'At Homildon Met'

'That some night-tripping fairy had exchanged/ In cradle clothes our children where they lay/ And called mine 'Percy' and his 'Plantagenet'/ Then would I have this Harry, and he mine'.

Shakespeare: King Henry IV First Part, I:i

King Robert II of Scotland died in 1390, and was succeeded by his son John, earl of Carrick, Lancaster's old sparring partner who adopted the name Robert, thus becoming King Robert III, ('John' had unfortunate connotations of John Balliol, 'Toom Tabard', who nobody wished to be reminded of). The new king suffered from an old malady, leading to degrees of incapacity, not helped by having been kicked in the head by his brother's horse. That brother, the earl of Fife, effectively ruled as quasi-regent. But a weak king means internal troubles, or as Bower puts it, 'under a slack shepherd the wolf fouls the wool, and the flock is torn to pieces'. The border and borderers would still be in a foment of anarchy.

Percy & Sons

His star status undimmed, Hotspur was soon appointed governor of Carlisle and West March Warden, sweetened further with a hefty annuity of £6,000. The family business was flourishing with, as yet no revived competition from the Nevilles. The Percies, father and son, were enjoying a virtual monopoly. John Neville's convenient demise pretty much cleared out the field for now though his son Ralph, 1st earl of Westmoreland from 1397, would mature into a formidable player. In 1391 Ralph was granted a warrant along with a clutch of English knights to perform 'feats of arms' after being challenged by Alexander Lindsay, a Scottish opponent. This was a form of proxy war in peacetime, no fears of swords getting beaten into ploughshares.

There's a lot of myths clustered around the Battle of Homildon and even some modern writers fall into the old trap (refer to map five). Those, who've never seen the ground, assume that the Scots drew up on the summit of the hill which stands at just under 1,000 feet (298 metres), while the English faced them across from another rise Harehope, standing due north. This is a virtual impossibility. Deploying medieval forces on such steep-sided terrain would have been a mammoth task and to no purpose, as the distance between would be far more than even the most powerful archer's best shot.

For the Scots, the dawn of a new century brought a severe blow. Canny George Dunbar defected to England and brought his vast experience and many talents with him. Losing so resourceful a commander was both damaging and, in the circumstances, foolhardy. Marriage alliances were at the root of it. Dunbar had contracted to marry his daughter to David, Duke of Rothesay, King Robert III's eldest son, a mercurial and rather unstable character, at odds with his authoritarian uncle Albany. So far so good. But the Duke changed his mind, or Dunbar was outbid, and Rothesay opted for a Douglas bride instead. Bad enough, but he refused to hand back the advance on the proposed dowry he'd already pocketed to seal the bargain. You could see Douglas' hand in this as well, but any triumph turned sour when Dunbar, understandably peeved, embarked on treasonous correspondence with Henry IV [1].

It was around Christmas 1400 when, on the death of the 3rd Earl, Archibald, Master of Douglas, and lord of Threave, scooped the whole inheritance [2]. Dunbar's sequestered lands boosted his rent roll and the marriage alliance with an heir to the Scottish throne set the seal on what looked very much like a Douglas hegemony in southern Scotland. Despite such an apparently auspicious beginning, the 4th Earl only ever earned the unfortunate cognomen 'Tineman' or 'loser'. He'd earn it, fighting numerous battles and invariably coming second. His last was Verneuil in 1424 where he died championing France against John, Duke of Bedford.

Dunbar was a useful turncoat and Henry IV appreciated his worth. The earl signed an indenture at Newcastle to serve the King of England and was rewarded by a grant of the Manor of Clippeston (Clipstone) in Sherwood Forest [3], boosted in spring 1402 with a handsome annuity of £400 for as long as hostilities lasted, though he was contracted to provide a dozen men-at-arms plus a score of mounted archers. His son Gavin was similarly retained at £40 per annum [4].

Despite Dunbar's defection, his eclipse was only partial. He kept control of Lochmaben, Cockburnspath, and wild Fast Castle, his own fortified dowry.

England still held on to Jedburgh and Roxburgh. Taken together, these were the keys that could yet unlock the Marches. This provided Henry IV with an opportunity. If he could march into Scotland and use these stepping stones to resurrect the English Pale, he'd score a major success, one that had, like so many others, eluded his predecessor. The King was already in negotiation with the Lord of the Isles [5] to open a second front in the north and west of Scotland. This was bold talk indeed for a monarch with an empty bank account, but it gave him the chance to carve out rewards for such loyal supporters as the Percies. To give the First Earl of Northumberland his due, nobody ever called him charitable. Kingmakers expect payback.

Henry may have led a force up to 13,000 strong [6], supported by a powerful fleet which cruised up the east coast, nabbing any Scottish vessels which couldn't sail fast enough. Still, the expedition came to nothing. Henry found out, as Richard had before him, the wily Scots preferred Fabian tactics: inglorious, frustrating, and highly effective. The English king ravaged the borderland during the last two weeks in August and then gave up, his stores exhausted and his wallet thinner than ever. His navy might have enjoyed some profitable raids, but his captains were soundly beaten off Strangford by the Scots [7].

Now, had Dunbar still been on side, the Scots might have landed an effective riposte, but Douglas was no Dunbar and the Council fumbled. What might have been a masterly counterstroke turned into a series of feeble probes, all easily seen off. Umfraville beat up raiders trespassing on his turf in Redesdale, capturing Richard Rutherford, their commander, and a move against Bamburgh fared no better. There was perhaps now a real chance to coordinate operations with Glyndŵr in Wales, but this too was frittered away.

It didn't take Dunbar long to illustrate the cost of his defection. In February 1401, accompanied by Hotspur, the pair launched a big raid into the Lothians though Douglas, to his credit, chased them back to the line. The 4th Earl was a significant player, but it was the King's ably unscrupulous brother Albany, who was in effective control of the Scottish polity and at odds with the rebarbative Rothesay. Albany, who was de facto regent owing to his brother's incapacity [8], was not inclined to continue war with England, so Douglas and Northumberland brokered a fresh truce which was to endure for a further year once the current term expired that November.

Rothesay too, as his thin power base shrank, veered towards conciliation. He might be the King's son and heir, but his uncle held the reins of power and had no intention of letting go (he would hang on until into his eighties). Besides, the troublesome duke lacked any solid affinity. Douglas, uninterested in peace, neatly switched to Albany's faction, side-lining Rothesay but at the same time drawing

Albany himself in with the hawks. Not that he wanted war but that was the price of Douglas' support.

A RUMBLING OF HAWKS

Douglas prevaricated over the proposed truce and was already having another go beating up country around Bamburgh before negotiations finally foundered on 23 October. From the next month onwards, English border officials were paid at 'war' rates. Nobody was placing much reliance on truces [9]. Henry IV had problems too aside from cash-poverty. It was now that trouble in Wales kicked off again and Glyndŵr captured Sir Edmund Mortimer who also appeared to be infected by the defection bug (see following chapter). The Scots were seeking, through aggressive diplomacy, to secure French aid through the 'Auld Alliance' once again and the piratical Earl of Crawford was planning joint naval operations in the Channel.

During the early months of 1402, Rothesay continued to stumble but then he died, in circumstances never properly explained but his uncle's hand was suspected, and the gloves were off [10]. Douglas, in February, had written to complain, if disingenuously, to King Henry that Northumberland and Hotspur were violating the truce. In late May, the King ordered a general muster against the Scots, but all available resources had to be shifted to Wales where the situation continued to deteriorate.

On the borders both sides were riding hard. That outwardly unlikely partnership between Dunbar and the Percies, father and son, offered tremendous potential. Northumberland had clout and guile, and Harry dash, elan, energy, and affinity while Dunbar brought wisdom and strategic nous. He effectively filled the perceived gaps in Hotspur's character, though these may have been overstated. Meanwhile, Douglas must have thought he'd properly got one over on his rival Dunbar, but that glee would soon turn to ashes.

Thomas Haliburton, Lord of Dirleton, had another crack at Bamburgh while Patrick Hepburn of Hailes struck deeper into the English East March. Dunbar had Hepburn in his sights, however. On 22 June and leading 200 soldiers from the Berwick garrison he and Hotspur tracked them back over the line and sprung their trap at Nesbit Muir (Moor) in the Merse. Despite odds of 2 > 1, the duo won their fight. Hepburn fell with 'The flower of the youth of Lothian' [11]. Haliburton, who'd beat up Bamburgh, was captured along with his brother John, Robert Lauder, William, and John Cockburn [12]. Winning was always made perfect by a nice cash crop of ransoms.

Subsequent correspondence suggests Northumberland was present, but this is unlikely, as West March Warden he is more likely to have been keeping an eye on

Carlisle. De Fonblanque asserts he was yet doesn't mention Dunbar, and he also alleges Hepburn had blitzed down as far south as Durham, which seems unlikely [13]. Hotspur was warden in the east and Dunbar, as Andrew Boardman points out [14], had proprietorial scores to settle with both Douglas and Hepburn. The fight is classic Hotspur, even if advised by Dunbar, a lightning dash and surgical strike. Not a big scrap by any means but a definite win for Harry Percy and one that shouldn't be overlooked. There's no sign of recklessness here and, as warden he'd no compelling need to listen to Dunbar unless he chose to do so.

This fortuitous if eccentric partnership between Dunbar and Percy is an odd anomaly. Previously they were enemies, both key players on their respective sides and now they were working together in a handy if essentially uneasy alliance. Both would have understood that Dunbar's present defection wasn't likely to be permanent and his overriding interest lay in recovering and retrenching his own position. Thereafter, they'd be foes again. For the moment, whatever damaged Douglas suited both admirably and that common aim was about to bear fruit and perhaps far more so than anyone could, at that time, have foreseen.

In his capacity as Warden of the West March, Northumberland wrote a dispatch to which King Henry refers in a letter to his council: '[Percy] has informed the King that he and his son with the garrison of Berwick upon Tweed to the number of 200 have defeated 400 Scots. John Haliburton, Robert Lewedre [Lauder], John Cokbourne, and Thomas Haliburton, Scottish knights were captured, and Sir Patrick Hepburn and other Scots killed and taken to the number of 240. There is also news from the letters of the Earl of Northumberland and reports from the bearer of these that 12,000 Scots have been near Carlisle but have done little damage. The earl says that the Scots are proposing to enter the kingdom with so great a power that it appears that they wish to give battle and the King urges that reinforcements be sent' [15].

Undeterred by this ill-omen, which oddly presages Lord Home's defeat, the Ill-Rode, before the disaster at Flodden in 1513, Douglas went ahead to plan a bold stroke for late summer. English sinews were stiffening for this inevitable onslaught all through July and August. Yet the army Douglas mustered was formidable, between 10,000–12,000 strong [16]. With him, under his symbolic banner of the 'bludy hert' [17] rode the regent's son Murdoch, the earls of Moray, Angus, and Orkney, lords Montgomery, Graham and Erskine, John Edmonton, and William Stewart, together with those two tough fighters Adam Gordon and Sir John Swinton (the latter of Otterburn fame). Also present was Patrick of Biel, George Dunbar's brother! The rank and file were made up of Gallowegians, Marchers, and Clydesdale men, bolstered by a detachment of 30 French knights eager to win renown. As Alistair Macdonald points out, while Douglas enjoyed high status as a public official, an agent of the Scottish polity, his army was raised primarily on the back of more traditional, personal, and feudal obligation, rather than on any concept of 'national service' [18].

Meanwhile, Dunbar and both Percies were gathering their own forces at Bamburgh. They'd be in no doubt as to the magnitude of their task. They scraped together every fighting man they could from the marches and co-opted a detachment of those renowned Cheshire archers (see next chapter), initially recruited to fight Glyndŵr. Northern gentry, as ever, were ready to ride alongside them; Ralph, Baron Greystoke, Sir Henry Fitzhugh, Sir Ralph Eure, William Lord Hylton, those hardy Umfravilles, the Lieutenant of Roxburgh plus Constable of Dunstanburgh [19], beefed up with some Lincolnshire levies, a smattering of Welsh marchers and Newcastle's militia [20]. At best, however, they might be half as strong as their opponents. Who commanded overall? It had to be Northumberland himself with Hotspur as his deputy. Dunbar's exact status was uncertain probably as much then as now. Temporary ally he might be, but his reputation was extremely high and his advice always worth heeding.

BATTLEGROUND

Walsingham, no friend to the Scots, recounts: 'At that time the Scots, made restless by their usual arrogance, entered England in hostile fashion; for they thought that all the northern lords had been kept in Wales by royal command; but the earl of Northumberland the Lord Henry Percy, and Henry his son, and the Earl of Dunbar … with an armed band and a force of archers suddenly flung themselves across the path of the Scots who, after burning and plundering, wanted to return to their own country, so that the Scots had no choice but to stop and choose a place of battle.. They therefor chose a hill near the town of Wooler, called Halweden [Homildon] Hill …' [21]. At the outset, Douglas had it all his own way. Marchers hid what they could and just got out of the way – at least they'd had a whole century to practice. The Scots penetrated fully down into Northumberland, possibly as far south as Newcastle and were retreating, or rather returning, roughly along the line of the current A697, passing Wooler and marching north when they discovered a most unwelcome surprise.

If you're following their footsteps and once you pass the market town, land on your left begins to rise while the Glen flows to your right, quite a narrow alluvial belt before the higher ground swells up. Homildon (Humbleton) and Harehope rising beyond are outriders of the Cheviot Massif which dominates the central borderland and is almost impassable for large armies. Most of the battlefield terrain is presently cultivated and not accessible, though there are good views of the ancient Bendor Stone (said to mark the field but it's prehistoric, but happens to be in the right place), from the roadside and a track to your right leading down to modern somewhat banal sewage works gives a nice appreciation of the field. Both Humbleton and Harehope Hills can be climbed via public footpaths, steep going but the views repay the effort. The UK Battlefield Trust website has some helpful maps but I 'd say the deployment of both armies as shown is still incorrect [22].

This rather leisurely withdrawal (obviously the Scots were slowed by their four-footed booty) suggests that Douglas may have been overconfident and/or misled by his spies in assuming, as Walsingham asserts, the border had been stripped of fighting men to bolster a precarious situation in Wales. In any event he had blundered. His scouting had to have been faulty, since he shouldn't have failed to detect such a large body of troops approaching nor, as it seems he did, should he have assumed his enemies would be cowed merely by superior numbers. He had grossly underestimated both Dunbar and the Percies. His followers were now about to reap that whirlwind and it would be a bitter harvest.

Having checked the Scots retreat by establishing a block across the road home, I'm suggesting the English deployed on flat ground with the line of the Glen on their right flank which was effectively refused and the Till some distance behind. The ground generally would have been wetter by far than now, but this was mid-September (14th) so would have dried out after summer's warmth. The English were now the cork in a narrow-necked bottle. Whether the archers were massed in front, billmen and men-at-arms behind or whether detached wings of archers stood ready to enfilade we can't say. Walsingham's account of English bowmen taking ground in the re-entrant between the two hills, suggests this may have been the case. I feel both Armstrong and Boardman show the Scots' initial deployment too far up the hillside, any infantryman would say so. I tend to opt for Colonel Burne's axiom of IMP here and assume the Scots deployed at the very base of the hill where ground forms a natural shelf sitting above the plain. Armstrong has them occupying the hillfort itself which was unlikely [23].

Andrew Boardman, quite rightly, notes that Walsingham describes the English leaving the road and ascending 'another hill facing the Scots' – clearly Harehope. It's easy to see how this confusion arises but it's simply not a practical proposition. My take is that the chronicler is referring to a move by the English away from the alluvial plain to bring the Scots, deployed at the base of Homildon, within range. It seems certain that a detachment of English, Hotspur's cavalry and maybe a body of commanded archers did occupy the gap between the two hills and this I think is what Walsingham is talking about. I'm also working on the assumption that the men of the grey goose feather began shooting at say 200 yards (183 metres). Boardman is confident that greater ranges were perfectly possible and whilst I appreciate this, I suspect that volleys would not be shot at extreme range – the arrow supply was always finite, so it made sound tactical sense to ensure causing maximum damage.

A PERFECT (ARROW) STORM

Was the Earl of Northumberland present, in which case he would surely have been in charge? Opinion varies, though John Hardyng who claims he took part in the fight is emphatic that he was: 'To Homildon, where on Holy Rode Daye, the earl them met in good and strong array/ His son also, Henry Percy, was there' [24]. I'm not so sure. It may well be Northumberland had directed operations and the overall muster beforehand but I'm doubtful he was present on the field. Hardyng also gives Douglas a huge army of 40,000, a wild exaggeration [25]. It's a shame he barely mentions the battle itself at all!

Bower, our most informative chronicle source, is as biased towards Scots as Hardyng to English: 'The new Earl of Douglas, (the second Archibald), who had custody then of the castles of Edinburgh and Dunbar and who was the king's son-in-law wished to seek revenge on the English for the slaughter of the Scots at Nisbet. He approached the governor of Scotland, the Duke of Albany, for his help in strengthening his army, because he said it was [only] with the duke's advice [and backing] that he would be willing to go to England. The duke gave him his eldest son Sir Murdoch with an augmented force of knights and brave men'.

'He therefore assembled a large army in the same year to the number of 10,000 fighting men, including the earls of Angus and Moray as well as the Master of Fife (the governor's son), and entering England they plundered it as far as Newcastle. As they returned Sir Henry Percy the younger (otherwise Hotspur) with Sir George de Dunbar Earl of March and a large army reached Millfield before them. [The master of Fife and] the earl of Douglas climbed to some rising ground called Homildon where they waited for the arrival of the English. As they stood on the plain facing the Scots, the English were impatient to attack them on Percy's order; but the Earl of March reined Percy back, saying that he should not move, but should send archers who could easily penetrate the Scots as targets for their arrows and defeat and capture them' [26].

Hotspur, leading the arme blanche, was positioned on the English right, ready to exploit any crumbling of the dense packed Scottish schlitron now massing to face the impending storm. Douglas had been neatly out-generalled and appeared to have no idea what to do next. His men had to just stand there and take it. Seldom had the men of the grey goose feather been offered such an obliging target. They nocked, drew, and loosed, deluging the exposed ranks. Knights, encased in fine plate, had some measure of protection, spearmen in jacks had virtually none and down they went in droves [27].

Walsingham says that the Scots did have archers and that these tried to compete but failed and gave way beneath the English barrage [28]. Bower doesn't mention these, and Walsingham goes on, gloatingly: 'The Earl of Douglas, who was the leader of the Scots, saw their flight, and did not want to seem to desert the battlefield; so, he seized a lance and rode down the hill with a troop of his horse, trusting too much in his equipment and that of his men, who had been improving their armour for three years, and strove to rush on the archers. When the archers saw this, they retreated, but still shooting, so vigorously, so resolutely, so effectively, that they pierced the armour, perforated the helmets, pitted the swords, split the lances, and pierced all the equipment with ease'.

'The Earl of Douglas was pierced with five wounds, notwithstanding his elaborate armour. The rest of the Scots who had not descended the hill turned tail and fled from the flight of arrows. But flight did not avail them, for the archers followed them, so that the Scots were forced to give themselves up, for fear of the death-dealing arrows. The Earl of Douglas was captured; many of those who fled were captured, but many were drowned in the river Tweed [in fact the Glen], so that the waters devoured, so it was said, 500 men. In this fight no lord or knight received a blow from the enemy; but God Almighty gave the victory miraculously to the English archers alone, and the magnates and men-at-arms remained idle spectators of the battle' [29].

It was slaughter, Western Front stuff, and Douglas stayed supine, poetically imagined by A. G. Bradley in his 'Romance of Northumberland': 'In blind red clouds the sun arose/ Which saw that fatal day/ where breathless on the green hill side/fu' mony a braw Scot lay/ For sair the English bowmen gall'd/ the van that ungeared stood/nae thirsty shafts 'een reached the earth/ unstained in Scottish blood'. Dunbar kept Hotspur's riders in check until their charge could achieve maximum effect while Douglas did his best to help the English. Galling for him his rival was guiding the opposing army, satisfying for Dunbar he was wreaking his revenge, even if the victims were his own countrymen.

At one point the Scots were either ordered to advance by Douglas and Murdoch or those erstwhile rivals Gordon and Swinton just charged anyway. It made no difference. Their initiative was a stillborn thing, the arrow storm beat too hard, that rain of death incessant, neither of the paladins survived. Bower gives them a glorious send-off: '… [Swinton] shouted out in a harsh voice as if he were a crier saying: "Illustrious comrades! Who has bewitched you today that you do not behave in your usual worthy manner? Why do you not join in hand-to-hand battle nor as men take heart to attack enemies who are in a hurry to destroy you with their flying arrows as if you were little fallow-deer or young mules in pens? Those who are willing should go down with me and we shall move among our enemies in the Lord's name, either to save our lives in so doing or at least to fall as knights with honour'".

'On hearing this the most famous and valiant Adam de Gordon of that Ilk who indeed for a long time had cultivated mortal enmity against the said lord of Swinton following the death of stalwart men-at-arms from both sides in various fights, knelt down before him to ask pardon from him in particular (as the worthiest knight in arms in the whole of Britain, as he claimed) so that he might be girded as a knight by the hands of the same Sir John. This was done, and a band of a hundred respected knights followed these leaders who had thus been reconciled. They contended intrepidly with a thousand Englishmen; and that whole Scottish group fell dead, though not without a great slaughter of English. It was assuredly believed, and it was sworn on oath by some Englishmen, as I have heard, that if the other Scots who had stood on Humbleton Hill had fallen on them with like vigour, either the English would have fled, or the Scots would have achieved victory over them' [30].

As we saw, Walsingham credits Douglas with leading this doomed charge (or perhaps another). With a company of mounted knights, he spurred forward – this clearly shows the Scots were nowhere near the top of the hill, no downhill charge would have been possible. Obviously, in good quality harness, these Scottish horsemen stood a better chance than their workaday comrades, falling in such disheartening numbers around them but Walsingham brags gleefully of their fate and the comprehensive havoc and destruction wreaked by those terrible English bowmen.

As the great mass began to shiver and splinter, the English line advanced, Hotspur's riders finally touched spurs, but they barged into a rout not a battle. If Dunbar was responsible, as we might assume, for timing, he got it exactly right. Scottish morale had collapsed, perhaps 700 had already died and as many if not more drowned in the mad scramble to get over the Till [31].

Douglas, minus one eye, was taken as were Murdoch, Angus, Moray, Orkney, Montgomery, Erskine, Stewart of Innernethy, Sir Patrick Graham, Sir Robert Logan, and Sir Adam Forster. In addition to Gordon and Swinton, the butcher's bill featured Sir John Livingstone of Callendar, Alexander Ramsay of Dalhousie, and 'about 80 other knights'. The same correspondence refers to only five dead on the English side [32]. While this may be disingenuous, casualties had clearly been exceptionally light. After all, the English didn't come to contact until the enemy was already running, more a fox hunt than a fight. Walsingham states that 500 Scots drowned trying to cross the Glen and/or Till but the Evesham chronicle suggests twice as many [33].

To swell the cash value of the bag of prisoners, several notable French knights, come to slake their ardour, were also netted. These included Sir Jacques he Heilly and Pierre de Essarts. Charles VI laid out 3,000 francs towards the former's ransom and the Duke of Burgundy coughed up another 600 towards the latter's [34]. The path of the Scottish rout, where so many casualties would have been sustained, as they pelted towards the Till, is today sombrely known as Red Riggs, an innocuous looking field but a proper slaughterhouse on the day. Hardyng pens their epitaph: 'Six earls taken and XL, thousand plainly/ some fled, some died, some maimed there for ever/ that to Scotland again then came they never' [35]. Losers tend to get short shrift from chroniclers!

This Scots defeat was a major game-changer. By supreme irony it was the founder of the Scots resurgence and increased military hegemony, George Dunbar who helped undo the whole show. Hotspur too must get significant credit; their partnership had already produced a neat little victory at Nesbit Muir and we've no reason to suppose that Dunbar was the sole presiding genius. Victory at Homildon was the zenith of a remarkably effective partnership. Macdonald, rightly, is in no doubt as to the resonances: 'Defeats like … Humbleton deprived the Scots of leadership and brought a collapse of resistance in their wake, especially in the south. The English were given an opportunity to capture strongholds and force the submission of local men to the English king. They also gained prisoners … as a source of ransoms and, more importantly, a means to exert political leverage on Scotland' [36]. Homildon might have been the destruction of a largely magnatial force, but Macdonald goes on to assert '… Humbleton was the annihilation of the Scottish nation in arms' [37]. It's hard to disagree.

Wyntoun brushes over the whole debacle as rapidly as he decently can. He tells us Douglas, as Lord of Galloway, invaded England with a great power but was stopped at 'Homyldoune in to Glendaille' where Sir Henry Percy defeated him, 'Scottis men mony slayn war there' [38]. This was more than just a Percy/Dunbar victory. It was validation of the entire system of borderland defence originally instituted by Edward III. Now, Henry IV was the inheritor not an innovator. From the outset of the Scottish wars, the Percies had been major players. Yes, they'd done mightily well out of their service, but they had fought steadfastly, conscientiously, and well.

Despite the increased tempo of Scottish aggression since 1370, these northern lords had held their own and now, with little or no assistance from the King, they'd trounced the Scots and trashed their chances for a generation. Hotspur and his father, albeit ably abetted by Dunbar, had forged a strong and successful partnership. Otterburn ranks as a defeat, but Homildon had washed that stain away and now they'd won the most complete and, from an English perspective, near bloodless victory, the most perfect and effective use ever of the English warbow. And their success opened up the Scottish border like a magic wand.

Two of the captives proved of special interest to Hotspur; both Sir Walter Stewart of Forest and Thomas Ker, knights of Teviotdale, had been Percy adherents who'd since reverted. Yet a jury on day of truce had acquitted the pair of March Treason on account of their alleged oath-breaking. But this wasn't enough for Harry Percy, who had both men killed without trial. This rather nasty bout of vindictiveness seems to have been a Percy characteristic, allied to a casual contempt for due process which must have raised more than a few eyebrows, and not just on the Scottish side [36]. In this hour of his greatest triumph, Hotspur's blindness and hubris marred his success. Nonetheless, he was the man of the hour and his star was firmly in the ascendant: 'In faith it is a conquest for a prince to boast of' [39]. And it would be the death of him.

Hotspur's descent from 'hero to zero' and a traitor's death at Shrewsbury was a classic fall from grace, the product of vaunting ambition and it must be said some royal duplicity. His old fox of a father just about weathered that storm but learnt nothing and fell in a silly little battle at Bramham Moor five years later. The Percies were down but very far from out. If life on the border for gentleman and commoner alike bred one common trait, it was resilience!

NOTES:

[1] Macdonald, op. cit., p. 137.
[2] He followed the aptly named Archibald the Grim, a bastard son of the famous James the 'Black' Douglas, Bruce's ferocious and able lieutenant. Archibald did well in the Scottish service and David II, in 1369, appointed him Lord of Galloway. With the death of the legitimate 2nd Earl at Otterburn in August 1388, Archibald scooped up the other Douglas lands and titles becoming 3rd Earl, the most powerful man in Scotland.
[3] This was quite a plum, site of King John's Palace and utilised by kings from Henry II – Richard II, thus it was in Henry IV's gift, royal heart of Sherwood Forest.
[4] Ridpath, op. cit., p. 256.
[5] The Lord of the Isles was head of an ancient Norse-Gael confederacy under the hegemony of the chiefs of Clan Donald, whilst nominally vassals of the Scottish crown, they were largely autonomous until 1493.
[6] Macdonald, op cit., p. 139.
[7] Ibid., p. 141.
[8] Robert II had mental health issues and appears to be both depressive and incapable, so he relied on his very able and ambitious younger brother.
[9] Macdonald, op. cit., p. 147.
[10] Douglas was tried for the Duke's murder more for the sake of form than any prospect of a conviction.
[11] Cockburn-Hood, Thomas H., The House of Cockburn of that Ilk and Cadets Thereof (Edinburgh: n. pub, 1888), pp. 43-44.
[12] Paul, Sir J. B., The Scots Peerage (Edinburgh: David Douglas, 1905), pp. 137–138, where it is stated that the Sir Patrick Hepburn of Hailes who died at this battle was 'younger of Hailes', the son, not the father who survived him.
[13] De Fonblanque, op. cit., p. 206.

[14] Boardman, op. cit., p. 128.

[15] Kirby, J. L., ed., Calendar of Signet Letters of Henry IV and Henry V 1399 – 1422 (London: HMSO, 1978), letter 77; see also De Fonblanque, note p. 206.

[16] Bower suggests this figure and it's generally agreed upon. Hardyng as we saw gives the much higher and wholly improbable total of 40,000!

[17] A powerful talisman, signifying Black Douglas' final doomed charge to retrieve a casket containing Bruce's heart in Spain en route to the Holy Land.

[18] Macdonald, op. cit., p. 154.

[19] CDS, 620, p. 403.

[20] Ridpath, op. cit., p. 371. Newcastle Militia – these had probably marched north up the coastal route either before or as the Scots invaded (we know Douglas penetrated as far south as the Tyne).

[21] Walsingham, p. 251.

[22] http://www.battlefieldstrust.com/media/488.pdf, accessed 11 February 2021.

[23] Armstrong, op. cit., p. 83.

[24] Hardyng, p. 359.

[25] Ibid.

[26] Scotichronicon, Book XIV, pp. 45–47.

[27] Numbers: According to Bower, as mentioned, the Scots numbered 10,000; the only other authority to make an estimate stated that the Scots 'assembled atop the hill of "Hamilton", near the town of "Vallor" (Wooler), to the number of about twelve of thirteen thousand fighting men'. The same source, the History of the Life and Reign of Richard II, computed the English at 12,000 lances and 7,000 archers, see Stow, G. B., ed., Historia Vitae et Regni Ricardi Secundo introduced (Pennsylvania: University of Pennsylvania Press, 1977), p. 174.

[28] If the Scots did possess a missile arm, these would likely be using the short bow rather than the more powerful English warbow, insufficient 'firepower'.

[29] Walsingham, p. 251.

[30] Scotichronicon, Book XIV, pp. 45–47.

[31] CDS, letter from Henry IV 20 September, no 620, p. 403.

[32] Kirby, op. cit., no. 81; see also Ridpath p. 371.

[33] Given-Wilson, C., Chronicles of the Revolution 1397–1400 (Manchester: Manchester University Press, 1993), p. 121.

[34] Moranville, H., ed., Chronographia Regum Francorum, iii (Paris: n. pub., 1897), p. 203; Macdonald points out that Heilly had been a comrade of the Earl of Crawford in his naval actions.

[35] Hardyng, p. 359.

[36] Macdonald, op. cit., p. 154.

[37] Ibid.

[38] Wyntoun, p. 401.

[39] Shakespeare: King Henry IV First Part, I: i.

[40] De Fonblanque, op. cit., records that an entry in the Syon House papers records that when Dr. Thomas Percy, the family's chaplain and chronicler, visited the hamlet (c. 1605) the street was still known as Percy's Row, note p. 206).

[41] https://historicengland.org.uk/content/docs/listing/battlefields/homildon-hill/, accessed 11 February 2021.

[42] Ibid.

CHAPTER FIVE: GAMES OF THRONES

'If the cycle of violence that had engulfed the English Crown for nearly five decades seemed finally to be coming to an end, it was only because there were so few candidates left to kill!'

Dan Jones, The Wars of the Roses: The Fall of the Plantagenets and the Rise of the Tudors

Just possibly, none of it ever need have happened anyway if it wasn't for those two great houses in the north of England. When, in the north, Percy adherents tried to ambush a Neville wedding party, the affair on the surface, may appear as little more than a local, bloodless brawl. Nonetheless, it could be said to represent the first significant, armed clash between these two pre-eminent northern affinities which were also active in the wider movement to reform and ultimately remove the Lancastrian administration [1]. That policy, begun by John of Gaunt, of buttressing the power of the Nevilles as a counterweight to the Percies, was continued by Henry VI and the rise of the former was, not infrequently, at the expense of the latter [2]. Neville prestige was particularly high in County Durham, where the influence of their rivals was noticeably weaker.

RUMBLINGS IN THE NORTH

Richard, Earl of Salisbury, inherited the bulk of the Neville holdings in Yorkshire, centred on the valuable estates of Middleham and Sheriff Hutton. The worth of this legacy, Salisbury as the son of the Earl of Westmorland's second wife, sparked a deep division with the senior branch, which retained the title and lands in the north-west. Undisturbed by this family rift, Salisbury went on to steadily build up the scale of his holdings. His own eldest son, another Richard, added the dazzling Beauchamp inheritance and the earldom of Warwick to his titles and was to mature into a key figure of the political landscape, bringing the power of his name to its ultimate zenith before crashing to ruin.: 'Warwick the Kingmaker'.

The three ridings of Yorkshire were parcelled out, in terms of land ownership, between four of the greatest magnates of the real, including the Crown as Duchy of Lancaster, the Percies, Nevilles, and the Duke of York, Salisbury's brother-in-law. The Percy holdings east of the Pennines were interspersed with those of Salisbury and York, though the latter showed little interest in his northern estates [3]. Having taken the years from 1416–1440 for the Earl of Northumberland to recover the bulk of his father's lost inheritance, Salisbury, who had been elevated to his earldom in 1429, had had ample time to consolidate his hold on manors in Cleveland, Westmorland, Cumberland, and the important lordship of Raby [4].

Most aggressive of the Percy brood was the Earl's second son Lord Egremont who had threatened the life of the Sheriff of Cumberland, Thomas de la Mare, an adherent of Salisbury [5]. Egremont, who had gained his lordship in 1449 at the age of 25, typified all the adverse traits of his name: '... quarrelsome, violent and contemptuous of all authority, he possessed all the worst characteristics of a Percy for which his grandfather [Hotspur] is still a byword' [6]. Salisbury's sister, Eleanor, was married to Northumberland, but the ties of blood counted for little in a game with such high stakes. Both families possessed mature and ambitious patriarchs, and each had a brood of young, restless, and potentially lawless sons, with no shortage of available manpower [7].

When Thomas Neville married Maud Stanhope, this proved a provocation too far for the volatile Egremont. The bride had been married before, to Robert, Lord Willoughby of Eresby, who had died the previous summer. She was also, and significantly, the niece and co-heiress of Ralph, Lord Cromwell, a choleric character himself but one who had acquired the leases on two choice manors at Wressle and Burwell in Lincolnshire, previously in the hands of the Percies.

In February 1440 Cromwell had purchased the reversionary interest. Northumberland, whose line had spent lavishly on Wressle, had litigated in vain. When Cromwell married his niece to a Neville, he was adding insult to injury [8]. Tension had been mounting throughout the early summer of 1452. In June the King had summoned both Egremont and John Neville, by the end of that month, Neville was laying plans for an ambush of his own. On 2 July, Henry dissolved Parliament and journeyed north to confront his quarrelsome vassals. He proposed that Percy and his affinity should be ready to serve in Gascony which would have got them nicely out of the way. However, the proposal came to nothing.

The King established a commission of Oyer and Terminer, the membership of which included both the rival earls, Viscount Beaumont, and some 14 others [9]. A fortnight later, the commission was re-issued but to little effect. Salisbury, who unlike Northumberland, sat in the Council, undoubtedly used his influence to pack the membership with allies, including such Neville stalwarts as Sir James Pickering, Sir Henry Fitzhugh, and Sir Henry le Scrope of Bolton [10].

Despite the commission's excellent credentials, it proved ineffective amidst a rising tide of disorder and, by the end of July, a new and perhaps less overtly partisan body was set up under the guidance of Sir William Lucy, a knight of Northamptonshire and Council member, his leadership supported by leading counsel. Immediately Sir William set to work, summoning Ralph Neville, Sir John Conyers, Sir James Pickering, Sir Ralph Randolf, Sir Thomas Mountford, Richard Aske, Thomas Sewer, and John Alcombe. On 10 August nine Percy adherents were summoned, together with both Sir Ralph and Sir Richard Percy [11].

Undeterred by the failure at Heworth, Richard Percy and a band of thuggish adherents now embarked on a spree of vandalism, culminating in the kidnapping of Lawrence Catterall, the bailiff of Staincliff Wapentake, who was roughly dragged from his devotions in Gargrave Church on 9 September. He was subsequently incarcerated, at first in Isel Castle and, latterly, at Cockermouth; obviously the luckless man had, in some unrecorded way, offended the Percies [12]. The unrest continued; on 25 September a brace of Percy retainers, a John Catterall and Sir John Salvin, pillaged the house of William Hebdon, vicar of Aughton. This may have been in reprisal for John Neville's plundering of the Earl of Northumberland's property at Catton [13].

On 8 October King Henry wrote plaintively to both earls, asking them to exercise some degree of control over their headstrong siblings. At this time the King's mental health was already causing concern, he had no history of instability and his Queen, with the court faction, were not inclined to advertise the fact. The exact nature of the King's malady has never been definitively diagnosed, though catatonic schizophrenia has been suggested.

Whatever the cause, the plain fact was that Henry's deteriorating mental condition contributed to his administration's weakening grip on law and order. By 17 October Egremont had assembled perhaps 50 'tooled-up' retainers, who mustered at Topcliffe. Rather less than half of these were from the Percy heartland of Northumberland or Newcastle upon Tyne [14]. Heedless of feeble royal admonitions, both sides were squaring up for a scrap and a confrontation of sorts probably occurred at Sandhutton on 20 October.

Here, Salisbury and Warwick, joined by Sir John and Sir Thomas Neville, were bolstered by such trusty friends as Sir Henry Fitzhugh and Sir Henry le Scrope.

Not to be outdone the Percy affinity were led by the Earl and Lord Poynings, Lord Egremont, and Sir Richard Percy. The standoff seems to have amounted to little more than bravado on both sides but the magnates themselves had now clearly shown their hands in the fracas. Battle lines had been drawn, even if very few blows had yet been struck [15].

As the tempo of strife rose the King's grasp on reality declined and it had, by now, become impossible to hide the fact of his condition. Matters were further stirred by the birth, on 13 October of a son, Edward of Lancaster. With this York's hopes of securing the succession from a childless monarch vanished like the mist. Increasingly vociferous, the Duke, as the senior magnate, was clamouring to be appointed as regent during the term of the King's illness, a demand the Queen and Somerset were equally determined to resist. On 25 October the Council convened at York with both Salisbury and Warwick in attendance. Both Northumberland and Lord Poynings were pointedly absent [16]. The Duke of York had married Salisbury's sister, Cicely, the celebrated 'Rose of Raby'. As a man he was: '... a somewhat austere, remote, and unsympathetic figure, with little capacity of inclination to seek out and win support from his fellow noblemen or from the wider public' [17].

York had no love for Somerset, whom he perceived, almost certainly correctly, as the main block to his inclusion in the King's inner circle. No sooner was York in office than his former rival was consigned to a sojourn in the Tower [18]. Meanwhile Lord Cromwell, notoriously litigious, had been at odds in the courts with Henry Holand, Duke of Exeter. The matter had become so heated between these two choleric peers that, in July 1453, both had been temporarily incarcerated. With the Neville marriage Cromwell found an ally in Salisbury, Exeter, inevitably, sought common cause with the Percies [19]. On 27 March 1454 the Duke of York was formally installed as Protector and, less than a week later his brother-in-law was appointed as Chancellor. Secure in his high office, Salisbury summoned Egremont and Richard Percy to attend upon his convenience on pain of forfeiture and outlawry [20].

Whereas the Percies might disdain the King's feeble complaints, Salisbury, in the mantle of Chancellor, could not be ignored. York's appointment marked a period of more decisive governance, though the Nevilles were clearly, as ever, motivated by self-interest. Sensing the mood, Sir Thomas Neville of Brancepeth (not Salisbury's son but a younger brother of the Earl of Westmorland, and no friend to his cousins) took the opportunity to 'take up' the property of Sir John Salvin at Egton in Eskdale. This was accomplished with a body of two dozen armed retainers who lifted some £80.00 worth of 'gear' [21].

In May 1454 York, as Protector, sent a strongly worded summons to the Earl of Northumberland, ordering him to appear before the Council on 12 June.

Lord Poynings and Ralph Percy were summoned to appear ten days beforehand. Already, on 3 April, Exeter had been removed from his lucrative and prestigious post of Lord Admiral [22]. Not unsurprisingly, Percies were not famed for following the path of humility.

On 6 May, they showed what respect they had for the new Chancellor by vandalising his house in York and roughing up one of his tenants, John Skipworth. Many of these now involved in this fresh rash of disturbances had been 'Out' on Heworth Moor the previous summer. By the middle of May Egremont was mustering his affinity at Spofforth and there, on the 14th, he was joined by Exeter, bridling at his humiliation. Riotous behaviour broke out in the streets of York, alarming the burgesses, especially after the mob had brutally assaulted the Mayor and the Recorder.

A wave of anarchy now swept through the North Riding, whilst Exeter, not to be outdone, busily stirred up trouble in Lancashire and Cheshire [23]. Needless to say, the invigorated Council, supported by York as Protector, were not minded to remain inert whilst these troubles flared. Sir Thomas Stanley, the Duchy of Lancaster's Receiver for the counties of Lancashire and Cheshire, ably assisted by Sir Thomas Harrington, saw Exeter off in short order. The Protector himself entered the City of York on 19 May – the rioters fled the streets [24].

Exeter, whose thuggish traits matched those of Egremont, was, nonetheless, one of King Henry's closest blood relations, tracing his line through John of Gaunt. It is conceivable he perceived, in this localised brawl, the chance to light a fuse that might unseat York and see him appointed in his stead [25]. On 21 May, with Egremont and his affinity, he reappeared in York and set about further intimidation of the much-abused mayor and burgesses. Disorder flared once again through the shire. Egremont was sufficiently inflamed to solicit aid from James II of Scotland. The Scots had recently violated the previous year's truce and the herald dispatched to Edinburgh to register the Council's protest was kidnapped at Spofforth. This smacked of rebellion and the rebels, as they could now be termed, planned to lure the Protector into an ambush beneath the walls of York [26].

York summoned both the ringleaders to appear on 25 June and used the interval to consolidate his position and build up local forces. By the 15th of the month, he was reinforced by Warwick and Lord Greystoke, a week later Lord Clifford, the Earl of Shrewsbury, and Sir Henry Fitzhugh added their retinues. Several summonses had been issued and, several individuals suffered forfeiture or even outlawry, Exeter, Egremont and Sir Richard Percy all failed to appear [27].

For all their violent posturing the rebels had completely failed to achieve any serious objective. Exeter crept back to London. By 8 July he was in captivity, and by the 24th he had been safely incarcerated in Pontefract Castle. The snake might appear to be scotched but was still writhing. York did not feel sufficiently secure in the north with the Percies still at large to return to the capital [28].

Matters continued in this tense vein until the autumn when a further confrontation took place; this time at Stamford Bridge, heavy with ancient blood, some miles east of York and held by the Nevilles. Whether any actual fighting occurred is doubtful, but the Percy faction were confounded by treachery, when one of their own bailiffs, Peter Lound, with some two hundred followers deserted. The Nevilles, led by Thomas and John, pounced on their discomfited enemies and captured both Egremont and Sir Richard Percy.

If the Nevilles felt they had cause for satisfaction, their triumph was short-lived for, in December 1454, Henry VI recovered his wits and was deemed able to resume the reins of government, the office of Protector was thus redundant. On 7 February Somerset was freed from the Tower and reinstated to all his many offices. A month later Salisbury bowed to the inevitable and resigned as Chancellor. A mere seven days after his departure Exeter was set at liberty. Somerset and the Queen would be in the mood for retribution rather than compromise, a further and greater trial of strength now appeared inevitable.

What had changed since that earlier showdown at Blackheath was that York was not now entirely isolated – true the Courtenay's, disgruntled at the Duke's handling of their feud with Bonville, had switched their allegiance to the court faction. Now, however, York had the powerful support of the Neville earls, Salisbury, and Warwick with their large affinities. Somerset had blundered in allowing the alienation of the Nevilles who, with York, now believed the Duke with Wiltshire, Exeter, Beaumont, and Northumberland, was at the head of a faction now intent upon their destruction. The situation was considerably more volatile than it had been in 1450; the scene was thus set for armed confrontation. On 22 May 1455, the first armies clashed in the streets of St. Albans; Northumberland was amongst the dead, as were Somerset and Lord Clifford. First blood had been drawn.

The Scots, who might otherwise be expected to capitalise on England's turmoil, had plenty problems of their own. The fifteenth century was plagued by a succession of minority kingships, with all the intercnine squabbling of over-ambitious regents and factional sparring. James I inherited as a minor, spent a long time in English captivity, yet emerged as something of an Anglophile before being done in by his own magnates at Perth. James II, he of the 'fiery face' (on account of a livid birthmark), was also a boy king and spent much of his unsatisfactory reign settling scores with the House of Douglas, most overmighty of overmighty subjects. James II, whose reign proved even unhappier, also came to the throne as a minor.

On Palm Sunday (29 March) 1461, on a sleet slashed moor above Tadcaster, young Edward IV of England won a hard fought, hugely bloody battle at Towton. The Act of Attainder, passed by his victorious Parliament, attainted all the northern lords who had fallen in the slaughter, the Earl of Northumberland, Lords Clifford, Neville, and Dacre. Many others from the region also found themselves dispossessed [29]. In his correspondence to Coppini, George Neville had been at pains to stress the magnitude of the victory: 'The armies having been formed and marshalled separately, they set forth against the enemy and at length, on Palmsunday, near a town called Ferrybridge, about 16 miles from out city, our enemies were routed and broken in pieces' [30].

Though the Lancastrians had been grievously beaten, the Milanese ambassador to the court of Charles VII, Prospero di Camulio, writing a mere four days after George Neville, sounded a shrewdly cautious note: 'Firstly, if the King and Queen of England with the other fugitives mentioned above are not taken, it seems certain that in time fresh disturbances will arise' [31]. This observation was to prove grimly prophetic as the focus of the war moved northward into Northumberland and where it was to fester for the next three years.

WAR IN THE NORTH

The county of Northumberland was a different region from North Yorkshire where the troubles of the preceding decade and the battles of that phase of the wars which occurred between 1459 and 1461 had been centred. There is, perhaps a tendency amongst historians to point generally to the 'north' as though the land north of the Trent was a single region. This is, of course, not the case, nor was it so in the fifteenth century. The cultural, topographical, and social fabric of the north embraced 'a kaleidoscope of overlapping regions and localities' [32]. Northumberland is the most northerly of English counties and shares a long border with Scotland. Northumbrians and Scots had been embroiled in endemic warfare since the late thirteenth century [33].

To the west Carlisle, with its great red sandstone Norman Keep, had been the gateway to the English west for centuries, defying every effort by the Scots. The city was a flourishing port, from where ships plied the busy routes to Ireland and Man. Naworth and Askerton castles stood along the West March, the Scots frequent choice of incursion route. A number of these fortifications were to prove significant in the struggles of 1461–1464 but none more than the three great east coast fortresses of Alnwick, Bamburgh, and Dunstanburgh. Of these, the first was a jewel of the Percies and much improved by them over several generations [34]. Bamburgh occupies a spur of the Whin Sill, rising 150 feet from the flat coastal plain. The ancient seat of the Northumbrian kings, it was said to be the

'Joyous Garde' of Arthurian legend [35]. Begun by Thomas, Earl of Lancaster, Dunstanburgh also occupies a dolerite outcrop, much rebuilt in the later fourteenth century by John of Gaunt, who held the wardenship in the 1380s [36].

After receiving the dire news of her defeat at Towton, Queen Margaret fled north into Scotland. With King Henry in tow, her young son Edward of Lancaster and a scattering of survivors including Somerset, Roos, Exeter, and Sir John Fortescue, she sought sanctuary in the northern kingdom. Margaret might have shared the view that Northumberland was solidly Lancastrian in sentiment, following the lead of the Percies who, as it has been argued 'have the hearts of the north and always have had' [37]. Whilst the Earl of Northumberland found his hegemony challenged in Durham and North Yorkshire by the Nevilles, Salisbury and his affinity had little influence in the most northerly shire.

On 22 April 1461, some three weeks after Towton, King Edward IV progressed northwards to Newcastle where on 1 May he attended the demise of James Butler, Earl of Wiltshire whose happy knack of slipping unscathed from a few tight spots had finally deserted him. With him was John Neville, Lord Montagu, who had previously been held captive in York. He had escaped the fate of the Yorkist lords taken at Wakefield when he himself was captured at 2nd St. Albans. His brother Richard had Somerset's younger sibling Edmund incarcerated at Calais, so a form of quid pro quo had obtained. Having established his authority, however, the King soon tired of the north, pressing matters awaited him in London and he was pleased to delegate mopping up operations to the Nevilles.

James II, King of Scotland, had led a six-day chevauchee through the English borderland in 1456 and had attempted to retake Berwick in the following year. His interest in the dynastic struggle unfolding in England was largely opportunistic and he had petitioned Charles VII of France to launch an assault on the Calais Pale. When James heard of the Yorkist victory at Northampton and the capture of Henry VI, he began a siege of Roxburgh, the last bastion of the former Pale. On 3 August, with his batteries sited, he was to be joined by his Queen, Marie de Guelders. The King ordered a cannonade to herald his consort but one of the great guns burst, a not infrequent peril, and James was fatally wounded when a fragment smashed his thigh [38].

His heir, now King James III, was only eight and Scotland was again subject to the uncertainties of a regency council. This body quickly split into factions – the 'Old' lords led by Bishop Kennedy of St. Andrews and the 'Young' who championed the widowed Queen. Margaret of Anjou was desperate for allies, to the extent that she would trade both Carlisle and Berwick. On 25 April, the keys of Berwick were handed over, but the citizens of Carlisle would have no truck with Scots and grimly barred their gates, refusing the Queen's summons.

A joint Scots and Lancastrian expedition was dispatched to besiege the city and the Yorkists perceived the threat sufficiently potent for Edward to bring forward the date of his coronation to 28 June, so he would be free to lead a march northwards. In the event this proved unnecessary as the resourceful Montagu, raising local forces, saw the besiegers off. Margaret had demonstrated not only the measure of her desperation but an epic disregard for the sentiment of the very northerners she sought to woo, to whom the Scots were a despised and frequent foe. Berwick upon Tweed was destined to remain in their hands until 1482 when it was retaken by Richard of Gloucester, at which point it had changed hands no fewer than 14 times [39]!

There were further disturbances; the French were said to be about to descend on the Channel Islands, led by Queen Margaret's fervent admirer Pierre de Breze. With the death, however, on 22 July of Charles VII, the likelihood of French intermeddling diminished. The new sovereign had little time for the gallant de Breze who was effectively put out to grass [40]. Warwick won the loyalty of a Burgundian captain, the Seigneur de la Barde who, having succumbed to the Earl's charisma and the attractions of his pay chest, led a company of hand gunners previously in the service of Duke Philip, joining the Yorkist ranks after the disaster at Wakefield [41].

In England the spark of rebellion flared briefly in East Anglia and, more seriously, in Wales where, as in Northumberland, the Lancastrian lords still held several major castles. By the autumn the Welsh adherents had been bested in the field and their strongholds systematically reduced, by the end of the year only mighty Harlech still held out. Feeling themselves relatively secure in Northumberland the Lancastrian lords, Dacre, Roos, and Rougemont Grey, launched a raid into Durham, advancing their banners as far as Brancepeth, King Henry present in their train. True to his fresh allegiance, Lawrence Booth, the Prince Bishop, previously a staunch supporter, but now converted by the great victory at Towton into an equally enthusiastic Yorkist, mustered the county levies and saw them off: 'The problem here [the north] was a complicated one, Henry VI and his supporters were sheltered and aided by the Scots, and, to a lesser extent, by the French. The region itself was remote, difficult of access and dominated by the great fortresses' [42].

ALARUMS AND EXCURSIONS

In July Warwick was appointed as warden for both East and West Marches, ably assisted by his brother Montagu. The Nevilles continued mopping up until September, by which time Alnwick surrendered and a garrison of one hundred men-at-arms installed. In early October Dunstanburgh capitulated; the terms of surrender were negotiated by the Lancastrian castellan, Sir Ralph Percy. It might be presumed that the Yorkist triumph was complete but for as long as the defeated court had a base in Scotland, the border would be troubled.

Edward IV, painfully aware of the narrowness of his own affinity and his fragile grip on the sceptre, was prepared to be accommodating and overlook past affiliations, a bold if risky strategy, in contrast to Warwick's approach which was considerably more and ruthlessly pragmatic. The King was disposed to permit Sir Ralph to remain in charge at Dunstanburgh, a mistake, for the Percy soon reverted. Another Lancastrian, Sir William Tailboys, emerging from Scotland swiftly re-captured Alnwick, whilst, in the west, Lord Dacre seized Naworth [43].

Both Edward and his lieutenant perceived that a diplomatic offensive against the Scots, aimed at depriving the Lancastrians of their foothold in the northern kingdom, was the only sure means of establishing firm control over the English border marches. Warwick thus held preliminary talks with Marie de Gueldres in April 1462, followed by a further meeting in July but the Scottish council, already divided, seemed determined to sit on the fence and wait upon events. In March Somerset and Lord Hungerford had returned empty handed from a begging mission to the French court. Undeterred, Margaret of Anjou borrowed £290 from the Regent and sailed from Kirkcudbright in April; she was prepared, as a measure of her desperation, to trade Calais as she had done Berwick [44].

Whilst Warwick sought an accommodation with Marie de Gueldres, his forces in Northumberland resumed the offensive; by July Montagu had compelled Dacre's surrender and regained Naworth, a vital bastion in the west. In the east Tailboys surrendered the keys of Alnwick to the Yorkist triumvirate of Lord Hastings, Sir John Howard, and Sir Ralph Grey, whilst Bamburgh was taken by Sir William Tunstall [45]: 'The support and sympathy of the local population worked against what was regarded as a hostile government and enabled even small forces of active rebels to defy it for months on end' [46].

The detail on the surrender of Alnwick is somewhat confusing. Worcester is the only chronicler who mentions the event whilst the Paston correspondence places Lord Hastings at Carlisle with Warwick in July, though this would not necessarily have prevented him from accepting the surrender. Equally, there is no reason to doubt the appointment of Tailboys as castellan, he remained a staunch Lancastrian till diverted by greed and misappropriated the funds placed in his care [47].

The Paston Letters also place Sir William Tunstall at Bamburgh in the autumn of 1462; his brother, Sir Richard, sat in the opposite camp and had been in the castle that summer. The collapse of the defensive chain of great border holds and the lack of any material support from either France or Scotland appeared to sound the final knell for King Henry's faltering faction. Queen Margaret remained unbowed, however, and proved able still to fan the dying embers of her cause. On 25 October she made landfall possibly, as Worcester asserts, at Bamburgh; the expedition was led by the faithful de Breze and comprised some 2,000 French mercenaries.

These invaders marched inland to Alnwick which, being but poorly provisioned, promptly surrendered, Hungerford and de Breze's son were left in command. Somerset based himself at Bamburgh where, by the fortune of war, Sir William Tunstall was taken by this brother Richard; Dunstanburgh also changed hands. Though these achievements passed control of the border fortresses back into Queen Margaret's hands, there was no popular upsurge in favour of her house. Whether she intended simply to foment local anti-Yorkist sentiment or whether she was seeking, in the larger game, to open a bridgehead for Scottish intervention, remains unclear [48].

What is certain is that having secured these three key bastions she, with the bulk of her expeditionary force, immediately took ship presumably heading for Scotland, there to press for significant intervention. Though she and de Breze did complete the sea passage, many of the ships were wrecked by adverse weather in the cold North Sea; men were scattered, while stores and cash were lost. Some four hundred French were stranded on the Northumbrian coast; foiled in their attempt to enter Bamburgh they fell back towards Holy Island, firing what remained of their boats. Though they overawed the few defenders they soon found themselves under determined assault from Yorkists led by the Bastard of Ogle and 'One Maners, a squire'. Falling back and barricading the Priory the French were soon obliged to seek terms [49].

Though clearly wrong-footed by the Queen, Warwick soon recovered and marched his forces into Northumberland by 30 October, with the King following on 3 November. Though he reached Durham by the 16th Edward was debilitated by a bout of measles which enfeebled him for the short, remaining span of the year [50]. Meanwhile the Earl vigorously prosecuted siege operations against the northern castles. Establishing his forward command post at Warkworth, he entrusted the Duke of Norfolk with responsibility for supply and logistics through the port of Newcastle. The earl of Kent was charged to reduce Alnwick with Lord Scales, the Earl of Worcester, and Sir Ralph Grey before Dunstanburgh; Montagu and Ogle leaguered Bamburgh. This was Warwick at his best, a war of attrition, free from the uncertainties and snap decisions necessary in open field, the Earl rode around his outposts daily, the supply from Newcastle moved smoothly despite the onset of winter conditions and the desperate state of the roads.

The tactical initiative had swung the other way. From Bamburgh Somerset and the turncoat Percy looked out over the besiegers' lines, Sir Richard Tunstall and Thomas Fyndern held Dunstanburgh. John Paston recorded that William Hasildene, Matilda Walsh, and John Carter acted as purveyors for the Yorkists before Bamburgh and the King's Pavilions were erected by William Hill, a servant of the Master of the Tents. Paston goes on to suggest Warwick had mustered some 10,000 soldiers whilst Somerset had fewer than 300 defenders [51]. Thorough as these siege preparations had been, the mere show of strength was sufficient to overawe the defenders, there was no bombardment, the great guns never progressed further than the dockside at Newcastle.

Even the lighter field pieces were not deployed, these would have been turned against Scottish forces had any intervention occurred. There was a natural reluctance to reduce the vital border holds by gunfire, since they were vital, in normal circumstances, for the defence of the northern shire and borderland. The prospect of campaigning throughout a miserable Northumbrian winter had scant appeal: 'Tough, hardy and used to discomfort as they were, medieval soldiers had a deep distaste for winter campaigning ... Henry V had forced his armies to maintain winter sieges in Northern France, but no one had yet attempted them in the even bleaker conditions of Northumbria in December' [52].

On Christmas Eve the Lancastrian Lords negotiated the surrender of both Bamburgh and Dunstanburgh; for the abandonment of their allegiance to Henry VI both Somerset and Sir Ralph Percy were to be restored to their titles and property. Both swore fealty to Edward IV. This capitulation may reflect a loss of morale – neither fortress was yet seriously threatened, but there appeared little hope of relief and Somerset may possibly have been resentful of the Frenchman de Breze being given overall authority over his head. Edward, for his part, was prepared to exercise a fair measure of pragmatism; the feud with the Beauforts ran deep, the blood of his father, brother, uncle, and cousin stained Somerset's hands [53].

In the meantime, the remaining garrison at Alnwick maintained their continued defiance. They had cause for comfort as the indefatigable de Breze was leading a Scots relief force. Warwick was caught off-balance and appears to have been seized with that dangerous indecision which gripped in moments of crisis where his careful planning and rigid control of events was suddenly undone. He withdrew his forces before Alnwick with such indecent haste that the Scots were led to believe that they were being lured into an ambush. This produced a near-farcical denouement as the Scots, in turn, speedily withdrew, leaving only a skeleton force and the discomfited besiegers re-occupied the lines they'd so recently abandoned [54]. The depleted garrison wasted no time in coming to terms and Warwick appointed Sir John Ashley to command with Ralph Grey as deputy, a demotion the latter bitterly resented believing the senior post should have been his. As was so often the case, this personal grudge would bear bitter fruit [55].

By the end of 1462 the position appeared to have returned to that which had obtained in the summer, prior to Queen Margaret's return but the Yorkist grip was flimsier than the tactical position would suggest. Percy was at heart a Lancastrian and Grey was nursing his resentment. In the spring of 1463 Percy reverted, opening the gates of Bamburgh whilst Grey seized Alnwick by a coup de main: 'And within three or four months after that false knight and traitor, Sir Ralph Percy, by false treason, took the said Sir John Astley prisoner, and delivered him to Queen Margaret, and then delivered the castle to the Lord Hungerford and unto the Frenchmen accompanied with him' [56].

Having neatly reversed the position in Northumberland the Lancastrians now concentrated their efforts against Norham, that 'Queen of Border Fortresses' held by the Prince Bishop and a prize which had, for decades, eluded the Scots. Frustrated by the loss of Alnwick, Bamburgh, and now Dunstanburgh which Sir Ralph Percy had also gifted, Warwick was constrained to move swiftly and raise the siege of Norham, with Lord Montagu scattering Queen Margaret and her marchers after a lightening march.

So swift and sure was this riposte both she and King Henry were nearly taken. The Lancastrian garrisons made no attempt to interfere. Despite this success the Earl did not propose to sit down, once again, before the great walls of the coastal castles. He now preferred to bring further diplomatic pressure to bear on the Scots and thus cut off the Lancastrians' aid at source. Warwick could undoubtedly sense that enthusiasm for the House of Lancaster was waning; the Scots efforts at Carlisle and now Norham had been contemptuously repulsed. Henry, sensing the changing mood of his hosts, transferred his truncated court either to Alnwick or Bamburgh [57].

Edward had, by now, obtained a further grant of taxation revenues from the English Parliament to be expended against the Scots (though the Commons approved the funds it was some time before the king came into possession of the cash). Warwick had, however, precipitated offensive action, with the support of the Archbishop of York, by launching a destructive chevauchee into the Lothians [58]. Margaret and de Breze were both presently engaged in the siege of Norham; their forces were surprised and scattered by Montagu.

After the debacle at Norham, Queen Margaret, fearful for her son's safety and accompanied by de Breze, took ship for Flanders where she proposed to solicit aid from Duke Philip. These wily Burgundians, the Duke and his son, the Count of Charolais (later famous as the mercurial Philip the Bold), were prepared to make encouraging noises and Charles wrote reassuringly to Henry immured within Bamburgh's stout walls (this correspondence was carried by a John Brown and William Baker, the latter one of Exeter's affinity). No practical assistance was, however, forthcoming.

Gregory [59] asserts that the Lancastrians sailed immediately from Sluys, having escaped from the trap at Norham, pursued, as the chronicler avers, almost to the walls of Bamburgh. Margaret and her shrunken contingent, which included Exeter, Fortescue, and the remaining Frenchmen, filled four 'balynggarys' (ballingers = large, sleek, double ended, and oared galleys). Gregory also recounts that a French drummer boy refused to embark and waited calmly on the shore. This disenchanted youth demanded, vociferously, a place in Warwick's retinue and the Earl accepted the request; the renegade doing good service for several years [60].

Unmolested by either Warwick or his brother, King Henry maintained the façade of dominion over his tiny Northumbrian domain. In December 1463 he issued letters of protection to William Burgh, Constable of Prudhoe, seeking to consolidate his faction's grip in Tynedale where Lancastrian sentiment remained viable. Early in the New Year he issued a charter to the burgesses of Edinburgh. The French ambassador who attended this shadow court was Pierre Cousinot and whom the King used as a messenger to his wife in Burgundy. Henry's proposed strategy comprised a tripartite alliance between himself, as titular King of England, the Count of Charolais, and the Duke of Brittany. He pleaded with the great lords of France to work against any understanding that might be brokered between Edward and Louis.

He begged aid from the Burgundians. He begged aid, particularly ordnance, from Rene of Anjou his father-in-law. He entreated the Bretons to exploit unrest in Wales and join with the Earl of Pembroke [61]. Henry's main difficulty was lack of funds, and all his entreaties included a request for cash. Deprived of parliamentary grants, destitute of lands and treasure, he had no fiscal base to fund aggressive action, his faction had no real leadership and the prospects for 1464 seemed bleak. The single rogue card was John Beaufort, Duke of Somerset, the erstwhile champion of Lancaster. His decision, taken in that spring to revert to his hereditary allegiance, would spark the final, dramatic denouement of the campaigns in the north.

NOTES:

[1] Griffiths, R. A., 'Local Rivalries and National Politics; the Percies, the Nevilles and the Duke of Exeter 1452–1455', Speculum, 43 (1968), p. 589.

[2] Weiss, H., 'A Power in the North? The Percies in the Fifteenth Century', Historical Journal, 19.2 (1976), pp. 501–509.

[3] Griffiths, op. cit., p. 589.

[4] Ibid., p. 590.

[5] Griffiths, op. cit., p. 592.

[6] Ibid., p. 591.

[7] Ibid., p. 592.

[8] Ibid., p. 594.

[9] Ibid.

[0] Ibid., p. 595.

[11] Ibid.

[12] Ibid., p. 602.

[13] Ibid., p. 603.

[14] Ibid., p. 604.

[15] Ibid., p. 605.

[16] Ibid.

[17] Ross, C., Edward IV (London: Yale University Press, 2002), p. 28.

[18] Ibid., p. 29.

[19] Griffiths, op. cit., p. 608.

[20] Ibid., p. 609.

[21] Ibid., p. 610.

[22] Ibid.

[23] Ibid., p. 611.

[24] Ibid., p. 612.

[25] Ibid., p. 613.

[26] Ibid., p. 616.

[27] Ibid., p. 620.

[28] Ibid., p. 621.

[29] Rot. Parl. 1st Edward IV 1461 vol. v fols 477–478.

[30] Calendar of State Papers and Manuscripts existing in the Archives and Collections of Milan, ed. and trans. by A. B. Hinds (London: HMSO, 1912), pp. 61–62.

[31] Ibid., pp. 74–77.

[32] Pollard, A. J., 'Characteristics of the Fifteenth Century North', in Government Religion and Society in Northern England 1000–1700, ed. by C. Appleby & P. Dalton (Oxford: Oxford University Press, 1977), p. 131.

[33] Hepple, L. W., A History of Northumberland and Newcastle upon Tyne (London: Philimore, 1976), pp. 14–15.

[34] Pevsner, N. & Richmond, I., Northumberland, The Buildings of England (London: Penguin, 1992), pp. 135–136.

[35] Pevsner & Richmond, op. cit., pp. 155–156.

[36] Ibid., pp. 258–259.

[37] Charlesworth, D., 'Northumberland in the Early Years of Edward IV', Archaeologia Aeliana, 4th Series (1953), p. 70.

[38] Lynch, op. cit., pp. 146–151.

[39] Lomas, R., op. cit., pp. 45–50.

[40] Murray Kendall, P., Warwick the Kingmaker (London: Weidenfeld & Nicolson, 2002), p. 86.

[41] Ibid., pp. 202–203.

[42] Ross, op. cit., p. 56.

[43] Gillingham, J., Wars of the Roses (London: Weidenfeld & Nicolson, 2001), pp. 140–141.

[44] Scottish Exchequer Rolls, vii Ramsay ii p. 290.

[45] Gillingham, op. cit., p. 141.

[46] Ross, op. cit., p. 60.

[47] Worcester, 'Annales', p. 470.

[48] Ibid., p. 480.

[49] NCH, vol. 1, p. 48.

[50] Worcester, 'Annales', p. 480.

[51] Paston Letters, no. 464.

[52] Ross, op. cit., pp. 62–63.

[53] Gregory's Chronicle, p. 219.

[54] Ibid., p. 219.

[55] Ibid., p. 220.

[56] Ibid., p. 221.

[57] The Yearbook de Termino Paschae 4 Edward IV in Priory of Hexham, Surtees Society p. cviii gives Alnwick as the location but NCH, vol. 1, p. 46 claims Bamburgh – the latter seems more likely being on the coast and closer to Scotland.

[58] Ross, op. cit., p. 65.

[59] Gregory's Chronicle, p. 222.

[60] Ibid., p. 222.

[61] NCH, vol. 1, p. 46.

CHAPTER SIX: SEASONS OF DISCONTENT

> Methinks truly/ Bounden am I/ And that greatly/ To be content/ Seeing plainly/ Fortune doth wry/ All contrary/ From mine intent.

> *Anthony Woodville, Earl Rivers, written 23 June 1483*
> *when Rivers had learned his brother-in-law Richard of*
> *Gloucester planned that he'd face the axe for treason,*
> *yet another 'high profile' casualty of the era!*

Henry Beaufort, his brother-in-law, Sir Henry Lewis, and Sir Nicholas Latimer had all been attainted in 1461 and all three were in Dunstanburgh when the fortress was surrendered on 27 December 1462. In the circumstances they with Sir Ralph Percy were treated with extreme leniency. Percy was confirmed as castellan of both Dunstanburgh and Bamburgh; on 17 March in the following year, he received a commission to accept the submission of other rebels.

This clemency reflects an element of realpolitik – Percy was still a name that carried great weight in Northumberland, if Edward could secure their allegiance, he effectively kicked away the greatest Lancastrian prop in the north. Somerset fared even better. He appears to have served with some distinction against his former associates, having all the charisma and fortitude of the Beauforts. King Edward made much of him, hunting with his former mortal foe, who even enjoyed the signal honour of acting as a knight of the bedchamber. The Duke received cash subsidies and the hefty annuity of a thousand marks. Tournaments were mounted in his honour and the King personally intervened to save Somerset from certain death at the hands of an unruly mob in Northampton [1].

HEDGELEY MOOR

Why then did the Duke defect and resume his former allegiance? He could, presumably, have accepted a safe conduct and withdrawn north of the border as other members of the Dunstanburgh garrison chose, though whether Warwick would allow the former commander-in-chief this option is uncertain. There is a suggestion he'd already approached the Earl some months beforehand to explore terms. On 10 March 1463, his attainder was reversed and yet, by December he and Percy had both reverted. Hicks has asserted, probably correctly, that this was not due to hubris or an unwillingness to accept reality, Somerset was neither fool nor dreamer – he must know the odds were long and that no second chances would be forthcoming.

What occurred was, therefore, a crisis of conscience, the pull of his affinity, the oath given to Henry VI was too compelling and triumphed over expediency. The cause might be hopeless, but honour outweighed the odds [2]. Possibly both Percy and Somerset regarded their earlier compromise as nothing more than a necessary ruse to gain time whilst matters turned more favourably, having said that there were scant grounds, in December 1463 for imagining the prospects for Henry VI were improving. The Duke and Sir Ralph were not alone; both Sir Henry Bellingham and Sir Humphrey Neville subsequently defected. Some commentators, particularly Ross, regard Edward's policy of 'hearts and minds' as naïve and culpable, a political blunder [3].

This may be too censorious. Edward had won the crown by the sword, but his affinity amongst the magnates was narrow. To survive and establish a stable regime he needed, urgently, to broaden his platform of support. To achieve this, it was clearly necessary to win over former opponents. Simply killing them was not, as recent history showed, an effective policy. That blood spilled on the streets of St. Albans had pooled into a legacy of hate and resentment that had led to the carnage of Towton. The effects of this titanic fight should not be underestimated; the Yorkists had won, but only by a whisker, it was a field that could have gone either way. No Prince would consider having to repeat such an epic campaign, since the drain on blood and treasure was simply too great, the stakes too high. Edward had judged that suborning his former enemies not only brought new friends but demoralised the remaining diehards and, by the close of 1462, he could have been justified in thinking that the flames of resistance had guttered out [4].

Edward's contemporaries certainly took the harsher view. Gregory, no friend to Somerset, observed that: 'the savynge of hys lyffe at that tyme cuasyd mony mannys dethys son aftyr, as ye shalle heyre' [5]. Hicks views Percy's defection as the more serious because of the power of his name in Northumberland, notwithstanding the fact the King still held both Somerset's brother and Percy's nephew as hostages [6]. Edward's policy of conciliation was at best a gamble and one which, in these leading instances, clearly failed [7]. At the time it seemed a risk worth taking if the prize was a lasting peace, but this was not achieved and the Lancastrian cause in the north was to enjoy a final, brief revival in the spring of 1464 [8].

Early in the year sporadic unrest erupted throughout the realm. In 15 counties, from Kent to Cornwall and as far north as Leicestershire, the disruption was sufficiently serious for the King to delay the state opening of Parliament. There is evidence from the contemporary record that Somerset might have, mistakenly, perceived that King Henry had received some fresh impetus and supply: 'herynge y King Henry was comynge into the lande with a newe strength' [9]. It is uncertain where these fresh troops were coming from and how they were to be paid, perhaps there was a hope the French might intervene or even the Scots.

Somerset began his reversion by attempting to seize Newcastle, a considerable prize, as it was the Yorkists' forward supply base. A number of his affinity formed an element of the garrison, but the attempt did not succeed. Lord Scrope with some of the King's household knights frustrated the scheme. The rebel Duke was very nearly taken at Durham where he was obliged to flee from his lodgings in no more than his nightshirt. Gregory reports that a few of his retainers were captured, together with their master's 'caskette and hys harneys [helmet and armour]' [10]. Others attempted to slip through the net and escape Newcastle; any who were caught suffered summary execution.

There is also some further doubt as to the fugitive King Henry's whereabouts. The 'Yearbook' claims he was at Alnwick, though this may be incorrect for the same source claims Margaret and de Breze were with him when we can, in fact be certain both were in Flanders at this time [11]. NCH still places his diminished court at lordly Bamburgh, and this seems more credible. Alnwick was nearer the Yorkists at Newcastle whilst Bamburgh had access to the sea [12]. Somerset may have proceeded directly to Henry or, equally possible, he may have made for Tynedale, where a crop of castles, Prudhoe, Hexham, Bywell, and Langley, remained staunch. As some point, either in February or March he was joined by his former comrades, Ralph Percy, and Sir Humphrey Neville of Brancepeth, with their retainers. With the Duke's defection a new sense of urgency infuses the faltering cause of the House of Lancaster.

And urgency there was for the Scots were showing willingness to treat with Warwick who had detailed his brother Montagu to march north and provide safe passage through the uncertain reaches of the frontier for a team of Scottish negotiators. These talks were initially scheduled to take place at Newcastle on 6

March, but the increasing tempo of alarums caused the start to be delayed until 20 April and the venue shifted southward to calmer pastures.

Edward, on 27 March, announced his intention to travel north and organise a suitable escort for the delegation waiting at Norham [13]. The success of any such mission would be fatal to Lancastrian hopes, so Somerset was placed in a position where he was bound to take the field, with such forces as he could muster and stake everything. Consequently, he dispatched a commanded body of foot, 'four score spears and bows too' [14], under Neville, to lay an ambush 'a little from Newcastle in a wood' [15]. Forewarned by scouts or spies, Montagu easily avoided the trap and chose a safer route into the city where he was reinforced by 'a great fellowship' [16]. He then set out to march northwards to the border.

Somerset's best chance now lay in forcing a decisive encounter; causing a defeat in the field that would leave the Scots immured and show the Lancastrians still had teeth. By mustering every spear he could find and stripping his handful of garrisons the Duke might, as Gregory suggests, have been able to muster 5,000 [17]. This seems a very generous estimate notwithstanding he could count upon his own affinity with those of Percy, Neville, Bellingham, the turncoat Grey, Lords Hungerford, and Roos. We have no note of the force Montagu was leading north but it would certainly have been the equal of anything his enemies could deploy. As the Yorkists marched north from Morpeth, the Lancastrians sallied from Alnwick, both sides probing with a screen of light horse or 'prickers'. Nine miles west of Alnwick Somerset drew up in battle order blocking the way northwards to Norham.

Though the chronicles provide only scanty details of the battle which ensued, a careful perambulation of the ground that, save for the spread of cultivation, remains largely undisturbed, indicates the fight took place on the shelf of rising ground just north of where Percy's Cross now stands. This is the area between, to the south, the stand of timber known as Percy's Strip Wood and the monument ("Percy's Leap"). Here, the ground is roughly level, slightly undulating rising toward the northern flank. In the spring of 1464, the land was not under plough but an expanse of open moor, largely devoid of trees. With the Lancastrians facing south, in front of Percy's Leap, the Yorkists most probably carried out their initial deployment on the line of the present woodland.

As they approached from the south the main body of the Yorkists would have had no opportunity to view the strength of their enemy until they ascended the slight rise, which swells from the lower ground. The Lancastrians would not have wished to deploy to the south of the position suggested as this would be to lose the advantages the field conferred. Haigh [18] shows the Yorkists drawn up somewhat to the south of this position and indicates the Lancastrians advanced to contact over open ground. I think this unlikely. Yorkist morale was most probably higher, and Montagu may have enjoyed greater strength, he was, by nature, a confident and aggressive commander. This is, however, conjectural as the chronicles remain frustratingly silent as to these initial dispositions and the numbers certainly cannot be assessed with any degree of confidence [19]. Somerset may, like Warwick, have been prone to indecision at key moments (his failure to reinforce Clifford at Dintingdale stands as a clear example) [20].

It could be assumed that the fight commenced with the customary duel of arrows (though there is no evidence) and Yorkist supremacy was swiftly asserted. Before ever striking a blow, the whole of the Lancastrian left or rearward division, commanded by Hungerford and Roos, dissolved in total rout, leaving the centre under Somerset, Bellingham, and Grey, together with the right or vaward, under Percy, horribly exposed. Montagu ordered the advance to contact [21].

Most probably the melee occurred in the vicinity of Percy's Leap, a short, savage, and largely one-sided encounter. The Lancastrian centre soon joined their fellows on the left in flight, Somerset and his officers swept along, unable to stem the rot. Percy by now was virtually surrounded; fighting bravely, he sustained mortal wounds seeking to break the ring. An enigmatic legend lingers over his last moments – 'I have saved the bird in my bosom,' he is said to have uttered as his mount stumbled the dozen yards between two low outcrops. What was meant by this remains uncertain, perhaps he referred to his true loyalty to Lancaster, ironic then, from a man who had changed sides with such facility [22].

Montagu's victory was complete and, though the chronicles give to hint of losses, probably cheaply bought. Aside from Percy and those retainers around him who held their ground, most of the defeated escaped unscathed. Morale was clearly a major factor in the Lancastrian defeat. Despite his humiliation on the field Somerset was able to rally many of the Lancastrians and retreat, in reasonably good order, into Tynedale whilst Montagu was fully occupied with the diplomatic game; King Henry's kingdom had shrunk further but was not yet extinguished [23].

With the Scots now in negotiations, and the French in talks at St. Omer, which had begun the previous autumn, the Lancastrians' diplomatic isolation was all but complete. As Northumberland was no longer viable as a bridgehead, then there was little incentive for Somerset to disperse his forces in isolated garrisons, simply holding ground was pointless. With the Scots set to change horses, bargaining chips like Berwick and Norham had no further currency [24].

Henry's prospects appeared brighter in the west, for in March there were some fresh disturbances in Lancashire and Cheshire. Resistance flared briefly in Skipton in Craven, seat of the Cliffords who, with their local affinity, had bled so liberally for Lancaster. None of these alarums developed into a serious threat [25]. However, King Edward continued to feel insecure in the north and west; commissions of array were sent out to the midlands and Yorkshire, but no writs were issued in Northumberland, Cumberland, Westmorland, Lancashire, or Cheshire [26].

THE BATTLE OF HEXHAM

Both sides were short of cash. Edward had been granted subsidies to prosecute the war in the north, and Norham had been relieved but beyond that little achieved bar Montagu's notable success in the field. Parliament's subsidies and a further grant from convocation had been gobbled up by existing commitments, particularly the garrison at Calais [27]. The Yorkist administration was surviving on loans and was substantively in the red, raising taxes built resentment in all quarters, and this was exacerbated when there was no tangible gain. So vociferous was this dissatisfaction that the King felt constrained, in November 1463, to remit some £6,000 of the subsidy granted in the summer [28].

Somerset was under even greater pressure. He had no taxation revenue, no grants, nor other subsidies; he was obliged to beg, borrow, and steal, even when monies could be scraped together, these could disappear through misappropriation. When captured, hiding in a coalpit, after the final defeat at Hexham, Lord Tailboys was loaded with pilfered funds: 'He hadde moch money with hym, both golde and sylvyr, that shulde hav gon unto King Harry; and yf it had come to Harry, lat kynge of Ingelonde, hyt wolde have causyd moche sore sorowe, for he had ordynyd harneys and ordenance i-nowe, but the men wolde not go one fote with hym tylle they had mony' [29].

Henry now appears to have moved his lodgings to Bywell Castle, where he was in residence by the latter part of April. After the rout to come the victors found evidence of a hurried departure, the King's helmet or 'bycoket' (a coroneted cap), 'richly garnysshed wt ij crownys, and his followers trapped wt blew velvet' [30]. There was a suggestion that the Lancastrians might have been bolstered by 'a great power out of Scotlade' [31], more likely these were riders from Liddesdale and Teviotdale, drawn by the scent of booty. Bywell was not a significant castle and possessed no strategic value [32]. Both Tynedale and Redesdale were administered as 'Liberties' – franchises where the crown sub-contracted the business of local government to franchisees, which led to a fair measure of autonomy. The Lancastrians still had a foothold in Tynedale [33], holding Hexham, Prudhoe, and possibly other centres [34].

How much local support the Lancastrian cause enjoyed is questionable? The northern lords, Percy, Dacre, and Clifford had all bled freely, their affinities thinned and leaderless. Much had changed since the halcyon days of 1459–1460; even then Queen Margaret had offered free quarter and plunder as incentives, now her cause was depleted by the disaster at Towton and three more years of attrition [35].

There is no indication of how long King Henry remained at Bywell. Probably he shifted westwards to Hexham, then fled deeper, he was likely gone before the battle and, therefore, the story of a precipitate flight from Bywell is almost certainly fanciful. Somerset would have been a fool to leave the king so exposed; Henry, however diminished, was his only trump. Montagu left Bywell undisturbed on his approach march. He would not have done so had he entertained any notion of Henry's presence there. Hexham was a larger castle and further west, in the fifteenth century the enceinte comprised the Moot Hall and Gaol, linked by a strong curtain wall [36].

Montagu, by the end of the first week in May, had returned from York to Newcastle, and being aware, through scouts and agents, of Lancastrian activity in Tynedale resolved to take the offensive. On this occasion he would not be hamstrung by diplomatic duties and could concentrate his considerable abilities toward achieving a decisive outcome. Thus: 'on xiii of May, my lorde Mountague toke his jornaye toward Hexham from Newcastelle' [37].

Advancing with his forces strung along the north bank of the Tyne, Hexham was his immediate tactical objective; his strategy being to expunge the Lancastrian presence, once and for all. Somerset would have been aware of this and though some Tudor chroniclers assert King Henry was present on the field, this is clearly fanciful. Gregory avers he fled north back into Scotland but, as this was no longer safe, it is more probable he slipped further into the west, to Lancashire. Montagu crossed the Tyne either at Bywell or Corbridge; only the line of the Devil's Water now stood between him and the Lancastrian base of Hexham [38].

Devil's Water follows a meandering course from the high ground of the Shire toward the Tyne. From Hexham the ground shelves markedly toward the crossing at Linnels Bridge, some two miles distant, then, on the south side, rises steeply in the direction of Slaley. The traditional site for the battle of Hexham, challenged by Dorothy Charlesworth, lies south of the present B6306, on low ground by the banks of the stream and as featured on the OS 1:25000 map.

As the best contemporary source, the Yearbook describes the actual field as 'un lieu appelle Livels sur le ewe Devyls' [39]. Worcester says a hill one mile from Hexham [40]. Ramsay, who had visited the location or talked to someone who had, observes tellingly that '[the site] is a nice, sheltered camping ground … but a very bad battlefield' [41]. The Yearbook, which also states the fight occurred on 15 May, merely points to Linnels as a general area. Worcester refers to a hill, suggesting, quite pointedly, rising ground and Dorothy Charlesworth observes that the low ground is indeed most unsuitable [42]. It appears clear from a perambulation that the traditional location for the battle is badly flawed. To the rear it is hemmed by the water and, to the front, by steeply rising ground which impedes visibility and inhibits manoeuvre, making a gift of the heights above to the attacker.

Later writers have accepted this view [43] without re-examining the topography and considering the implications. Ms. Charlesworth argues, compellingly, that whilst Somerset may have camped on the Levels, he did not deploy for battle there rather, on the morning of the 15th, he drew up his forces on the higher ground along the crest of Swallowship Hill. Had he not done so, Montagu could have outflanked him and gained Hexham from the ford over the Devil's Water directly below the hill. The chroniclers do not really give us any assistance here [44], we are in 'inherent military probability' as advanced by Colonel Burne.

If, as Dorothy Charlesworth supposes, the defenders occupied the rise of Swallowship Hill, no such outflanking move would have been possible, with the stream circling the base, the crest of the hill commands all the viable crossings. As the ground, on both elevations, drops quite sharply toward the Devil's Water, it would be possible for Somerset to refuse both flanks and channel the attacking Yorkists against his centre. It may therefore be that his line was curved to conform to the contours, Grey and Neville commanded on the left, Hungerford, and Roos the right.

The Lancastrian left thus dominated the ford which lay below them and that to the north by Earl's Bridge; from the right it was possible to cover Linnels and the more southerly ford by Newbiggin. This is conjecture, but the nature of the ground clearly favours Dr. Charlesworth's view. This was the deployment which confronted Lord Montagu, who then made his own dispositions accordingly. Whilst he probably fielded more troops, with higher morale, both his flank commanders, Lords Greystoke and Willoughby, were former Lancastrians. The former, on the left, had fought at 2nd St. Albans, where the latter, now on the right had served with him, losing his father Lord Welles in the wrack of Towton. Willoughby had made his peace with Edward at Gloucester in September 1461 and had done good service since [45].

Whether this fight began with a duel of arrows is not recorded, the Yorkists may have advanced swiftly to contact and the melee was both swift and certain of outcome. Hungerford and Roos, on the Lancastrian right, were the first to give ground, and the line dissolved in precipitate rout. Somerset may have tried to cling to the crest and rally, but he was swept away in the confusion of panic; the fords soon choked with fleeing men. With the brief fight over, only the business of pursuit remained [46]. Casualties in the combat were most likely very light, since the chroniclers do not mention any knights killed on the field, more gentle blood by far was spilt by the executioners in the killing spree which followed. Worcester argues that Montagu fielded 10,000 men against Somerset's 500 [47] but no commander would accept battle against such odds, perhaps the Duke could count on no more than half a thousand retainers of his own immediate affinity.

Conversely, Warkworth argues that the Lancastrians had 'gathered a great people in the north country' and that the Yorkists were outnumbered, having no more than 4,000 [48]. Looking at the ground, the position on Swallowship Hill covers a front of around 1,000 yards, allowing one man per yard and a gap between divisions, a force of at least 4,000 would be needed to give substance to the deployment. For his part, Montagu would surely have been less enthusiastic to engage had not his army been equal to or greater than that of his opponent.

Unlike the immediate aftermath of his previous victory Montagu was not encumbered by distractions and was fully able to harry the fleeing Lancastrians. Somerset, Hungerford, and Roos were all taken, captured 'in a wood faste by' [49]. Henry Beaufort, 2nd Duke of Somerset, could not anticipate any further clemency; Montagu, like his brother, was not interested in reconciliation. It was now time for retribution and the Duke was executed the following day in Hexham, while Hungerford and Roos were conveyed to Newcastle where they too faced the axe 'behedid at Newcastle' [50]. Others, including Sir Philip Wentworth, Sir Edmund Fitzhugh, John Bryce, Thomas Hunt, and a reiver called 'Black Iaquys' ('Black John' or 'Black Jack'), were given appointments with the headsman at either Hexham, or perhaps Middleham, 'after some writers' [51]. At least one captive, Sir Thomas Hussey, was executed at York.

THE SIEGE OF BAMBURGH

Lancaster in the north was ruined; Somerset and the rebel lords hunted out; their retainers scattered. Humprey Neville managed to escape the hounds, like Beaufort his attainder had followed on from Towton but he, too, had been subsequently pardoned. Previously he'd escaped from the Tower and possessed a genius for survival, with Sir Ralph Grey and the odd remnant he regained Bamburgh, where the reduced garrison maintained a show of defiance. The embezzling Lord Tailboys was also netted, and his hoard provided a handy bonus for Montagu's soldiery: '... the sum of 3,000 mark. And the lord's meinie of Montagu were sore hurt and sick, and many of him men were slain before in the great journeys, but this money was departed among them, and was a very wholesome salve for them' [52]. Tailboys was chopped at Newcastle on 20 July, the last of the crop of prisoners to face the axe.

Barely two weeks after Hexham, John Neville, Lord Montagu before King, and court at York and in the presence of both of his brothers, was elevated to the Earldom of Northumberland. This was the high-water mark of his house, the zenith of the Nevilles. Whilst at his northern capital Edward ratified the treaty with the Scots, concluded on 11 June and which secured a truce of 15 years duration. Warwick, as the King's Lieutenant, was charged, once again, with the recovery of the three border fortresses.

To assist in these operations Edward had assembled a formidable siege train, 'the great ordnance of England', the bombards ''Edward', 'Dijon', 'London', 'Newcastle' and 'Richard Bombartel' [53]. The sight of these great guns was sufficient to overawe the shaken defenders at Alnwick, which capitulated on the 23 June, followed, the next day, by Dunstanburgh. Bates, however, maintains that the latter was, in fact, stormed and that the governor, John Gosse, of Somerset's affinity was taken and sent southwards to York to face his execution [54].

Bates continues to assert that Warwick maintained the feast of St. John the Baptist at Dunstanburgh while Henry VI was still within the walls of Bamburgh. He further claims that Henry made good his escape with the aid of Sir Henry Bellingham. NCH concurs and suggests Sir Thomas Philip, Wiliam Learmouth, Thomas Elwyk of Bamburgh, John Retford of Lincolnshire, all described as gentlemen, together with John Purcas of London, a yeoman, Philip Castelle of Pembroke, Archibald, and Gilbert Ridley, from Langley, Gawen Lampleugh of Warkworth, also a gentleman, John Whynfell of Naworth, yeoman and Alexander Bellingham from Burneside in Westmorland, were all in the King's reduced household during this episode [55].

This is most certainly inaccurate; none of those mentioned appear to have fought at Hexham and, if so, avoided capture. It is more likely that these individuals were in the King's service before the debacle on Devil's Water and fled westwards at the same time. Bates, with the NCH, suggests Sir Ralph Grey also escaped back to Bamburgh before the rout, rather than after [56]. Once again this seems unconvincing, Grey and his retainers would be needed on the field. Bamburgh was very much a last resort for a defeated captain who was all too aware that his duplicity excluded him from amnesty.

Though perhaps the greatest of the Northumbrian fortresses Bamburgh was not built to withstand cannon and the deployment of the royal train before the massive walls, gave ample notice of deadly intent. The earl of Warwick dispatched his own and the King's herald, Chester, to formally demand the garrison's surrender. Quarter was offered to the commons but both Grey and Neville were excluded from any terms, 'as out of the King's grace without any redemption' [57].

Grey, with nothing to lose, breathed defiance; he had 'Clearly determined within himself to live or die in the castle'. The heralds responded with a stern rejoinder and one can perhaps hear the words of the Earl of Warwick resonating through the chronicler's account: 'The King, our most dread sovereign lord, specially desires to have this jewel whole and unbroken by artillery, particularly because it stands so close to his ancient enemies the Scots, and if you are the cause that great guns have to be fired against its walls, then it will cost you your head, and for every shot that has to be fired another head, down to the humblest person within the place' [58] (author's emphasis).

Thus began the only siege bombardment of the Wars. The bombards 'Newcastle' and 'London' were emplaced, sighted, loaded, and began firing, the crash of the report like the crack of doom, with a great sulphurous cloud of filthy smoke drifting over the embattled ramparts. Whole sections of masonry were blasted by roundshot and crashed into the sea [59] A lighter gun, 'Dijon', fired into the chamber wherein Sir Ralph Grey had established his HQ in the eastern gatehouse, he was injured and rendered insensible when one of these rounds brought down part of the roof [60].

Humphrey Neville, ever the survivor, seized the moment of his ally's fall to seek terms, securing clemency for the garrison and, cleverly, for himself. The dazed Sir Ralph was tied to his horse and dragged as far as Doncaster to be tried by Sir John Tiptoft, Earl of Worcester and Constable of England. One of the indictments lodged against him was that he 'had withstood and made fences against the king's majesty, and his lieutenant, the worthy lord of Warwick, as appeareth by the strokes of the great guns in the king's walls of his castle of Bamburgh' [61]. Grey was executed on 10 July – the war in the north was, at last, over.

BROTHERS AT WAR

Poor King Henry was captured next year and banged up in the Tower where he languished, scruffy and largely forgotten until Warwick's amazing volte-face in 1470; having fallen out with Edward he stirred the post in his great northern fiefdom setting Sir John Conyers up as his agitator under the brand of 'Robin of Redesdale'. Montagu who'd kept out of his brother's intrigues was finally and fatally drawn into the net and both died on the field of Barnet on 14 April 1471.

Having beaten his enemies (Edward of Lancaster was killed at Tewkesbury and sad, old King Henry quietly disposed of just after), Edward IV embarked on a Yorkist age. He'd only his brothers to worry about, fractious George and ever loyal Richard who scooped up Warwick's great northern fiefdom. Clarence remained a problem till Edward finally dealt with him in 1478, leaving Richard of Gloucester as his only surviving sibling and one upon whom, he must have thought he could rely totally. And indeed, he could, if he remained alive.

Dominic Mancini, Milanese ambassador and a pretty astute judge, wrote of Richard: 'He very rarely came to court. He kept himself within his own lands and set out to acquire the loyalty of his people through favours and justice. The good reputation of his private life and public activities powerfully attracted the esteem of strangers. Such was his renown in warfare, that whenever a difficult and dangerous policy had to be undertaken it would be entrusted to his direction and his generalship; by these arts Richard acquired the favour of the people and avoided the jealousy of the queen, from whom he lived far separated' [62].

King Edward wasn't alone in having ambitious and mercurial younger brothers; James III of Scotland was in the same boat but lacked the English king's successes and ruthlessness. James wasn't what the Scottish nobility wanted in a king; any more than Henry VI had satisfied the English. A great patron of the arts and clear Anglophile, he built much, ornamented more and might, if he'd won victories, have modelled for the Renaissance Prince. But James didn't share his magnates' love of military pomp, their obsession with skill at arms and dangerously, his sexuality was open to question. He surrounded himself with an artistic set of low-born favourites who came to exercise far too much influence and incur the enmity of his fractious lords. This rage reached its very nasty finale in the murderous cull at Lauder in 1482, as James stumbled towards an attempted relief of Berwick.

James' two brothers both fitted the more conventional bill, particularly the Earl of Albany who cultivated a beau sabreur image, tailored to more match expectations. Like Clarence he was also fickle and treacherous. It was said of him: 'he lowit [loved] nothing so well as abill men and a good horse and maid gret cost and expenssis thairon; for he was wondrous liberall in all thingis pertaining to his honour' [63]. James made him Lieutenant of the Borders, Gloucester's equivalent but he did not possess that steady acuity and self-discipline which ruled Richard, though outwardly more ambitious. By 1479 he was very possibly in treasonous communication with Gloucester and both he and his other brother the Earl of Mar were arrested. Albany, now a Duke, was accused of fomenting bother at a truce day and encouraging his marchers' scrapping, not it has to be said, a difficult accomplishment [64].

Mar died in captivity, not necessarily because of foul play but Albany preferred not to take chances and broke out of gaol, heading for safe harbour in France. Edward toyed with the idea of using Albany as a pawn to control Scotland and recover Berwick, a project dear since Margaret of Anjou had traded the town in 1461. James dithered and tried to broker a marriage alliance but when that failed finally stirred himself to action, sending Angus' riders to tear up Northumberland, torching Bamburgh in time-honoured style. Gloucester, controlling his vast northern satrapy, didn't take kindly to such intrusions and received formal confirmation of his role as Lieutenant of the Marches, immediately launched his own riders across the Tweed, tit for tat.

For his proposed major campaign of 1481, Gloucester made thorough preparations, his ships saw action, but his soldiers didn't. Edward already appeared, despite the fact he wasn't yet 40, to be failing, the long years of excess finally taking their toll of his Herculean frame. Like his grandson Henry VIII, he slid into obesity and lethargy. Richard was ablaze with energy and appeared to cooperate well with the 4th Earl of Northumberland – though as he'd find out no Percy ever put loyalty above self-interest. For the next season, 1482, Gloucester had a clear objective to retake Berwick.

He struck in that spring, beating up Dumfries and bringing the exiled Albany under his banner as counterfeit king, he launched his main assault in July. This was a meticulously planned assault on Berwick, his army said to number 20,000 [65]. James' feeble riposte ended in the wholesale murder of his metrosexual cabal at Lauder. Berwick was still besieged while Albany, as mascot, marched effectively unopposed into Edinburgh. Within a month, Berwick fell, changing hands for the fourteenth and (to date) final time. It was a very satisfactory conclusion and Albany, the viper, was lodged in the bosom of Scottish polity. Gloucester had done well yet there were still jealous murmurings from the ever-unpleasant Woodvilles. If they'd had the wit to realise what was in the heart and mind of the King's younger brother, they'd have had much to murmur about.

Still, on paper, Richard did well enough with his writ extended to re-creating a wide English Pale across the border, an impressive enough commission though he had no resources allocated. Moreover, should Albany have managed to supplant his own brother, he would have been obliged to part with a considerable dowry to his sponsor. Within the year the political landscape in both realms shifted again. Edward IV died, and Albany was back in exile. James III had survived the Lauder crisis and regained control of the helm of state. For once events moved in his favour, the rebel Earl of Douglas was captured in 1484 and Albany died in a bizarre jousting accident in Paris the year after.

James had survived but hadn't learnt much. Albany had successfully turned the Queen, Margaret of Denmark, and her eldest son the Duke of Rothesay, later James IV, against the king. Margaret died in 1486 but the younger James' suspicions stuck deep. When James III advanced a junior child at the start of 1488, his older boy slipped the net and allied himself with a growing rebel faction. The Duke became the talisman of a swelling tide of opposition. His father had always been grasping and high-handed. On the border he clashed with both Humes and Hepburns who challenged his intermeddling in the affairs of Coldingham Priory. He declared them traitors, so they instantly defected to Rothesay.

Both factions begged aid from England and Denmark, but Henry VII was too canny to get directly involved. The Scottish king turned to his half-uncle James Stewart, Earl of Buchan, arguably the least popular man in the kingdom, a move which just sufficed to antagonise waverers and direct them firmly toward the rebel camp. Matters deteriorated pretty quickly after that and soon standards were unfurled, drums beaten, and a spluttering civil war bubbled. James was as bad a general as he was king.

Father and son clashed near the hallowed site of Stirling Bridge, a far less noble fracas in which the younger claimant was beaten. James decided he was the new Bruce and hurried towards a new Bannockburn. What he got at Sauchieburn on 11 June 1488 was more an Alamo. It's said he even carried Bruce's sword and if true, a fat lot of good it did him. A much larger rebel army scattered his and the magic sword was left on the field. Casualties were few but they included James himself, killed somehow in the rout, largely unnoticed and certainly unmourned. Any list of usual suspects would have been a very long one, besides nobody was asking. James IV began his reign in violence and despite a quarter century of exemplary rule would end in just the same way but at far greater cost to Scotland [66].

NOTES:

[1] Hicks, M. A., 'Edward IV, the Duke of Somerset and Lancastrian Loyalism in the North', Northern History, 20, p. 24.
[2] Ibid., p. 25.
[3] Ross, C., Edward IV (London: Yale University Press, 1998), pp. 51–52.
[4] Hicks, op. cit., p. 31.
[5] Gregory's Chronicle, pp. 221–223.
[6] Hicks, op. cit., p. 32.
[7] Ibid., p. 33.
[8] Ibid., p. 34.
[9] Fabyan's Chronicle, p. 683.
[10] Gregory's Chronicle, p. 224.
[11] Yearbook of Edward IV, p. cviii.
[12] Gillingham, op. cit., p. 180.
[13] Gregory's Chronicle, p. 224.
[14] Ibid., p. 224.
[15] Ibid., p. 224.
[16] Ibid., p. 224.
[17] Ibid., p. 224.
[18] Haigh, op. cit., p. 80.
[19] Gregory's Chronicle, p. 224.
[20] Boardman, op. cit., p. 75.
[21] Haigh, op. cit., p. 80.

[22] Brenan, G., The House of Percy (London: Wentworth Press, 2016), vol. 1, p. 93.

[23] Gillingham, op. cit., p. 152.

[24] Ross, op. cit., p. 56.

[25] Ramsay, Sir J. H., Lancaster and York (Oxford: Clarendon Press, 1892), vol. II, p. 302

[26] Paston Letters, no. 252.

[27] Ramsay, op. cit., vol. 2, p. 302.

[28] Ross, op. cit., p. 55.

[29] Ibid., p. 56.

[30] Gregory's Chronicle, p. 226.

[31] Fabyan's Chronicle, p. 654.

[32] Chronicles of London, ed. by C. L. Kingsford (Oxford: Clarendon Press, 1905), p. 178.

[33] Long, B., The Castles of Northumberland (Newcastle upon Tyne: H. Hill, 1967), p. 76.

[34] Lomas, op. cit., p. 136.

[35] Ibid., pp. 154–155.

[36] Boardman, op. cit., p. 38.

[37] Charlesworth, op. cit., pp. 62.

[38] Gregory's Chronicle, p. 224.

[39] Ibid., p. 232.

[40] Charlesworth, op. cit., p. 63.

[41] Worcester's Chronicle, p. 779.

[42] Ramsay, op. cit., vol. 2, p. 303.

[43] Charlesworth, op. cit., p. 64.

[44] Haigh, P., The Military Campaigns of the Wars of the Roses (Gloucester: Sutton, 1995), p. 84.

[45] Gregory's Chronicle, p. 224.

[46] Ramsay, op. cit., vol. 2, p. 303 n.

[47] Ibid., p. 303.

[48] Warkworth's Chronicle, p. 4.

[49] Fabyan's Chronicle, p. 654.

[50] Chronicles of London, p. 178.

[51] Fabyan's Chronicle, p. 654.

[52] Gregory's Chronicle, p. 219.

[53] 'Edward' is alter listed in an inventory of 1475; the Master of the Ordnance, John Sturgeon, handed into store at Calais, 'divers parcels of the King's ordnance and artillery including a bumbartell called "The Edward"'; see Blackmore, op. cit., p. 33.

[54] Bates, op. cit., p. 202.

[55] NCH, vol. 1, p. 47.

[56] Worcester's Chronicle, p. 280 n – the assumption may be based on a misreading of the Latin text: 'Radulfus Gray fugit de Hexham ante bellum inceptum ad castrum Bamburghe et post bellum de Hexham multi ex parte Regis Henrici fugerunt in eodem castro'. It is more probable the chronicler is describing Grey's flight as the battle opened rather than beforehand.

[57] NCH, vol. 1, p. 48.

[58] Warkworth's Chronicle, pp. 37–39.

[59] NCH, vol. 1, p. 48.

[60] Warkworth's Chronicle, pp. 37–39.

[61] NCH, vol. 1, p. 49.

[62] Sadler, D. J., The Red Rose and the White (Harlow: Longman/Pearson 2010), p. 227.

[63] Ibid., p. 226.

[64] Ibid.

[65] Ibid., p. 229.

[66] Watson, C., 'The Battle of Sauchieburn', Battlefield Trust Magazine, 24.4 (spring 2020), pp. 9–11.

CHAPTER SEVEN: FLOWERS OF THE FOREST

> And on the ridge of Braxton hill the Scottish army lay,
> All beautifully arrayed, and eager for the fray,
> And nearby stood their noble king on that eventful day,
> With a sad and heavy heart, but in it no dismay.
> William Topaz McGonagall: The Battle of Flodden Field

This is a modern version of a classic border balladry, a sad lament for all those who died in James IV's ill-judged Gotterdammerung at Flodden. It's sentimental tosh of course, but still calculated to show just how badly the English have behaved towards the Scots even though, yes, theirs was the invading army. I remember a solemn rendition in the splendidly restored hall of Stirling Castle which had American visitors devouring whole boxes of tissues – shame about reality. Now, there's a good display board by the monument on Piper's Hill which explains the action quite clearly and this vantage provides an Englishman's view of the Scottish line along the crest in front. You've just got to imagine ground heaving with the great weight of Scottish pikes, points glinting in a pallid sun, the crash and roar of the great guns. It's a daunting prospect.

FLODDEN EDGE

Step down into the line of the dip, look toward the English line and you can appreciate how so mundane a feature could lead to so total a disaster. Think about that innocuous burn, spread with marshes, swelled by the rains, and churned by tramping feet, muddy waters turned red by so much blood. A Scottish king who, if he failed as a general, did not fail as a knight, nor did he desert those who followed him and they, true to their oath, fell around. To be fair they didn't have many other options as the English weren't taking prisoners, red mist was boiling that dank afternoon.

Apart from increased levels of cultivation and effects of improved land drainage in the eighteenth and nineteenth centuries, the field remains remarkably unchanged. All the principal features can be easily identified [1]. The present line of the B6352 runs westward from its junction with the A697 and skirts the base of Flodden Edge. The great strength of this first Scottish position is at once apparent. This rise completely dominates Millfield Plain below and the task facing any attacker would be a decidedly risky one, particularly with those great Scottish guns securely dug in and so largely protected against counter battery fire.

At West Flodden, a right-hand turn leads past the flank of this position and continues over the saddle beyond leading towards Branxton Edge. This, the lowest point, is traversed by a very minor road running east to west through Branxton-moor and Blinkbonny, a pretty farmhouse in restrained estate gothic style. The road then breasts the lip of Branxton Edge, and the field opens out before you. The apparently formidable Scottish second position lay astride this ridge. Here, you're standing where those massed pikes of Errol, Crawford, and Montrose's Division were deployed on 9 September 1513. For many, this was to be both their first and last battle. As a brisk wind plays over the brow of the hill, it's not at all difficult to visualise that great phalanx of serried staves, men shuffling nervous and uncertain. Skeins and eddies of smoke from burning rubbish, a rush of stinging, cold rain driven by an east wind, then a tentative sun, men turning to empty bladders, throats dry.

As you go down this undemanding hill, the line of that fatal burn is clearly visible. Now much tamed by ploughman and drain-layer, the nature of this obstacle is still apparent, a marked dip with an uphill struggle to reach the English line beyond. Westwards and the drop evens out, merges into smoother contours that fronted Home and Huntly. Here topography creates a far more level descent, and you can see how, on this wing, ground so favoured the Scots. At the base of the ridge, the terrain swells left toward the monument beyond that, Windy Law, and a drop into the shallow valley of the Pallinsburn, again much drier now than then. Further north and east, toward Twizel Bridge, stretches the line of the English approach march.

To follow this, take the B6525 which branches eastwards from the main A697 at Wooler. Stay on this road through Doddington, keeping the golf course and Iron Age settlements on high ground to your right. Barmoor Castle (much later and now a shell) is on the left, as is Watchlaw as you pass over the crossroads just west of Lowick. Bear left at Bowsden toward Duddo. Remains of the sixteenth-century tower, a lone defiant gable, make a good landmark. From Duddo head due westward to the Till, that delightful bridge at Twizel and Heaton Fords. This is truly wonderful.

A new bridge now isolates the beautiful arch of the elegant original, aesthetically dazzling if not suited to the weight and volume of modern traffic. Northwards the river curves in a lazy bend, lined by bluffs on the east bank. Above that is the softly hidden shell of a much later folly, wrapped around a far earlier tower, very possibly here at the time. It's worth the scramble up through the woods, sort of place you'd expect to meet the Woman in White or, on a bad day, the Woman in Black.

At Etal Castle where the shells of both gatehouse and keep survive, English Heritage has mounted a splendid series of tableaux depicting the events of the battle. Ford Castle also still stands, though much modified, and is not generally open to the public, more on that below. 'The Queen of Border Fortresses', great Norham Castle remains [2], also in the care of English Heritage. The great, square stone keep is formidable, if denuded, as is the circuit of the walls. Mons Meg, which predates the battle and although not used in 1513 is not untypical of guns that were, remains impressively housed in Edinburgh Castle.

LEGENDS OF A FALL

One of the legends of Flodden is James IV's supposedly dangerous dalliance with Lady Heron of Ford and her equally handsome daughter – her husband was a wretched hostage in grim Fast Castle answering by proxy for the many crimes of his wonderfully dangerous half-brother the notorious and rather glorious Bastard Heron. It never happened but, when I and my co-author were researching an earlier book on Flodden for the 500th anniversary (available from all good bookshops), we took photos at Ford Castle.

It's a smashing place; most of what you're looking at is nineteenth-century restoration, remodelled by the talented improver Lady Waterford around 1860. She gave the whole village, now owned by Lord Joicey, a full makeover while she was on and the result is both charming and unique, a real jewel of this 'Sceptered Isle'. The castle has been through many vicissitudes, damage by the Scots in 1513 had, when we visited, been emulated by County Council workmen hacking great gaping holes in partition walls. Paul Thompson, who will recur in the chapter on World War Two and was then the custodian, showed us round. Our photographer the cheerfully artistic Adam Barr took excellent photos and we saw nothing unusual at the time. These were digital of course yet when we saw them on the screen (can't call 'em prints anymore I suppose), a clear and ghostly apparition of what appeared to be a knightly figure emerged! And that's a true story – honest.

If Lady Heron was not the key player, she's built up to be, then there is one woman who was. It takes local knowledge and a bit of luck to happen across Isabella Hoppringle, Prioress of Coldstream. Although, of course, once identified you find a host of intriguing references start to crop up. Thomas Grey, 2nd Marquess of Dorset, records Margaret Tudor's description of her and his own assessment, 'her grace reported that the Prioress had been very goode and kind to her … another cause which moved us to assure the sayd house was by cause the prioresse there is one of the best and assured spyes that we have in Scotland' [3]. Margaret might have been less positive had she known of Isabella's opinion of her, she is 'very fickle: therefore, counsel the man ye know not to take on hand over-much of her credence'. Thus, reports Sir William Bulmer to Earl Surrey on 7 October 1523, a report Surrey forwards on to Wolsey [4]. Surrey mentions another prioress, (that of Eccles), who was also providing information; perhaps another tantalisingly, under-reported female occupation of the sixteenth century!

Isabella was a member of a well-known reiver family, firmly Scots by this time but with affiliations and affinities on both sides of the border. Their grand impossibly romantic tower at Smailholm which we encountered earlier is now administered by Historic Environment Scotland; the family name was shortened from Hoppringle sometime in the course of the century. Isabella was just one of a series of Hoppringle prioresses at Coldstream, an institution whose proximity to the border crossing made it a location of interest to both countries. Letters of protection were issued by Henry VII, advising the English wardens that servants of the Priory were to be allowed into England to buy lead (not untypical of cross-border commerce). Isabella had been prioress for four years when James IV issued a licence to 'intercommon with Englishmen in the buying of vitallis, sheep, horses... and other lawful goods' [5].

Fiscal records suggest Coldstream had rights at Plesset Mill and Shipley in Northumberland as well as extensive holdings in the immediate area. A 1589 plan reveals church, chapterhouse and cloister nestled next to what was, presumably, accommodation for the prioress. It also reveals a range of ancillary buildings including a guesthouse and service facilities (most likely, kitchen, brew house, bakery, and malt kiln), in addition to burial grounds, orchard, and farm buildings; all of it substantial enough to merit attention from raiders as well as armies on the march.

We know that the Scots sacked the priory in 1310, maybe following the inspiring example of Edward 1 in 1296, (although the damage he left behind is perhaps better expressed as the consequence of too lively a set of house guests). English armies certainly dispersed the nuns in 1543 and 1545. Isabella was concerned enough about potential raids in 1515, when the Priory was sheltering Margaret Tudor, to seek assurance from Lord Dacre that he would do her house no harm. Margaret wrote on their behalf and was guaranteed safety as long as the house were not supporting any who would harm the king, 'nor keeping nor receiving into hir hous any Scottishemen of war' [6].

Local difficulties are underlined by a comment in a note to Bulmer in 1523, in which Isabella asserts she dare not come out of doors for fear of her neighbours at Wark. She seems to have been even handed in her distribution of information leaving this author with the clear impression that what really mattered to her was the protection of her house. Nor is it hard to understand the necessity.

We hear her voice quite vividly in 1523 talking about life on the borders: 'Lately heard from her that the Queen is gone to Stirling and has taken with her all the Frenchmen that were about her son. Monday after Palm Sunday the lord Lieutenant was with Dacre at Morpeth. The latter has undertaken that the Riddisdale [Redesdale] men shall make redress for all the robberies committed by them since lord Rosse's departure, by the 1st of May. Ralph Fenwick has done the same for the Tynedale men and brought in half a score of them as sureties. My lord Lieutenant and himself have made proclamations for injured persons to bring in their bills to them, since his coming hither, strange to say, there have been no offences on either side, seldom has there been peace so long' [7].

It's said on the morning after the battle, wagons were sent from the Priory to gather up the noble dead and provide a burial for them. Sadly, no record remains to confirm or deny this story. However, we do have a tantalising glimpse from Robert Chambers, "Picture of Scotland" 1827 which refers to 'many bones' unearthed on the priory site. Even more interesting is a report by a Captain McLaren in the 1834 issue of "Gentleman's Magazine" which is quoted in "Second to None", 'On a spot said to have been the burying ground of the Priory of Cistercian nuns, immediately below the surface discovered a great number of human skeletons, which seemed to have been buried in the greatest confusion' [8]. It is impossible to tell, of course, without access to the burial, what period these bones belonged to. But it does set the imagination working.

MARTIAL DREAMS

'God is not on the side of the heavy battalions but of the best shots'.

Voltaire

There was, within James IV of Scotland's character, a fatal fascination with the art of war. Though he had partly subdued his rebellious Highlanders, quelled troublesome Borderers and dreamt of the great crusade, he was no general. His interest in the navy was mirrored by his interest in the science of gunnery and by 1508 he was casting his own guns in Edinburgh Castle. He attempted, but was never successful, to establish a standing army along Continental lines, though by 1502, he was nonetheless able to send a force of two thousand men to Denmark. A portion of his inheritance was the 'auld alliance', which he had renewed in 1491–1492 [9]. In England, the victorious Henry Tudor still did not sit easy upon his throne and during the early years of his reign he was beset by a series of pretenders.

Henry couldn't really afford to fall out with his powerful Scottish neighbour and as early as 1493 the English king hinted at a marriage alliance. In September 1497, at Ayton, James and Henry came to terms and a seven-year truce was agreed. By a further treaty, signed in 1502, the English king pledged his eldest daughter in marriage to James and the nuptial agreement was supported by a further treaty for 'Perpetual Peace', the first such mutual undertaking since 1328. On 8 August 1503 the fourteen-year-old princess married King James in the Abbey Church of Holyrood, and for the rest of Henry's reign the two countries existed in amity [10].

His son and successor, Henry VIII, was a man of a very different stamp, outwardly jovial and good-humoured but ruthless, bombastic, and aggressive as numerous of his wives were to discover. At a very early stage, he headed for a collision with France by allying himself to the wily Ferdinand of Spain. France was obviously anxious to avoid English interference in the seemingly endless Italian wars and James was effectively employed as a diplomat to find an understanding between the warring parties. In November 1511, Henry joined the Pope, King Ferdinand, and the Venetians in a Holy League against France.

James was now in a difficult position. He was allied to France through the 'Auld Alliance' and yet was equally tied to England by the accord of 1502, though these agreements now appeared mutually exclusive. A more unscrupulous and more cynical man than James could have exploited this situation to his advantage. He certainly used best endeavours to remain above the struggle in Europe, but the French were naturally anxious that their old ally should support them against England. Henry was determined to enjoy his hour of glory and accordingly prepared to invade France, which he did in the summer of 1513. Prior to this he had taken good care to ensure that the northern shires were in a state of defence and had appointed the ageing but competent Earl of Surrey as commander-in-chief.

The king now felt bound by his relations with the French to intercede on their behalf and on 24 July he began to summon the shire levies. On 12 August he made a last-ditch attempt to negotiate with Henry and sent his chief herald Lyon, King-of-Arms, to deliver an ultimatum. This was curtly dismissed and on 22 August the Scottish host crossed the border [11]. Lord Home, with five thousand East March riders, led the first foray into Northumberland. Having wasted the valley of the Till he was ambushed, whilst returning, by a thousand English archers under Sir William Bulmer of Brancepeth [12]. In the ensuing melee the Scots came off worst with several hundred dead – not an auspicious start. Undeterred, James pressed on. His huge army is said to have numbered 30,000. His artillery train included several heavy siege guns, two culverins, four sakers, and six demi-culverins [13].

MORE THAN A WHIFF OF ROUNDSHOT

The first English castle to feel the punch of the Scottish cannon was Norham, after which came the turn of Etal and then of Ford which, once taken, the Scottish king made his headquarters. Before the age of artillery Norham had resisted a conventional siege for the best part of two years, but such was the firepower of James's train that the castle was hammered into submission in five days. Even at the outset, the very size of the Scottish force began to pose problems as small groups, full of loot, began to drift off homeward. This trickle of desertions was exacerbated by an outbreak of disease which further thinned the ranks. By the early part of September James had probably lost the best part of a third of his force [14].

Surrey, despite the weight of his 70 years, displayed considerable energy. By 1 September he had reached Newcastle and the shire levies of Lancashire, Cheshire, Yorkshire, Wensleydale, and Swaledale began to filter in. The quality of these often-unwilling recruits was at best indifferent and the only regular force upon which Surrey could count were the 1200 marines from the fleet under the command of his eldest surviving son Thomas Howard, the Lord Admiral. Surrey, who understood the vainglorious nature of his opponent's character, began a careful campaign of taunts and insults delivered through heralds though James was too smart to rise to the bait.

This daily barrage of gentlemanly abuse was carried by the English herald Rouge-Croix who found the Scottish king and his army drawn up in a strong position on the north-eastern slopes of Flodden Hill. James, alone amongst his nobles, having no apparent objection to giving battle, at least had the good sense to detain Rouge-Croix and avoid making Surrey aware of his dispositions [15]. Surrey now marched his army to Wooler, where he arranged an exchange of hostages to recover his herald. The intelligence brought back by Rouge-Croix can't have been encouraging. The Scots were in a position of considerable strength; their guns had been dug into the hillside effectively covering the passage between the east end of Flodden Hill and the line of the Till. A low-lying, waterlogged track was the only approach to the Scots position and any attempt to advance would be subject to galling fire from above [16].

It's uncertain who from Surrey's council of war suggested the idea of a flanking march to the north. It may have been the notorious Bastard Heron himself, whose useful bandits had swelled the English ranks. The next day the English army broke camp, splashed across the Till and headed north, marched past Doddington up towards the heather-clad moors and then out of sight of the watching Scots. This was an impressive and risky gambit, no easy stroll either, hard marching for hungry men.

That evening the English camped on Watch Law, invisible to the enemy who appeared baffled by the manoeuvre. From the top of the hill Surrey and his officers were able to get a far better view of the Scottish lines. The enemy position now lay to the south and a line of advance from the north, though equally precipitous, would be free from artillery fire. Local historian John Ferguson has now located the probable site of the English camp, shown on a hitherto unconsidered survey map from 1786 [17].

APPROACH TO CONTACT

Early on 9 September, the army was again on the march, abandoning all heavy baggage and gear and moving in battle order. To advance necessitated a further crossing of the Till. This proved difficult; the narrow bridge at Twizel could not accommodate the great array of men, horses, and guns. While the vanguard and the Lord Admiral's division crossed by this route, Surrey led the main body across the shallows at Mill-Ford [18].

By about 13.00 hours, the English deployment became all too visible, and the alarm was raised. The Scottish lords were all for caution, urging James to withdraw though he, throwing a violent tantrum, determined to fight. The Scots began the cumbersome task of moving their positions almost a mile to the north and redeploying along the ridge of Branxton Hill, heaving only the lighter cannon, which could be more easily shifted, with them. Although their new position was less strong it still gave them a substantial advantage in height, or certainly appeared to [19].

On the left stood Home and Huntly's division, then that of Errol, Crawford, and Montrose; in the centre the king and on the left the Highland brigade under Lennox and Argyll. Bothwell's division remained in reserve. In the Lowland divisions there were a number of French officers and the whole army had been largely re-equipped with pikes at French expense. As the Scots decamped the followers began burning the abandoned gear and refuse so that a great cloud of greasy smoke hung over the ridge effectively obscuring each side from the other [20].

Though clear of the Till the English were not clear of difficulties; that soft and marshy ground by the Pallinsburn was churned into a quagmire by marching feet. The van, under the Lord Admiral, was the first to clear the morass and in fact advanced too far, outstripping the main body. Had the Scots swooped down from the heights, the van would have been isolated and the army defeated in detail (see map six) [21]. Realising his error, but not losing his nerve, the Lord Admiral marched boldly on, along the southern bank of the Pallinsburn.

Despite his appearance of confidence, he was sending repeated messages back to his father urging the main body forward. When finally deployed the English right was under the command of Edmund Howard, Surrey's third son. The Lord Admiral stood left of him with Surrey himself taking the centre. On the English left the line was held by the experienced Edward Stanley or would have been except Stanley was trailing, apparently lost. In front of Surrey's position, in the centre, there was a moderate decline falling into the wet gap.

This was important for the Scots, to attack, would have to cross the mire and advance up this seemingly insignificant slope, losing that vital downhill momentum. James had schooled his levies in the latest Swiss pike tactics with the aid of his French advisers. The successful deployment of the pike phalanxes depended upon long and hard training, strict discipline, and determined ferocity. All three were lacking in the Scots and the choice of ground was disastrous. The Swiss also fought only for pay, whereas James' conscripts were unwaged; king and country was never such a strong incentive as hard cash.

Surrey was concerned about the position on his right. Apart from Howard, a handful of retainers, and a hardcore of Cheshire knights such as Bryan Tunstall, this division was made up of raw levies from Lancashire and Cheshire [22]. This scratch-built brigade was facing Home's tough Borderers bred to endemic warfare. Moreover, as these were Stanley retainers, they expected to fight under their own Eagles' Claw standard. Such things mattered. English guns were sited between the bodies of foot and very soon began to make their presence felt. Coolly directed by Sir Nicholas Appleyard and William Blackenhall, the English gunners methodically raked the Scottish line and a furious artillery duel developed. It was now that the relative inexperience of the Scottish gunners began to tell and one by one, they were silenced. With his guns disabled and his gunners dead, James's line was exposed to the full fury of the English cannonade. This was probably very short in duration, but the fight was effectively decided before either side advanced to contact [23].

FLOWERS OF THE FOREST

The Scottish king, whatever the shortcomings of his leadership, had detected the weakness of the English right and he launched Home and Huntly's division upon them. These tough Scottish Borderers cannoned into the English ranks and quite literally swept them from the field. The men of Lancashire and Cheshire dissolved in rout, leaving Howard and a few diehards to sell their lives as dearly as possible.

The heroic Tunstall flung himself upon the Scots, cutting down Sir Malcolm McKeen and several others before he himself was killed.

Despite this opportune beginning, James now proceeded to commit what appears to have been a masterpiece of reckless folly. Seeing his advantage on the right and thinking the battle won, he placed himself at the head of his own division and led them down towards the English centre. In so doing he effectively deprived the Scottish army of any vestige of leadership. For a king to abandon his position as commander-in-chief and to elect to fight as a common knight was an act of gross negligence and was to cost both king and country dear.

In James's defence his tactics were entirely consistent with the Swiss precedent, which asserted that commanders should lead by example. Besides, once the pike columns were committed there was little a commander-in-chief could do to determine the outcome. The Swiss also advocated attacking in echelon, launching divisions one after the other to deliver a series of hammer blows. So far this appeared to be working.

The men of the king's division were exposed to the aim of the English longbowmen as they raced downhill. Yet the Scots had finally devised a tactic to resist the cloth-yard storm, their front ranks now equipped with heavy wooden shields or pavises which could be raised as a protective screen and then discarded [24]. What did disconcert the Scottish soldiers was the swamp into which they descended at the base of the hill. Their momentum was checked and lost, so that it was they who now had to lumber uphill towards the English ranks. The two sides met with a terrific shock – Scottish pikes levelled against English bills. Momentum, mass, and cohesion, critical to the success of Swiss tactics, were irretrievably lost.

This English bill – a basic but effective weapon – was a hybrid of the battlefield, born of a useful union between the agricultural implement, the billhook, and the military spear. Originally the peasants of the feudal levy had simply mounted their billhooks upon longer shafts until, around 1300, the weapon was developed with a hefty blade, a long spear-like head, and a shorter, narrower cutting edge at the back. The bill now proved lighter and more versatile than the cumbersome pike and Surrey's men were able to lop off the heads of the enemy's weapons and then hack down the pikemen.

Both sides fought with undiluted fury, casualties began to mount, the muddy ground puddled with blood. Errol, Crawford, and Montrose all fell at the head of their division and their levies could make no headway against Howard's elite marines. Increasingly, the king's division became isolated as Howard's lapped around the flanks. From one of difficulty the king's position deteriorated to one of desperation and, though the fight was to rage murderously for a further two hours, there was little doubt as to the outcome.

The Scottish right wing and reserve had been scattered by a bold if belated charge from Stanley's division which finally appeared on the English right. The Englishmen had cannily infiltrated the north-eastern slope of the hill from whence they were invisible to the Scots until they bounced them. English longbows made short work of lightly equipped Highlanders who, ill-suited to this form of defensive warfare, took to their heels. Both Argyll and Lennox, in the company of several clan chiefs, died attempting to rally their men [25].

King James, though defeated, remained undaunted and legend relates that, with his few surviving retainers, he launched one last Homeric charge against the banners of Surrey himself. Cut and slashed by bills, James fell dying, almost unnoticed by his men [26]. Dawn revealed the scale of the English victory. Surrey claimed he'd accounted for ten thousand Scots and the toll amongst the nobility had been frightful: one archbishop, one bishop, ten earls, 19 barons, and as many as three hundred knights had joined their king in oblivion. Whole counties and towns were stripped of the cream of their manhood. All the Scottish artillery, arms, and baggage fell to the English. The English themselves might have lost around 1700 [27].

RECKONING

That morning after the battle, a half-naked corpse was dragged from the pile of Scottish dead. Transported to Berwick, it was formally recognised as the mortal remains of James IV of Scotland; the body was disembowelled, embalmed, and sent, first to Newcastle and then, in a lead casket, to London. Catherine of Aragon debated sending the grisly trophy to her husband in France but finally sent the dead king's bloody surcoat instead (reminding anyone as prone to sulking as Henry of how much greater her victory had been might, in the long run, have been unwise). The body remained in the monastery of Sheen and was thrown into a lumber room after the dissolution. Years later, workmen in the house found the remains, cut off the head and used it for a macabre plaything. Thereafter it apparently came into the possession of one Lancelot Young, Elizabeth I's master glazier, who kept it as a curio at his home, until finally it was buried in an anonymous grave. Posterity sneers at losers.

A contemporary chronicle offered this epitaph for the dead king: 'How could the matter be, hitherto we want, quhen we want him, a stout, just and devote King, who won great honour both in peace and war when other princes of his day contracted ignominie' [23]. Bull Dacre might have thought himself shot of Scottish royalty, but he would have been mistaken. Sometime later he had Queen Margaret as a guest at Harbottle Castle and found her a most demanding and difficult VIP [28].

For Scots, Flodden seems to be a final flowering of an aspiring realm about to take its place on the European stage; the last chance in generations for an independent nation to act on its own behalf free from the shadow of domination. Flodden is a lost opportunity and a lost generation, or so it is portrayed. It is the death toll which seems to have made the greatest impact, yet Scots would go on to sacrifice thousands in the Great War. Not until 1914–1918 do we once again find a carnage that strikes at the Scottish psyche in this way.

Such high losses must have an inevitably greater impact on a small population (estimates put the total at around 500,000 in 1513). Everyone would likely know somebody who was there. Wood claims there was trouble and considerable rivalry over the filling of benefices left vacant by the death of their holders at Flodden [29]. Some of the fiction written about the event, (of which there is a significant amount), seems almost driven by that consciousness. Take Elizabeth McNeill, for example, who, in the afterward to her novel, Flodden Field questions whether the 1707 Act of Union could have taken place if men of power had not died on the battlefield: 'In 1513 the country was powerful, rich and on the crest of a wave, but everything crashed to disaster in only two hours'. She contends the disaster was worse than Culloden, because by that time Scotland was already subdued and had been sold out [30]. It's an interesting approach even if not wholly persuasive and comparisons with Culloden are wholly wrong, that was a very different war.

NOTES:

[1] For the visitor, refer to OS Landranger Map 75 and OS Explore Map 339 which show the field (NT895371 389596, 637112), its immediate environs and elements of the English flank march.

[2] As noted previously, Norham was held by the Prince Bishop of Durham, part of his North Durham holdings.

[3] Letters and Papers, Foreign and Domestic, of Henry VIII, 1519–23 cited in "Second to None: A History of Coldstream", Coldstream and District Local History Society, 2010, p. 38.

[4] Letters and Papers, Foreign and Domestic, Henry VIII, vol. 3 1519–1523, ed. by J. S. Brewis (London: HMSO, 1867), pp. 1421–1422, accessed at: British History Online (http://www.british-history.ac.uk).

[5] Cited in Second to None: A History of Coldstream, Coldstream and District Local History Society, 2010, p. 36.

[6] Ibid.

[7] Ibid.

[8] Letters and Papers, Foreign and Domestic, Henry VIII, vol. 3 1519–1523, ed. by J. S. Brewis, (London: HSMO, 1867), pp. 1421–1422, accessed at: British History Online (http://www.british-history.ac.uk).

[9] Sadler, D. J. & Serdiville, R. B., Flodden 1513 (Gloucester: History Press, 2010), p. 110.

[10] Ibid., p. 112.

[11] Ibid., p. 114.

[12] Ibid., p. 102.

[13] A saker or saker falcon was medium calibre artillery firing a 5.25 lb (2.7kg) ball; a demi-culverin was larger but smaller than a culverin.

[14] Sadler & Serdiville, Flodden, p. 117.

[15] Ibid., p. 119.

[16] Ibid.

[17] Ferguson, J., The Flodden Helm and events linked to the death of Thomas Howard in 1524 (Berwick on Tweed: privately published, 2009), p. 132.

[18] Ibid., p. 132.

[19] Ibid., p. 134

[20] Ibid., p. 141.

[21] Ibid., p. 147.

[22] Ibid.

[23] Ibid., pp. 149–150.

[24] Ibid., p. 156.

[25] Ibid., p. 169.

[26] Ibid., p. 170.

[27] Ibid., p. 180.

[28] It appears the ornate coffer chest Queen Margaret stashed her silks in was acquired at auction by a Coquetdale farmer and authenticated by NMS where it currently resides.

[29] Sadler & Serdiville, Flodden, p. 211.

[30] Ibid.

CHAPTER EIGHT: A VERY ROUGH WOOING

'Those to whom evil is done do evil in return'

W. H. Auden

'Avenge not yourselves, but rather give place unto wrath; for it is written, Vengeance is mine, I will repay, saith the Lord'.

Rom. 12:19

It's most unlikely the bible was preferred reading for our reiver ancestors, most of whom couldn't anyway but it seems equally unlikely they'd agree with that sentiment. Vengeance really was for the here and now. Do unto others as you would have them do unto you – just do it first was probably nearer the mark and the ethic of reciprocity or their version of it ruled constantly on the Marches.

A VERY ROUGH NEIGHBOURHOOD

Ask Percy Reed. Percival was a kind of deputy-sheriff or Keeper of Redesdale and owner of a decent spread at Troughend [1]. From the fine eminence his property provided, he kept an eye out for malefactors of which, in fairness there was never a shortage, and he was lively about his duties. As ever those Liddesdale names were high on the list and he managed, on one occasion, to nab young Whinton Crosier: 'The Liddesdale Crosiers hae ridden a race/ And they had far better stayed at hame/ For they have lost a gallant gay/ Young Whinton Crosier it was his name' [2]. This was brave, veering towards foolhardy as the Liddesdale riders would not take kindly and meddling with them could spark a feud. Crosier's heidman possessed the usual cross-border affinity and was in with Halls of Girsonfield, Redesdalers sure but no friends of Percy's.

What they did was pretty rough form even by highly malleable local standards. They asked Percy Reed to join them for a day's sport, ranging over Rooken Edge and Bateinghope, resting at the end of summer's day, flasks passed around. Silly Percy dozed off and his host set to work. They took the tack off his horse, poured water down the barrel of his long gun – soaking the charge, glued his sword into the scabbard and then woke Percy just in time to see five Crosiers hurrying up.

Reed still didn't get it; he entreated his three companions to stand with him and take the Scotsmen on. They advised they had pressing matters elsewhere and he was on his own. Their excuse was that they didn't want a feud on their hands 'the three fause [false] Halls' as they were branded thereafter. Off they went. Percy now found the odds rising in a most unfortunate manner. He couldn't ride effectively; his gun was useless, his hanger jammed. The Crosiers closed in felling him with 33 blows, his hands and feet were hacked off, his mangled carcass left littering one of those miniature valleys that flow down into Rede: 'They fell upon him all at once/ They mangled him most cruellie/ The slightest wound might caused his deid/ And they gave him thirty-three/ They hackit off his hands and feet/ And left him lying on the lee' [3].

His remains were so hacked up that what was left came back in several pillowcases. It was indeed a pretty rough neighbourhood, but those vicious and cowardly Halls weren't forgiven, hounded out of the valley. This was a nasty mix of, effectively, murder under trust compounded by siding with the enemy. Such things don't get forgotten.

BUSINESS AS USUAL

Despite the enormous loss which Scots sustained at Flodden, it was soon business as usual on the borders. There were big English raids that autumn and the riding names kept riding. The problem both sides had was that while both could mount large-scale incursions, warden raids, and the bloody trail of private enterprise, neither could hope to win any long-term strategic advantage. The old English Pale of Edward III no longer existed or appeared viable; Scotland was incapable of pursuing territorial ambitions south of the Tweed. To add to the northern kingdom's woes, James V was a minor and that implied the usual dismal intercnine squabbling of competing regencies.

Dowager Queen Margaret blew it completely by marrying Archibald Douglas, 6th Earl of Angus. He was nobody's favourite and despite being a tough fighter he would change sides with almost bewildering frequency, and he was often head of a significant pro-English faction. James IV had a cousin, John Stuart, Duke of

Albany who, despite having spent most of his life in France and speaking little Scots or English, was persuaded to accept the regency. Francis I was perfectly content to have such an ardent Francophile running the show. Albany's task was a most unenviable one and he defected across the sea to France in 1517 but returned four years later when Anglo-French tension escalated once again. Henry VIII was always dazzled by a return to the glory days of the Hundred Years War, as silly and pointless as it was. This obsession largely blinded him to Scotland in which he had no interest beyond keeping the back door bolted.

Henry allowed that wily old fox Lord Dacre significant licence in how he controlled the marches. The warden was good at what he did, the only trouble being the doing of it involved him in a lot of shady arrangements with dubious characters. He funded some riding names against others and used the royal purse to keep the pot simmering. This bribe/ divide and conquer strategy worked well enough in its own way but didn't please many on the English side and Dacre's Machiavellian doings would catch up with him later [4].

Once hostilities between England and France kicked off again in 1522, Albany was determined to assist and bring a large Franco-Scots army into play on the border. He was enthusiastic, his French officers were too but the Scottish lords were not. Memories of Flodden and the price of dancing to France's tune were far too raw and besides, Scots found the overweening arrogance of their guests intolerable. They refused to cross the border, full stop; period, as our American friends might say. Either way, they wouldn't budge across the Tweed. Dacre gave Albany an out by proposing an extension of the existing truce and the Duke had little choice but to accept. Henry was none too happy, but Dacre's pragmatic solution suited everybody [5].

Next year and it was back to normal. Dacre with Surrey pounded the Scottish marches. In his spring chevauchee the earl dragged light guns with his column to shoot up Scottish towers, normally safe from raids. He came up against squat Cessford a real blockhouse, up-graded with earth banks or rampires to soak up the effect of cannonballs. The siege stalled. In September he tried again, leading six thousand soldiers, and pouncing on Jedburgh. Undaunted, the townspeople fought back, a real mini Stalingrad, street by street, house by house till the place was finally flattened. Surrey was a hard man to impress but the grit shown by the Jedwardians won his praise if little else, as Ridpath records: 'The English incensed by this resistance burnt the town and demolished its ancient and beautiful monastery' [6].

Andrew Ker's stronghold of Ferniehurst was next on Surrey's 'must burn' list and the situation wasn't helped by the fact Albany had welcomed Richard de la Pole. A successful condotierre in his own right but, importantly Henry VIII's worst nightmare, the surviving Yorkist claimant to the English throne, a new and rather more convincing upgrade on Perkin Warbeck. Yet the Duke was constantly being undermined by the Queen and other disaffected lords who leaned more towards England, these planned: 'a project of putting the reins of government into the hands of the king, although not yet thirteen years of age' [7].

In a raid into the Merse that July, a substantial force of English riders led by Sir John Fenwick, Leonard Musgrave, and the Bastard Heron of legend ran into an ambush and were badly cut up, a couple of hundred were taken prisoner and the fight proved to be Heron's last [8]. Dacre was doing rather better, according to Edward Hall: 'appointed to keep the borders against Scotland, did so valiantly … burned the good town of Kelso and lxxx (80) villages and overthrew xviii (18) towers of stone with all their barmkins and bulwarks' [9].

That autumn Albany tried again bringing a large Franco-Scottish force down to the Tweed and again the Scots weren't having any of it. Determined to make some kind of effort, he led the Gallic contingent in an attack on Wark Castle, defended by Sir William Lisle [10] with only a single company of infantry. Their assault began well, breaking into the outer ward but Lisle led a near-fanatical counterattack, despite the odds and cleared the French out, killing three hundred of them. Albany might have done better had he had adequate artillery support from the Scottish guns but they'd already packed up and gone [11]. The Duke, disillusioned and bitter, left for France again and didn't return. Two years later a formal truce was agreed but Dacre whose past sins were catching up with him and whose enemies had grown loud also became a casualty of sorts, and was stripped of his offices by the Star Chamber [12].

Surrey was withdrawn and for a brief interval the border stayed calm or what passed for calm. With Albany gone, Henry worked to promote the Earl of Angus who was far more amenable. Both Arran and the young king distrusted Douglas. Never one for subtlety, he seized power in a bloodless coup, clinging to the reins until James came of age in 1528. Like James II before him, he had a hearty detestation of his stepfather and his uncle of England. Angus was soon on the run and sought refuge at the English court which Henry was happy to offer.

The wheel of history was shifting inexorably as the King, obsessed with his need for an heir, put aside Katherine of Aragon and took up with Anne Boleyn, lurching towards the Reformation and the stripping of the altars. In Europe the great Catholic powers, France, and the Empire, were temporarily reconciled and appeared to form a concert party. Scotland was still wedded, despite Henry's best efforts, to France. James sought a wife there, the King's daughter, though the Scottish climate quickly finished her off. He went back for a more robust model and married Mary de Guise, a handsome six-footer and no wallflower.

James was also under the influence of a rising star, David Beaton, Archbishop of St. Andrews (latterly a Cardinal), who fuelled the young man's inherent hostility to Protestantism, shoots of which were just emerging in Scotland. France and the Empire soon fell out and Henry was back in with Charles V. As ever, his ambitions were dogged by the threat of the Auld Alliance. Meanwhile on the borders, it was business as usual and what passed for peace couldn't endure. Henry had tried to persuade James to meet him at York, but his nephew stood him up, a monumental and self-defeating gesture. Henry didn't care to be humiliated. If the young man couldn't see reason, then it was out with the carrot and back to the stick.

Tension and trouble mounted. In August 1542, the Captain of Norham, Sir Robert Bowes, abetted by the renegade Angus and his brother George, blitzed Teviotdale. The Englishman commanded three thousand lances and following standard drill [13], stationed his main body at Hadden and dispatched two flying columns, one with rough riders out of Redesdale and Tynedale, and the other, more sedate, the regular complement stripped from the defences of Berwick and Norham. The Scots were ready; Sir Walter Lindsay of Torphichen [14] led a vanguard, around two thousand strong with their principal strike force under George Gordon, Earl of Huntly. Lindsay's fast-moving detachment interposed itself between the two flying columns and their main component. Random skirmishes flared as the riders clashed. This wasn't the kind of battle you could ever draw up a neat plan for, a snapping snarling savagery of bickering lances. Lindsay neatly nipped the salient created by the flung out English columns to get between them and the rest. Huntly received a handy reinforcement of four hundred additional riders led by Home.

What followed was a retreat so hasty it became a rout. Angus, a tough customer not given to panic, blamed the English dalesmen for thinking more of their loot than their honour (in fairness they usually did). Bowes, his brother Richard, with William Mowbray ended up as captives, along with many others, perhaps as many as six hundred [15]. Angus succeeded in hacking his way out but was chased clear across the Border. Some seventy-odd of the English riders were killed and Hadden Rigg, though small beer in overall strategic terms, ranks as a resounding tactical victory for the Scottish Borderers.

Retaliation was already planned even before the shambles at Haddon Rigg. A hefty chevauchée led by Surrey, now Duke of Norfolk, saw Roxburgh, Kelso, and a score of lesser townships reduced to ashes. On paper Norfolk's tally of destruction looked impressive but, in any strategic sense, he'd achieved next to nothing. The list was carefully primed to placate Henry who was expecting rather more bangs for his bucks and these shows cost big bucks. Norfolk encountered the classic hazards facing any English commander wanting to campaign north of the border, exacerbated by lateness; he hadn't set off till 23 October: lack of supply, lack of transport, bad weather, bad roads made worse by autumn mud and even worse, a serious shortage of ale [16].

The road to Solway Moss

James was determined to retaliate, though – despite his earlier exhortations, the victors of Haddon Rigg had declined to push their luck across the border. He summoned a levy to muster on Fala Muir about 15 miles (24 kilometres) from the capital, but nobody wanted to cross that fatal line and the levy plan foundered. Undeterred James, already chronically sick from an undiagnosed illness, raised an army from his magnates' affinities to be led by Robert, Lord Maxwell, West March Warden, a force possibly 18,000 strong [17], though I tend to favour lower estimates of say 10,000–12,000 [18].

The expedition got off to a bad start. King James proposed to lead in person but with his health failing, he got no further than Lochmaben. Maxwell might hold command and be best suited to exercise it, but James could not bring himself to trust his warden (the Maxwells were notoriously slippery) and gave secret orders to his favourite, Oliver Sinclair, that he was to assume command once the army had crossed into England. This was a very silly plan, swapping horses almost literally in mid-stream was bound to spread confusion and damage fragile morale. It was already late November when the invaders broke camp, very late in the season. Nonetheless, the king's overall strategy had been successful in that he had convinced Norfolk his blow would fall in the east, which left the back door through the western marches seemingly undefended.

In the wee small hours of 24 November 1542, the Scots were on the march, moving up from Langholm and Marston Kirk. Torching Graham steadings throughout the strip of Debatable Land as they advanced, the grey pall of smoke a familiar beacon and in the chill of that late autumn dawn, they splashed over the sullen waters of Esk, beyond which lay the barren waste of Solway Moss. Lord Wharton, warden of the English West March, was a veteran of countless border scraps and not prone to panic. A less aggressive captain might have been happy to hide behind Carlisle's massive walls, which had always successfully defied the Scots, but Wharton was determined to fight, having potentially around three thousand troops available [19].

Shadowing the invaders, Wharton commanded some of his patrols to harass the Scottish March behind them, by-passing the invading army to do some torching of their own [20]. As Wharton's riders pricked at the great mass of Scottish pikes, they were initially seen off by covering fire from their light guns, Maxwell was dragging a decent sized artillery train. Once across and on the English side, the attackers advanced past Oakeshaw Hill towards Arthuret Howes, following the line of the Esk. Their path was narrow and constricted, hemmed by river and marsh, the great wet swamp of Solway Moss. Wharton had gathered his infantry and moving from Hopesike Hill set up a blocking position.

At this point, Sinclair, like some second-rate magician, produced his authority to lead. James had just stage-managed his own disaster: 'by the King's immoderate affection for Oliver Sinclair'. He had appointed this minion Lieutenant-General of his army and his commission being produced at the critical appearance of a body of the enemy and Sinclair himself being elevated on two pikes to show him to the forces as their leader, a general murmur and breach of all order ensued [21]. A worse move could hardly be imagined; if Wharton was hoping for a miracle, his prayers had just been answered. Lord Maxwell's observations may best just be imagined.

Perhaps, almost at the very same moment, the English warden directed his deputy Musgrave to canter from the right of the thin English line and strike a blow against the Scottish left. Wharton, master tactician, could see how the extended enemy deployment could be hustled into that nasty wet ground by a timely attack. He wasn't wrong. With perhaps seven hundred riders Musgrove swooped, struck like lightning, and wheeled to re-form. Wharton knew how to best use his men, to keep pricking and avoid close contact. Maxwell was arguing with Sinclair who patently had no idea what orders to give so none were given, no dispositions made, the army remained inert whilst the Cumbrians hacked and harried their flanks.

Wharton, to his amazement, witnessed a rapid disintegration of the Scottish host. As always, the rot began at the rear as men witnessed the damage being done further forward and this trickle soon turned into a river and finally a tsunami. As the warden dryly noted, 'Our prickers... gatt them all in a shake all the waye' [22]. James had dreamt of avenging the catastrophe at Flodden but his own débâcle – though the loss of life was miniscule by comparison – was an even greater humiliation. His army simply fell apart.

Over a thousand Scots surrendered. Some hundreds died for the loss, according to Wharton, of only seven of his own marchers. It was said fishermen were yanking corpses out of the water for days afterwards [23]. The shocked and dazed survivors stumbling back through smouldering shacks on the Scottish side suddenly found the Grahams, emerging like hungry foxes, to avenge their losses. Le renard kills for sport, so did the Grahams and they now had scores to settle.

James's brittle personality, enfeebled by sickness, simply couldn't stomach such an outcome and, blaming his officers for his own folly, died at Falkland Palace on 14 December. He was only 30. Both his infant sons had predeceased him and his only heir was a baby daughter. Worse, the child's nearest male relative was her great-uncle, Henry VIII. The grim spectre that had harried Scotland after 1286 had returned. But with a difference, a doctrinal twist, one significant event in James's reign had been those first stirrings of religious discontent. New ideas and new thinking did not sit easily with the pomp and religiosity of the established church, where worldliness, nepotism, carnality, and corruption were rife. Cardinal Beaton perfectly embodied all that old style Borgia stuff, and his unpopularity was swelling.

A VERY ROUGH WOOING

After the disaster of Solway Moss and James's death, Henry appeared in an unassailable position. Wharton's victory won prestige and netted valuable prisoners; the queen was a minor and a strong Anglophile party existed. Arran, the current regent, was undistinguished. The English king, at last, had a son and a marriage proposal was soon on the table. This was anathema to the spirited royal widow, French by birth and staunchly Catholic. Aided by Beaton, she attempted a coup but failed miserably and the Cardinal, hat and all, was temporarily banged up.

One who was both witness and player in these events was my own (possibly) distant ancestor, Sir Ralph Sadler (1507–1587). The legacy of Thomas Cromwell didn't die with his execution in 1540, the protagonist of Wolf Hall & Bring up the Bodies, was succeeded in influence by his protégé Ralph. He, unlike his mentor, successfully served four Tudor sovereigns and survived to become the richest commoner in England. Sadler (sometimes spelt Sadleir) was a remarkable polymath and agile gymnast in the tricky survival stakes of the Tudor court and the dangerous maelstrom of Anglo-Scottish politics. For nearly half a century he was a key player.

His story, only briefly written up once in the 1960s, is the remaining saga of the era that has never really been told. Sadler was unique amongst Tudor statesman and diplomats, not just for his humble origins but the fact he served four successive monarchs, though his time under Mary was fraught. He also lived to a ripe old age and died both wealthy and in his bed. Given the attrition rate amongst men of ambition, these were achievements in themselves.

Ralph was now the fellow entrusted with that most delicate of missions, broaching the matter of a marriage alliance after James V's death. He managed to achieve a rapport with the formidable Mary of Guise and brokered the marriage alliance between the infants Edward of England and Mary of Scotland. Sir Ralph, as ambassador, had the tortuous task of growing the pro-Henry faction, championed by the slippery Angus. As he wrote to his master on 20 March

1543: 'The next morning I met with my Lord of Angus in the Blackfriars here, by appointment … I discoursed with the great earl at length, thereafter with the Earl of Glencairn and then with both together. I found them both assured to your majesty in my poor opinion, but they excused the not proponing [proposing] the matter for the government for your majesty "there was a governor chosen before" which they say "did change the case"' [24]: slippery customers indeed.

The Treaty of Greenwich, signed in August 1543, formalised the marriage deal and the throne of Scotland appeared within England's grasp. In this, his moment of near triumph, Henry proved his own worst enemy. His arrogance and condescension alienated many Scots and the pendulum of opinion swung towards France. By December, Beaton was free and Mary of Guise back in control. Henry wasn't a good loser and decided that if the Scots wouldn't listen to his kindly avuncular overtures, more direct means of persuasion were needed. His brief to Edward Seymour, Earl of Hertford, [25] for the 1544 campaign was as unequivocal as it was terrifying.

He was: 'to put all to fire and sword, to burn Edinburgh town, and do raze and deface it, when you have sacked it, and gotten what you can out of it, as that it may remain forever a perpetual memory of the vengeance of God lighted upon it, for their falsehood and disloyalty. Do what you can out of hand, and without long tarrying, to beat down and overthrow the castle, sack Holyrood-House and as many towns and villages about Edinburgh as ye conveniently can; sack Leith and burn and subvert it, and all the rest, putting man, woman and child to fire and sword, without exception, where any resistance shall be made against you; and this done, pass over to the Fife land and extend the extremities and destructions in all towns and villages whereunto you may reach conveniently and not forgetting amongst all the rest to so spoil and turn upside down the cardinals' town of St. Andrews, as the upper stone may be the nether, and not one stick stand by another, sparing no creature alive within the same, especially such as in friendship and blood be allied to the Cardinal' [26].

That's a very long sentence and expresses the kind of detailed sentiment Joe Stalin would have applauded. It's not quite an incitement to genocide but comes as close as you'd want. In May 1544, pursuant to his instructions a substantial force under Hertford, harnessing to the full England's amphibious capability, landed at Newhaven on the Firth of Forth and wasted both Leith and the capital. Edinburgh Castle on its jutting crag defied English guns but other ad hoc defences were swept away in a deluge of blood and terror. Citizens battled with all they had, a courageous but hopeless defence. Hertford carried out his instructions to the letter, though Fife at least escaped the holocaust. This was the 'Rough Wooing' and it would be very rough indeed over the next six years.

One feature of the era was the English policy of assurance, effectively buying in Scottish names as temporary allies. Gold was always persuasive, and it freed up the 'assured' Scots from harm. Many were happy to wear the cross of St. George for as long as it suited. But it would suit only for so long as the English maintained the whip hand. Once that grip was prised free, it could swiftly be broken and while money talked it was only ever a temporary conversation.

Distinguished, even in such ruthless company, by his greed was the English Middle March Warden, Sir Ralph Eure. Together with Wharton and Dacre, who were active in the west, he mounted a campaign of terror, targeting the Merse, Teviotdale, and Lauderdale. This was so effective that a royal warrant was reputedly issued ceding him all the territory he could conquer. This was unfortunate as these territories were largely in the ownership of Angus who was tempted to swap sides again: 'He swore that if Ralph Eure dared act upon the grant, he would write his sasine [now a 'title information document'] on his skin with sharp pens and bloody ink' [27].

So, Angus reverted to his Scottish allegiance, his wily and aggressive temperament was never more needed. He was appointed Lieutenant of the Border, past omissions overlooked, and declared his intentions by putting pressure on Eure's assured Scots, particularly Nixons and Crosers. It was their appeals for aid that led Eure with his deputy Brian Laiton to assemble a motley force of about three thousand, many of them foreign mercenaries: Germans, Italians, French, Spanish, Irish, and Greeks, the dregs of Continental armies. Crossing the Border, he picked up a few hundred Scottish riders who soon seem to have fallen out with the rest of the hired help.

The English ploughed through the marches like a whirlwind leaving Melrose in ashes, the abbey, with its Douglas tombs, wantonly desecrated. Such depredations could only stiffen Angus's resolve, but he didn't have enough men to risk a battle and had to be content with nibbling at the enemy flanks. He was joined by Arran but, even with these reinforcements; he had only three hundred, enough for Leonidas perhaps but Angus intended to win. Sometime later he was bolstered by another contingent led by the Master of Rothes; the odds were shortening. By this time the English were camped, stuffed with loot, on Ancrum Moor, hard by the banks of the Teviot and a bare five miles (8 kilometres) from Jedburgh.

Bolstered by Leslies and Lindsays, Angus's mini-army now numbered over a thousand and more were on their way, led by tough Walter Scott of Buccleuch. Though he'd initially drawn up his forces on a slight rise overlooking the moorland rim, Angus was persuaded, probably by Buccleuch, to withdraw and deploy both out of sight and dismounted, using lances as impromptu pikes: 'having dismounted from their horses and sent them to some eminences in their rear they drew up on a piece of low ground where they were in a great measure hidden from the English who, from the motion of their horses, imagining they had already begun to fly marched precipitately towards them' [28]. Eure's scouts and leading elements may also have been lured on by a fleeing gaggle of horsemen, the oldest trick in the book.

Prior to the battle and while 'taking up' the marchland, the invaders were said to have fired a tower at Broomhouse, incinerating the elderly owner and her dependents. At any event the cry of 'Remember Broomhouse' would ring the death knell for many who had watched the flames. Laiton hurrying on with the vanguard topped the rise and ran headlong onto those levelled lances. Blinded by the rays of the setting sun, the attackers floundered. Behind, Eure advanced with the main detachment, mounted men-at-arms in the centre flanked on one side by archers and on the other by harquebusiers [29]. The Scots fought hard, emptying saddles, and sending the vanguard crashing back against the middle. Seizing the moment, Angus ordered a general advance and the dogged files surged forward, chewing through the invaders' rapidly disintegrating ranks. On a good day, the fortunes of war can be slippery, for the English this wasn't a good day at all.

Eure and Laiton struggled to rally their polyglot army, knowing they couldn't expect quarter. Of the English 800 or so were killed outright, a 1000 more captured, 80 of these were gentry [30], a hefty cash dividend. Those assured Scots, Liddesdale names mostly, riding beneath English banners, selected the most judicious moment to revert to their national allegiance, swapping their crosses of St George for the Saltire (prudently they tended to wear one on top of the other, just in case). Assurance has its limitations. Neither Eure nor Laiton got out alive. Those dazed survivors who escaped the fight had little hope of ever seeing the border: 'The peasantry of the neighbourhood hitherto only spectators drew near to intercept and cut down the English ....' [31]. 'Remember Broomhouse' for sure!

One of the imagined heroines of the fight was 'Fair Lilliard' whose legend asserts 'upon the English loons [infantry] she laid many thumps/ And when they cutted off her legs she fought upon her stumps' [32], anticipating Monty Python by four centuries! Ancrum Moor was a significant tactical success and bigger morale booster for the Scots, though strategically nothing had changed. Henry plotted to remove Beaton from the scene by having the annoying Scottish prelate murdered, using the radical preacher George Wishart as his tool. Having studied at Cambridge and in Germany, Wishart was a prophet of the new religion, fervent and ruthless, but he proved less successful as an assassin and ended up at the stake. In May 1546, however, a gang of ruffians finally completed his mission and Beaton was nastily murdered [33].

After the burning of his mentor, the banner of Reformation passed to John Knox. Born near Haddington in 1514, he trained as a priest before being assailed by doubts and converting to the Protestant cause. The murder of Beaton did the Anglophile party little good, and the Dowager, Marie de Guise, chased the rebels back behind the walls of St Andrew's Castle, where they continued to hold out for a time. The death of Henry VIII and the accession of a sickly boy put paid to any hope from England and encouraged France in more overt support for the royalists. St Andrews was reduced by naval gunnery and the 'Castilians' were obliged to strike their colours. Knox was sent to the galleys where he languished till released through English influence. He remained a pensioner at the court of Edward VI until his return to Scotland in 1559.

It was on the night of 28 January that Henry VIII finally died, to the sorrow of few and the relief of many. One who was very relieved was Thomas Howard, Duke of Norfolk, victor of Flodden and uncle of two queens of England [34], both of whose death warrants he signed. Norfolk was due to his own appointment with the headsman that morning, but Henry's death saved him, an automatic amnesty. Ever the recusant, he'd go on to serve Bloody Mary and die in his bed at a ripe old age. Edward Seymour, now elevated to Duke of Somerset, was as Jane Seymour's brother the young king's uncle and appointed Lord Protector. Unlike Henry, he didn't see subjugating Scotland as a viable strategic objective. That didn't mean Scotland was no longer under attack, it just shifted the emphasis. What Somerset wanted was to win hearts and minds, a mix of stick and carrot, taking assurances and buying friends while building up an English Pale on the border.

PINKIE

This was nothing new of course; Edward III had attempted to do the same. What had changed was the landscape of faith. As momentum grew behind the Scottish Reformation, the Auld Alliance with Catholic France, which had always been pretty one-sided, became progressively less attractive. Nonetheless, Somerset's grand plan wouldn't ever work despite a promising start. Costs would be prohibitive, and construction, manning, and supply would always be a logistical nightmare and, finally, there'd be major French intervention to cope with.

Before any carrots were delivered it was time to put some serious stick about. Somerset gathered his forces around Newcastle throughout August and by 1 September was on the road north, heading for a muster at Berwick. At the same time, Wharton would lead a second pincer, more of a large-scale raid, from the west directed towards Annandale. Somerset's main strike force totalled just over 18,000 [35]: John Dudley, Earl of Warwick, acting as Lieutenant-General, effectively chief of staff [36] led the vanguard of three thousand; Somerset commanded the four thousand strong centre or main battle and Dacre a strong rearguard of another three thousand [37]. This was primarily a northern levy, though the men might be conscripts in name; they'd been in the field on and off for five years and campaigning against the Scots was in their blood.

Lord Grey of Wilton commanded the cavalry, a mix of 'light' and 'heavy' two thousand 'demi-lances' [38] under Sir Francis Bryan, half a thousand stripped from Boulogne's garrison with four thousand 'heavies' under Sir Ralph Vane, including Sir Thomas Darcy's Gentlemen Pensioners of the Royal Bodyguard [39] and Edward Shelley's 'Bulleners' [40]. This was very much an all-arms force – Somerset had hired in mounted harquebusiers led by the mercenary Pedro de Gamboa, with Italian specialists under Malatesta. Scouting was undertaken by Sir Francis Bryan commanding four hundred riders [41]. Fifteen big guns made up the artillery train and the army needed a tail of nine hundred supply carts and a multitude of assorted wagons [42]. Just moving this big a contingent through enemy territory on very bad roads was a major logistical feat: 1400 pioneers were needed, and the vast column would have extended for 20 miles or more. Scottish riders, like jackals, would be hanging on the flanks waiting for any chance to strike [43], Somerset's own light cavalry would have been constantly busy.

The Lord Protector, a fine soldier if an indifferent politician, was an active commander and spied out Eyemouth harbour as a potential forward operating base beyond Berwick. The Governor, Thomas Gower, was left to start digging foundations for a new fort [44]. This wasn't castle building. Old medieval walls could no longer withstand modern artillery so the new science of defence depended on timber and earth redoubts, designed to soak up roundshot and based on the trace Italienne model, wide flanking bastions that could be crammed with guns while also providing enfilade fire. Many such forts, such as the later construction at Haddington, were dug from scratch, others incorporated earlier towers, retained as blockhouses or modified as gun platforms. In the years 1547–1550, English strategy relied on such outposts and several later survived multiple sieges.

Four days later the army was approaching Cockburnspath, 16 miles north of the line and the narrow defile there known as the Pease. Somerset feared the Scots would be lying in wait where the outriders of the Lammermuir Hills slip down towards the coast. High cliffs along the ragged coastline would have sheltered defenders from naval gunfire, as an English fleet under Lord Clinton shadowed the army: 34 warships, 30 transports, one galley and a shoal of lesser vessels [45]. Arran chose not to fight for the gap and all the English found were abandoned trenches. That evening the invaders approached Tantallon Castle whose formidable defences seem to have deterred the Lord Protector despite his big guns. Smaller fortlets, like Dunglas which surrendered, or Thornton and Innerwick which had to be assaulted, fell after short but stiff exchanges [46].

Next dawn the English marched westward again through East Linton, making camp at Longniddry. On the 8th the march was resumed over ground since covered by Prestongrange Golf Course, behind which the land shears away from the coastal plain and rises to form Fa'side and Carberry Hills [47]. Always a prudent man, Somerset pulled his troops back to camp on the coast, pretty much where the present caravan park is located, undisturbed by the hostile garrison in Fa'side Castle. He had reason to be careful; deployed against him were those 30,000 Scots the Governor had managed to muster [48].

Arran had shown a shrewd eye for ground, his line fronted by the sweep of the Esk bellying out towards the sea with steep banks on the defenders' side. He controlled the only bridge where the road to Edinburgh crossed the Esk. Huntly, on the left of the line, had thrown up an earth parapet to shield his men from Clinton's naval guns, his division beefed up with Argyll's four thousand clansmen [49]. Arran took the centre, strongly positioned on Edmonstone Edge, while Angus the right, his flank covered by Home's 1500 border lances and shielded by wet ground on both banks of the river but with a wider marsh on the south side. Somerset convened a council of war; Clinton's seaborne vantage gave him a perfect view of the whole Scottish position. Meanwhile Huntly issued the standard chivalric challenge – daring Somerset to settle the issue with a combat of 20 a side, ten a side or just the two of them banging it out [50]. Somerset wisely declined.

On the 9th, Home's Borderers splashed across the Esk, trusting in their swift and sure-footed Border garrons and aiming to rattle their enemies. Lord Grey was all for the charge but Somerset preferred caution, for a long time the English line stood whilst the Scots postured. Grey insisted; Somerset relented; trumpets blared and his cavalry advanced. Caught completely by surprise, the Borderers soon fled and were hunted down; some were killed and perhaps eight hundred, including Home himself, went into the bag: 'after a skirmish of three hours the Scots were defeated and driven back to their camp with great slaughter' [51]. This outwardly minor setback robbed Arran of what effective cavalry he had.

A little after 08.00 on Saturday, 10 September the Lord Protector ordered the advance. His immediate goal was the hillock, though he was only thinking of this as that day's campsite and as a handy spot for his guns [52]. Sweating and cursing, gunners and matrosses manoeuvred their great cannon. He hadn't, at that point, realised the Scots were already marching. Arran had given the order to advance. Why did he choose to abandon such a strong defensive position? He may well have feared the broadsides from Clinton's ships but also saw a chance to catch the English unawares, possibly while still in camp.

Somerset was wrong-footed as his army sighted the Scots moving towards them, and fast: 'coming towards us, passed the river, gathered in array and well-nigh at this church [Inveresk] 'ere we were halfway to it' [53]. Though the armies were on a collision course, neither had been fully aware of the other but as Huntly's rearguard moved out of the cover of their earthworks the fleet began firing – the Master of Graham and 25 other ranks were pulped in an instant. Despite such losses and the morale-bursting effect of being under fire in the open, which rattled Argyll's Highland archers, the Scottish juggernaut rolled forward, a bristling steel tipped leviathan. Angus led with eight thousand spears and five guns, Arran followed with ten thousand, the cream of his army and Huntly started with another eight thousand, though a number were already wavering, and some had probably voted with their feet.

Somerset wasn't slow to work out the crisis he was facing, his carefully considered plans evaporating in the fog of war. Dense as the ranks were, the Scots came on at an impressive pace. It would be a race to see who could get to the high ground of Fa'side Hill first. Somerset couldn't allow the Scots to win. This called for another hasty council of war. To curb the rush of pikes Somerset had to commit his cavalry, relying on shock and impact to slow this forest of pikes and buy time to get his guns in action and his infantry into line, a real Light Brigade job.

One eyewitness who provides a comprehensive first-hand account was William Patten, Somerset's secretary. He could clearly see the Scots' pike brigades, who: 'Stood at defence, shoulders nigh together, the fore-rank stooping low before their fellows behind them holding their pikes in both hands, the one end of the pike against the right foot, the other against the enemy's breast, so nigh as place and space might suffer. So thick were they that a bare finger should as easily pierce through the bristles of a hedgehog as any man encounter the front of the pikes' [54].

Both sides were bringing more and more guns into action, the field already shrouded in a dense pall of acrid smoke, making command and control even more difficult. Cavalry attacking head on and unsupported had very little chance of breaking a pike formation and the Scots weren't overawed: 'Come here lounds [rascals]; come here tykes [dogs]; come here heretics', they jeered [55]. Grey and Shelley's Bulleners would advance from the east while Vane with D'Arcy's Pensioners would come at them from the west. To make matters worse, the agricultural land over which they'd have to ride was 'a fallow field', furrows lining towards the English, the ground bisected by a ditch which both slowed momentum and impeded many riders who got bogged down.

Artillery support was provided by guns drawn up on higher ground behind, as the cavalry charged. This would never be the mad gallop of movies but at best a sedate canter, mass and cohesion mattered more than speed. 'Herewith waxed it very hot', Patten commented [56]. The cavalry was unstoppable mass meeting immovable object and the pikes won. Horsemen were spitted on points, horses gored and brought down, a mass of human and equine corpses piling up (many of the heavy cavalry had left their horse armour with the baggage as they'd not expected to fight and now paid the price). Men and boys would dart from the phalanxes to hobble and hamstring horses, and cut the throats of riders. Steam rose like a cloud from the sweat, blood, entrails, and excrement puddling churned ground while the charnel house reek and satanic pall of gun smoke added a furious encore.

Recoiling, losses heavy, the English cavalry stumbled back up the slope to the catcalls of their unshaken enemies. To the Scots it seemed the battle must be won and the field theirs. Somerset and Vane had a job to rally their riders and reform on the flanks of the English infantry. Though apparently victorious, the pikemen were stalled and now being winnowed by continuing fire from Clinton's ships and Somerset's musketeers. No further advance was possible in the teeth of such a barrage, and Scots were hemmed in by the press of dead. Many of the cavalry had paid the ultimate price, including Edward Shelley and a slew of his 'Bulleners'. But their sacrifice was not in vain. From a range of two hundred yards (183 metres) and less, English guns raked the massed files, arrows and bullets peppered their ranks.

Swooping like vultures, De Gamboa's lethal harquebusiers nibbled at their flanks. As they couldn't advance and simply to stand was to invite destruction, the Scots attempted to withdraw, a difficult manoeuvre for pikemen. The phalanx shivered, stumbled and then like a torrent, broke, pursued by jubilant cavalry. As always, the rot began at the back, 'they fly, they fly', the English exalted [57], their pikes which had, only a short while before, dominated the fight left abandoned: 'The place they had stood like a wood of staves [pikes] strewed on the ground, as rushes in a chamber, impassable they lay so thick for either horse or man' [58].

Losses on the Scottish side were dreadful, perhaps as many as ten thousand failing to reach the north bank of the Esk. Amongst the rank and file sprawled many of the nobility, but wily Angus evaded both death and capture and slipped away with the mass of fugitives streaming towards Dalkeith. Huntly, who was also Scotland's Lord Chancellor, wasn't so lucky; he was captured. English losses barely exceeded 250, mostly, as noted, from amongst the cavalry – the infantry got off far more lightly.

STALEMATE

Pinkie was a momentous tactical victory but a strategic failure, the Scots had suffered another severe beating, but they soon bounced back, and Arran's credibility survived his running away. Somerset, however, felt he could now get on with his primary objective, turning the Scottish border into an extended outpost line. He wanted to blend hearts and minds with persuasive sharp swords but the two were uneasy bedfellows and the costs of his venture were prohibitive. Wharton had got off to a good start in the west after his successful 'taking up' of Annandale but in February 1548, it all went wrong for him. He was caught out in a well-staged ambush at Drumlanrig, where he suffered a humiliating near defeat. Raging against his assured Scots who'd turned out totally un-assured, he raged so far as to hang some of his hostages. That didn't do too much for hearts and minds either.

Somerset meanwhile had established a post on Inchcolm Island in the Firth of Forth and even pushed his line up to the Tay, taking over an assured castle at Broughty which, in theory, could control both the river and Dundee. Sir Andrew Dudley, Warwick's capable younger brother, was given command and he soon discovered he had been lumbered with a poison chalice, a regular Fort Zinderneuf where men, materials, horses, food, and ale were all in permanent short supply. Nonetheless, he saw off several siege attempts and was finally bolstered by a new sheltering redoubt in modern style. Dudley kept hanging on by his fingernails. When he was finally relieved by Sir John Luttrell who'd held Inchcolm, I doubt he even spared a backward glance.

Eyemouth was already being fortified, Home Castle was taken, and ancient Roxburgh remodelled. A new and impressive fort, state of the impromptu art, was thrown up at Haddington, big enough to house a garrison of two and a half thousand [59]. Somerset couldn't afford to keep the fleet in action, so the ships were sent home which vastly exacerbated his supply problem. His intention was that light cavalry stationed in his new bases could range freely and put some stick about whilst reminding assured Scots where their loyalties lay. To do that they needed healthy horses and unfed mounts don't stay healthy.

Somerset had bitten off more than he could chew, and the spectre of significant French assistance loomed closer in the early part of 1548. When the French did land, they brought a good general, D'Esse, with plenty of men, guns, and supplies. Their troops were all seasoned campaigners and they put heart into the Scots as well as boosting resources. Both sides still relied heavily on mercenaries, Pedro de Gamboa was still a player and each imported ensigns (a double company say three hundred+ strong) of German Landsknecht [60] who, tough customers as they were, didn't always get on too well with their respective host nations.

D'Esse hammered away at the English forts but was generally seen off. Baulked militarily, he managed to achieve a real diplomatic coup. Arran persuaded the Scottish Parliament to ratify Henry II of France's proposal that Mary should marry the Dauphin Francois. The Governor's reward was a French dukedom, a real plum while the Scots were happy to sacrifice their independence to France just to spite England. In August Mary sailed for France and any hope of reviving the Treaty of Greenwich sailed with her. Somerset's strategy had come truly unstuck; more fighting was now just an appendix to failure.

Yet nobody was quite ready to give up. Grey, utterly exhausted, was succeeded by the Earl of Shrewsbury as Lord Lieutenant in the North and lifted an epic siege of Haddington. The new commander retrieved a strong naval presence and French ships could no longer ply with impunity; some were sunk, while more became prizes. Undeterred, D'Esse made a further attempt on Haddington, hoping to seize the place by a coup de main or camisado (surprise attack/coup de main). He very nearly succeeded but not quite nearly enough and left several hundred of his men dead in the ditches [61].

Like two weary fighters locked in an exhausted embrace, the Franco-Scots and English stumbled on. The war was pointless yet infinitely bloody and merciless. The cruel English garrison at Ferniehurst were cut down wholesale by vengeful Scots whose bitter hateful fury astonished even their allies [62]. Northumberland didn't escape destructive raids either and Ford Castle was unsuccessfully invested. Meanwhile, Somerset had other worries; unrest and rebellion in the south-west of England, an increasingly hostile council who undermined his authority and finally wanted his head.

Warwick, his rival and successor, inherited an unwinnable and hugely costly war. Like dominos, those remaining English garrisons toppled and what was left was finally abandoned as untenable. There was bad news from France too, as Henry II threatened Boulogne. A treaty was needed and agreed. Both sides really had had enough and then the war, just like that, was over. Its legacy would linger forever. This Rough Wooing had been the bloodiest episode in a long saga of bloody episodes and the stains would soak deep into the souls of both kingdoms. They're still there yet.

MARY

Sir Ralph Sadler, during the war and ever versatile, became a soldier rather than diplomat; quartermaster for Hertford during the brutal invasion of 1544. The universal fixer, he did well in his new assignment and was soon back again as QMG for the English army that fought and won at Pinkie three years later. Again, Sadler outlasted his master and even Bloody Mary's vengeful spree. Elizabeth soon found use for his more subtle skills when she debated whether to help Scottish Protestants oust the last partisans of the Auld Alliance and the French spears that were propping them up.

Machiavelli would have been proud of the crepuscular logic Sir Ralph deployed to justify this intermeddling (August 1559): 'Q. Whether it be meet that England should help the nobility and Protestants of Scotland to expel the French, or not? A. (1) – It is agreeable both to the law of God and nature, that every prince and publick state should defend itself, not only from perils presently seen but from dangers that be probably seen to come shortly after; (2) – Nature and reason teacheth every person, politick or other to use the same manner of defence that the adversary useth in offence' [63]. In short there was every moral and practical justification for Elizabeth to support the Scottish Protestants. And this religious accord would, in due course, foster the Union of the Crowns.

In December 1560 the young and chronically unstable King of France died and his Scottish consort, Mary, found herself unpopular with her formidable mother-in-law, Catherine de Medici. The following year she returned to her native land, cold and impoverished. It was a poor substitute for cosmopolitan France. Mary had at least sufficient sense to ignore Huntly's dangerous overtures and make herself amenable to the Protestant clique, the Lords of the Congregation. She would not, however, agree to ratify the Treaty of Leith which had ended hostilities with her adopted country, as a clause in the draft excluded Mary from the English succession, a potential prize which she would not willingly relinquish.

I think it was George MacDonald Fraser who observed that wherever Mary went trouble was sure to follow. Her tenure in Scotland, no easy task, a Catholic queen of a now Protestant state, was not a happy one and her final failure at Carberry Hill saw her incarcerated in Lochleven Castle, forced to abdicate in favour of her infant son who was very much not being raised as a subject of Rome. She broke out of gaol but her short-lived comeback fell flat in the rout at Langside, and Mary was on the run. She fled to England which surprised everybody.

When the runaway queen and a tiny band of adherents landed at Workington on 16 May 1568, nobody had any idea what to do with her. The plain fact was that Mary was toxic; most of Catholic Europe recognised her as the rightful Queen of England, and saw Elizabeth as a heretic bastard. There was paranoia in the administration that she'd now be a talisman, a beacon for disaffected recusants in England. These fears were fully justified. Mary was met by Lord Scrope's deputy and escorted to Carlisle. Her status was unclear; clearly, she wasn't a prisoner, not quite, nor was she exactly on a state visit, she no longer possessed a kingdom to visit from. Her half-brother Moray, victor at Langside and now regent, was moving rapidly to consolidate his position and ready to cooperate fully with the English wardens.

THE NORTHERN EARLS

Her initial landfall, technically, placed her under the Earl of Northumberland's remit and 'Simple Tom' as Percy was rather unkindly badged wasn't so simple, he didn't see a valuable pawn when one was thrust under his nose. Moreover, though not a Catholic, he was part of a general disgruntlement of northern gentry. Scrope cannily denied Northumberland's request to take charge of Mary but at the same time his West March was too close to the border and Maxwell, still with the queen, had far too many confederates just across the Solway. Mary was an IED, ready to detonate and was soon moved south to Tutbury as her royal cousin wondered what to do with her. Mary wasn't, would never be, in irons but she'd never breathe free air again. That August, Elizabeth appointed Lord Hunsdon (her putative half-brother, bastard of Mary Boleyn and Henry VIII) as East March Warden and he'd prove a very sound choice. She'd have need of him.

Thomas Percy, 7th Earl of Northumberland, was the son of Sir Thomas Percy who'd lost his head in the clear up after the Pilgrimage of Grace (October 1536 – February 1537). The rebellion of 1569 was, in part, an aftershock. Henry VIII's stripping of the altars had alienated many devout Catholics in the north and a lawyer, Robert Aske, became unofficial leader of a popular insurrection which kicked off at Louth in Lincolnshire and soon spread to Yorkshire. This wasn't as much a revolution as a large-scale protest, fully armed though and as many as 30,000 strong. Initially Northumberland and the borders weren't especially involved, and Henry bought off the pilgrims with promises, secured their goodwill then dealt with them once they'd disarmed and dispersed.

Northumberland's uncle, the 6th Earl, was a rather dysfunctional character, an ex-boyfriend of Anne Boleyn. He managed to waste or alienate most of his vast patrimony before, to everyone's relief, dying in his thirties. One of the main beneficiaries of his largesse was Sir Reynold Carnaby of Halton, a proper jack the lad. No flies on Reynold; he abused Percy's generosity and participated enthusiastically in dismantling the abbeys, taking Hexham for himself [64], (Sir John Forster was his son-in-law and I'm sure they got on famously). Carpetbaggers make enemies and Carnaby had plenty. These included Percy's younger brothers Sir Thomas and Ingram.

In October 1536 the brothers hosted a gathering at Alnwick, ostensibly to muster support for the Pilgrims but in fact to arrange a concert party aimed at bringing the local upstart down. Heron of Chipchase who felt cheated of a traditional office as Keeper of Tynedale, another of Carnaby's captures, was keen to help. So effective was the reaction Sir Reynold felt obliged to hide behind Chillingham castle's thick walls [65] and his people were roughed up at Stagshaw Fair. Sir Thomas Percy was no fan of the king either who'd refused to recognise him as his brother's heir, despite being nearest. Thomas died a traitor's death at Tyburn and Ingram went to gaol for their part in the affair but family resentment survived.

Burghley had no particular love for the Earl of Northumberland. Even though Percy opposed a proposed marriage between Mary and Thomas Howard, 4th Duke of Norfolk, he was already suspect and his abortive bid to grab Mary set alarm bells ringing [66]. If Tom was dull, his beautiful wife, Countess Anne, was the life and soul but a convinced papist – daughter of Henry Somerset, Earl of Worcester. His younger half-brother Henry had already earned a reputation in the endless run of cross-border skirmishes as something of a beau sabreur. Meantime, Moray and Hunsdon got on very well indeed. The regent, who needed to keep control of his unsettled marches, found a willing and effective ally in Hunsdon. Moray's version of local justice was of the short, sharp shock variant, coming down hard on Liddesdale. This type of summary justice never produced any lasting calm, but levels of cross-border cooperation were at an all-time high.

Meanwhile an unlikely conspiracy was brewing. Tom Percy was talking to Charles Neville, Earl of Westmorland. Now Westmorland's countess, Jane, was a real firecracker, daughter of the Earl of Surrey who'd been executed for treason in 1547, a fervent Catholic. The third triumvir Leonard Dacre, 'Crookback' Leonard, that 'cankred suttil traitor', was motivated primarily by rage at being, as he saw it, cheated out of his Dacre inheritance at Naworth by the Howards (and they're still there). None of this unholy trinity was leadership material but Mary was their catalyst and letters were sent to Madrid and Rome seeking support.

These northern lords were not successors in title to Aske's pilgrims a generation before. Their grievances were more personal. They'd done well from Queen Mary but felt marginalised under Elizabeth. If neither of the earls was a born general, many of their adherents were strongly motivated by ingrained loyalty to the old ways [67]. Their treason was born of perceived grudges rather than conviction, but we should remember Elizabeth's version of Protestantism, the Church of England, was still an infant to be weighed against centuries of Rome. Besides and though the Queen had confirmed Percy in his office as East March Warden, his appointment was fettered by so many restrictions, he gave it up and Lord Grey of Wilton, a southerner, took over. Percy had to endure the humiliation of the new warden lording it over his family seat at Alnwick.

Burghley was watching all three, but the administration seemed wrong-footed when their rebel flags were raised that November. Thomas Radcliffe, Earl of Sussex, the Queen's representative in the north, perhaps fearful his friendship with Norfolk, might smear him, summoned the northern Earls to York and, on 9 October, they duly appeared. Despite their fulsome declarations of loyalty

Sussex thought it wise to ensure the major centres were put on alert and kept well supplied [68]. Queen Elizabeth had heard of this proposal that Mary should be married to the Duke of Norfolk which would join her into the English polity, an idea even some Protestants found reasonable. The Queen did not. It may be a letter written by the Duke of Norfolk to Westmorland on 1 October begging him not to rebel was the catalyst; the Duke was hoping he might marry the Scottish Queen and create a powerful papist bloc, but he'd lost his nerve by this point.

Sir Thomas Gargarve wrote to Burghley on 2nd November: '... news came that the Duke had left the court and gone to Norfolk and that thereupon the Earls of Northumberland and Westmorland had caused their servants to take up their horses and be in readiness, whereupon the people imagined that they would assist the Duke ... There was another bruit [rumour] that he confederates minded to deliver the Scottish Queen from the custody of the earl of Shrewsbury' [69]. Percy still bore the magic name and the dalesmen were happy to fall in with any cause that offered free licence. The rebels marched down to Durham and celebrated mass there, waving a two-fingered salute to Elizabeth, a cack-handed revival of the Pilgrimage of Grace. Mary was rapidly moved further south to Coventry while her northern adherents, holding Warkworth and Alnwick, wondered what to do next. For lack of any ideas, they settled for a siege of Barnard Castle.

Spanish aid was rumoured but never materialised, the rebels even sent a flying column to seize Hartlepool as a potential bridgehead. Meanwhile Hunsdon blamed their wives! Writing to Burghley on 26 November he sneered: 'I am sorry to hear of Westmorland's wilfulness in refusing to follow the advice of those who, for his house's sake, wish him well. The other [Northumberland] is very timorous and has meant twice or thrice to submit but his wife encourages him to persevere and rides up and down with their army, so that the grey mare is the better horse' [70].

Moray, however, had his own marchers on a tight leash while Hunsdon, Sir John Forster, and yes Henry Percy prepared a local counter-offensive. Lost castles were retaken, and the rebels scattered after a skirmish at Chester le Street. The earls fled west. Naworth's gates were shut, and Dacre didn't want to hear anyone knocking. They panicked into the Scottish marches where fugitive Northumberland and his spirited lady found a very different level of accommodation with betrayal and a traitor's death to follow. Younger brother Henry slipped effortlessly into his sudden inheritance [71]. Hunsdon was pretty scathing about the tardy response from the Queen's forces labouring up from the south '... Others beat the bush and they have the birds' [72].

Moray cooperated fully in the capture of Northumberland, though Westmorland got away and the Earl of Sussex, arriving belatedly in the north with reinforcements, hanged as many rebels as he could find. So far so good, but in January 1570, Moray was 'taken out' by a sniper while riding through Linlithgow. With his strong hand now cold and still, a froth of trouble rose immediately to the surface. Mary's supporters in Scotland and there were many found an ally in Dacre who'd kept out of the earls' folly but was still implicated. Scrope was after him, but Dacre fudged and managed to raise a substantial force from his own tenants with a promise of hundreds more from over the line. Combined, they could grip Carlisle in a vice; the warden didn't have sufficient manpower to hold, provided of course, they could combine.

As before Hunsdon and Forster came up trumps. The warden marched out of Berwick leading his garrison while Sir John raised as many riders as would follow him. Forster had charisma and courage by the container load and the names responded, besides there'd be loot. By winter's dusk on 18/19 February they'd marched as far as Hexham. Hunsdon could confront Dacre directly at Naworth or side-step to join forces with Scrope. He opted for the latter, but Dacre tried to block the road near the confluence of the little river Gelt and Hell Beck (well named), about four miles (6.5 kilometres) south of Brampton.

In a short, sharp fight Hunsdon and Forster scattered the rebels. As the warden reported: 'In a heath where we were to pass a river [the Gelt] his foot gave the proudest charge upon my shot that I ever saw; whereupon having left Sir John Forster with five hundred horse for my back, I charged with the rest of my horse upon his foot and slew between three and four hundred' [73]. Dacre managed to escape and got away to the Spanish Netherlands where he remained a nuisance till his death three years later. There weren't many mourners.

Though victory was won, it appeared only a respite; the Scottish marches were in turmoil. So, in the spring, Sussex launched a major warden rode to bang heads together. Seconded by both Hunsdon and Forster this was a thorough job. Buccleuch and Ferniehurst, leading Marians, were targeted; Hawick, Jedburgh, and Kelso all took a hammering. Scrope carried on the good work in the west, though Maxwell made him fight for it at Old Cockpole, a narrow English victory, abetted by the Armstrongs, who were never ones to let an opportunity slide by. Savage and unrelenting as such harrying would appear to the citizens of Hawick or Jedburgh, this was the last chevauchee, a curtain call for the major warden raids. Mary's failure meant a Protestant Scotland with a Protestant king and that would finally produce an outcome nobody could, at that point, have foreseen.

BEAU SABREUR

Long before Bamburgh Castle, in its ruinous condition, came into the capable hands of William Lord Armstrong and its subsequent Olympian makeover, it belonged to the Forsters. Sir John had acquired the castle in the mid-sixteenth century from the crown and retired there after his tumultuous five decades as Warden on the Middle March. He wasn't Wyatt Earp, much more a part of the problem than the cure. It could fairly be said he understood the nature of rampant criminality on his turf as he was the facilitator of most of it, more Mafioso than lawman. He took a cut on every act of thievery and there were many. It was on his watch that a border truce day in July 1575 degenerated into a mass brawl with dozens dead, 'Raid of the Reidswire'.

Sir John was persuaded to retire in the mid-1590s, and, in age, he ran with the century. He almost certainly clocked up a hundred plus years. His last were very nearly as turbulent as the rest when a posse of assassins sought him out even in his dotage at Bamburgh and only Lady Forster's quick thinking saved her husband's life. His descendants held the place for several generations. Dorothy Forster (1686–1767) became a romantic heroine of the doomed Jacobite Rising in 1715.

After Forster came Carey and a greater contrast would be hard to imagine; something of a culture shock for the inhabitants of firstly the East and then Middle March in England. Robert Carey, born probably in 1560, was the 10th son of that tough old bruiser Sir Henry Carey, who Lord Hunsdon described as 'an honest stout-hearted man … something of a braggart' [74]. Young Robert was well educated and spent an apprenticeship in diplomacy and was sent on several high-level missions to the court of James VI. He campaigned with Essex in France, fought against the Armada, and served as MP for Morpeth. A favourite of his aunt he fell from grace after his marriage in 1593 which led to a stormy session with an angry Gloriana but silver-tongued as he clearly was, he managed to re-ingratiate himself into royal favour.

Lord Scrope, the unfortunate West March Warden, precious son of a very able father, to be humiliated in the Kinmont Will Armstrong debacle, was Robert's brother-in-law and secured him his first role as a border law enforcer. Even better, uniquely for the time, Carey left us a detailed memoir. He served his probation as warden in the East March before being moved to the Middle, a much tougher assignment, hardly improved by Sir John's long and astonishingly corrupt tenure. It was in a dreadful mess and even Carey thought twice but finally acceded: 'I knew all things were out of order … and that the thieves did domineer and do what they pleased and that the poor inhabitants were utterly disabled and overthrown …' [75].

It was a monumental task, but Robert set to, moving his household and family into Alnwick Abbey, Forster's old pad and soon making his presence felt. His internship in the west under Scrope had taught him some valuable lessons. It was indeed a 'stirring World' and a dangerous one. When stationed at Carlisle, agents brought news that a brace of fugitives were being abetted by a man called Greene whose tower was a bare five miles (8 kilometres) off. The suspect lived in a 'pretty' house with the old tower handily adjacent. Carey with 25 troopers left in the early hours aiming to surprise the place at dawn.

Nice try but the Scots were too quick and got into the tower before they could be flushed out and ominously, a lad was seen galloping off. Carey's experienced deputy, Thomas Carleton (more on him later) warned the boy was off to raise reinforcements and the posse would soon have a major fight on their hands. That was a game two could play and Carey, on Tom's advice, sent off for more troopers. Within a few hours, scores more riders and finally infantry from Carlisle garrison pitched up. Carey now had a combined force of hundreds. To take the tower, men got up onto the roof with ropes and grapnels, prised free some of the stone flags and a squad dropped down into the upper storey. The defenders got the message and gave up [76].

Just as the Scots struck their colours and came out, a sizeable body of Scottish riders hove into view, perhaps as many as four hundred. The English West March lads were overjoyed, here was a prime opportunity to even a few outstanding scores: 'God hath put them into your hands that we may take revenge of them for much blood that they have spilt of ours' [77]. This was a tricky choice; Robert was half-inclined to let his lads do their worst but opted for the judicious course, telling them to hold off and if the Scots backed down to let them go. This wasn't the answer his marchers were hoping for but, even if with bad grace, they held back. The Scots took the hint and were off faster than Carey's messenger could speak. They had cause to be grateful for the young deputy's forbearance.

Inevitably, on his new patch, the Middle March, Liddesdale was the prime offender but King James, who was already acquainted with Carey, was happy for him to pursue offenders over the border. The king had no love for his own thieves. When a large raid struck, Carey sent a couple of hundred riders after them. Most simply took refuge in their towers: 'But one of the chief of them, being of more courage than the rest, got to horse and came pricking after them, crying out "what we he that durst avow that mighty work?" One of the company came to him with a spear and ran him through the body, leaving his spear broke in him, of which wound he died' [78]. We could be tempted to say the reivers got the point, but due notice had certainly been served. Things were changing.

Sim of the Calfhill, a notorious Armstrong, was the man killed and his kin vowed vengeance on the Ridleys, one of whom had run him through so effectively. As good as their word the dalesmen 'took up' the Ridleys settlement at 'Hartwessel' [Haltwhistle]. The raid was anticipated and the villagers in their strong-houses fully locked and loaded, blasting the reivers as they tried to fire the place. One marksman accounted for another leading Armstrong baddie. Sim of Whittram vowed the usual deep revenge and could command a couple of hundred horsemen of his own. It was time for a final solution to the Liddesdale problem.

Carey's remedy was to take his own 40 troopers with as many marchers as were up for it into Liddesdale and effectively lay siege to fearsome Tarras Moss, that primeval swamp which had always been the reivers last and hitherto impenetrable redoubt. But they'd not reckoned on Carey by now a superb border tactician, adept at fieldcraft. The net result was the netting of a handspan of leading offenders, including two of Sim of Whitram's sons [79]. The warden had got the better of Liddesdale and that didn't happen often.

While serving in the East March, Carey had to deal with his opposite number, Robert Ker of Cessford, a real throwback to the worst of the bad old days. One of his affinity was the notorious Geordie Bourne. This family weren't numerous which was a blessing but made up for lack of numbers with widespread thuggery and Geordie was the worst. Carey's riders caught up with the Bournes returning from a raid and shot dead Geordie's uncle while, after a stiff fight, capturing the man himself: 'After he was taken, his pride was such that he asked who it was durst avow that night's work' [80].

He soon found out and all Cessford's huffing and puffing wasn't going to save Geordie from the noose. But here's where Carey did posterity a second great service – not only did he leave us his story, but he also tells Geordie's as well. And this is it, the only actual recorded testimony from a reiver. We hear lots said and written about them but never from them, yet Geordie Bourne talked to Carey: 'After supper about ten of the clock, I took one of my men's liveries and put it about me … and came to the Provost Marshal's where Bourne was …' [81].

Bourne had no idea who he was talking to, assumed he was just an average trooper anxious to hear the story of the famous brigand's life before it ended. Bourne was happy to talk, villain but no coward, he knew his time was short. He boasted 'that he had lain with above forty men's wives … and that he had killed seven Englishmen with his own hands, cruelly murdering them' [82]. He'd spent his life, 'whoring, drinking, stealing' and pursuing petty grudges. He did ask for a priest however not understanding that the very frankness of his confession cancelled any hope of clemency. Local gentry were appalled not by the hanging, a near everyday occurrence but that Carey would risk humiliating Cessford who'd make their lives intolerable. But the 'Firebrand' had met his match and was forced to learn the lesson.

Humbling Lord Scrope

William Armstrong of Kinmont, known to history and to legend as 'Kinmont Willie', was a vicious ruffian with a record of lawlessness. From his tower at Morton Rigg on the fringe of the Debatable Lands, the wildest tract in the West March, he led regular raids across the Border, lifting sheep, beasts, and anything else that took his fancy. In the spring of 1596, he attended a truce at Kershopefoot on the Scottish side. After the formal business he rode, seemingly alone, along the north bank of the Liddel. On the far bank rode a squadron of English marchers. Safe in the knowledge that he was inviolate till sunrise the next day when the truce expired, Will felt free to indulge in some less than genial banter with his less than friendly neighbours over the narrow waters. Salkeld, 'a gentleman of that west wardenry' [83], Lord Scrope's deputy, was leading.

Exactly what happened next is unclear: in all probability, the English, stung by this arrogant posturing, and seeing their inveterate enemy so close, found the moment too tempting and spurred across the Liddel Water to take the astonished reiver captive. A principal primary source, the Shawfield MS, tells us that: 'they brake a chase of more than 200 men out of the English train' [84]. What is certain is that he was carted beneath the fortress walls of Carlisle and incarcerated. Such an act, occurring as it did on a truce day, was considered an outrage, notwithstanding the nature and misdemeanours of the alleged victim: 'O have ye na heard o' the fause Sakelde?/ O have ye na heard o'the keen Lord Scrope?/ How they hae ta'en bauld Kinmont Willie/ On harribee to hang him up?' [85].

It's probable Scrope was more embarrassed than elated. True, Will was a prize worth having and well worth hanging but that was never really on the warden's agenda. The catch was illegal and villain he might be, but law was law, and the warden couldn't flout such a powerful convention, one of those few slender threads that bound the marchers. Neither, on the other hand was he minded to let the Armstrong loose. If nothing else, he was a useful hostage to keep his nasty affinity in check. Scrope vaguely suggest Will had broken his assurance on the day but doesn't specify how and this does sound like rather specious justification, knowing full well his people were in the wrong [86].

Salkeld lodged his prisoner within the great castle but not in the massive keep or any dark dungeon. It seems Will was comfortably housed and not unduly confined. Outrage there was and none more outraged than Walter Scott of Buccleuch, at this point Keeper of Liddesdale. Now here was a force of nature, tough, efficient, brave, and murderous 'Bold' Buccleuch was the very model of everything a border official shouldn't be. He didn't like prissy Scrope to begin with and the dislike was entirely mutual. Kinmont's seizure was far more than a breach of protocol, it was a direct insult, a pointed two-fingered gesture aimed straight at him. From the start this was personal.

Buccleuch began properly enough; official letters demanding Will be set free. This was completely reasonable. The Keeper was clearly in the right and the fact Kinmont was probably a client and under his far more unofficial protection irrelevant, for the moment anyway. He wrote in the first instance to Salkeld and then to Scrope. If the English warden replied at all, it was in dismissive and suitably vague terms, probably like those he later used to explain himself to the Queen's Council (by no means on his side at that point) [87]. However, he actually worded any reply; it was perfectly plain he was hanging on to his prisoner.

Protocol was now out of the window; it was a grudge match between Scrope and Buccleuch. Bad blood ran deep, and Buccleuch certainly was addicted to the feud. He was as odds with the Tynedale Charltons (no strangers to a vendetta). A year earlier he'd led a force of three hundred Teviotdale men on a raid, torched a Charlton steading but found nobody to kill. Coming back a week later, he murdered four, promising at the same time 'he'd be back' [88]. So far, in the game with Scrope, he'd behaved entirely correctly and hearing nothing sensible from him wrote next to Sir Robert Bowes the English ambassador. Bowes was none too happy with Scrope either and his letter made it plain he wanted Will released forthwith. The Warden ignored him too.

Well, nobody could say Buccleuch hadn't played it by the book thus far but thus far wasn't going anywhere, so other means would be needed. Force was the only remaining option and force was something Scott understood but cutting up Charltons, while satisfying, wasn't the same as storming Carlisle Castle, still one of the strongest in the land. Any direct assault would need an army plus artillery and would be an outright act of war. King James would have a fit and would never allow it; he had his eyes on a far more glittering prize and the fate of some border toerag was neither here nor there.

An attack – no but a raid, might that be possible? Very long odds indeed unless of course it could be an inside job. On the credit side Buccleuch could easily find the right men, he had the experience and credibility to lead and the wit to plan carefully. Intelligence was the essential building block and given the numbers of Scots who traded freely in Carlisle, it was easy to build up a detailed plan of the castle. Interestingly, an isolated postern gate offered possibilities [89]: 'And for such purpose the lord of Buccleuch, upon intelligence that the Castle of Carlisle where the prisoner was kept was surprisable and of the means, by sending some persons of trust to view to view a postern gate and to measure the height of the wall very closely' [90].

Ritchie Graham of Brackenhill was happy to play dishonest broker and provide introductions to Lance and Thomas Carleton. Now these were men after Buccleuch's heart. Thomas was a prominent and able border officer, land-sergeant of Gilsland and, in the immortal words of MacDonald Fraser 'crooked as a corkscrew' [91], related by marriage to the Grahams (a partner in his blackmail racket) and ironically distantly connected to Will himself. Lance was every bit as corrupt and neither brother had any love for Scrope. The meeting lasted for four productive hours and guaranteed Buccleuch the inside track he needed. It's almost possible to feel sorry for the English warden. For all his posturing, he was a babe in the woods compared to the talent now ranged against him: Buccleuch, Old Wat (Walter Scott) of Harden, the Armstrongs, the Grahams, and now the Carletons, as distinguished a rogues' gallery as history ever produced.

As might be expected, the Grahams were key players, 'crooked as a corkscrew' doesn't do them justice. Not only were they facilitators, but they also had a material part to play; the raiders would have to cross Graham territory going both ways, so their complicity effectively unlocked the frontier. That part of the border didn't belong to English or Scots; it was the sole province of Ritchie Graham. If they were studiously looking the other way, any early warning system was disabled, and the great fortress was shorn of its frontline defence. Sunday 13 April was chosen, and that Saturday Buccleuch was at Langholm Races, not just for the winners, such meetings hosted more covert operations than CIA HQ at Langley Virginia and that Saturday was a very busy one. Buccleuch was tying up loose ends and giving orders; he'd arranged for some lifted Graham stock to be returned as a gesture of goodwill and down-payment for services rendered and about to be rendered (Grahams PLC wasn't a charitable enterprise).

Eighty borderers would ride out against Carlisle on that dark and stormy night, four score against the mightiest castle on the marches. This is high adventure and villains they might have been but this sheer dash and elan, this glorious hubris, well-seasoned by skill and experience, is the stuff of legend and rightly so. 'Who dares wins' might have been their motto. At the same time, they were all professionals who knew full well what they were about. Any Special Forces outfit today would have signed the lot of 'em up there and then. Scotts, Eliotts and Armstrongs, including Kinmont's four lads, were all in the saddle that night. A screen of scouts ranged in front – MacDonald Fraser supposes, correctly I think, that these were Armstrongs, a vanguard behind the prickers, assault group with all the kit, ladders, grapnels etc, then the main body and a strong rearguard behind [92].

They moved with stealth rather than speed, using the cover of darkness to ford the Esk, carefully, frequently halting to close up and maintain cohesion.

They only covered six miles but did so undetected; the slightest giveaway would have been fatal. By the time they sighted the squat, menacing bulk of Carlisle from the northward side, first light was only a couple of hours off. They likely forded the Eden a short distance below where the present bridge stands. The waters were frothing high and the dank night clinging like a wet cloak – proper reivers weather: 'And passeth the water of Eden about two hours before day, at the Stoniebank beneath Carlisle Brig' [93].

Nobody heard anything, perhaps the roaring of the spring wind drowned any noise or perhaps the watchers were trying hard not to watch or listen, but they got beneath the walls undetected, probably just a chosen assault group, the rest keeping watch, still in the saddle. Quite how they did get in is unclear. Maybe the postern was unlocked or had to be broken down, forced in some way. Ladders may have been used, probably were but if so, somebody had their sums wrong as those they'd carted with them proved too short [94]!

Buccleuch knew from a female agent that Will was kept in a domestic building, west of the keep, no close security. Whether he was in on the plot we can't say. The story he had to be carried out still in chains is clearly untrue. It's quite possible some of his hosts even helped him to the door: 'The prisoner was taken out of the house where he was kept, the which was known to the lord of Buccleuch, his sending a woman upon pretext the day before to visit the prisoner' [95]. Scrope seems to have had few supporters even among his own men.

Will was soon on horseback and still there was no general alarm. Buccleuch had posted the bulk of his riders between the narrow postern and the West (Irish) Gate, ready to take on any posse that came tumbling out. None did. Only the attackers' trumpet, blaring briefly to summon the company together disturbed the murky calm and off they went. And that was that, if there was any pursuit which is unclear, it was half-hearted at best, and they were back over on the Scottish side a couple of hours after sunrise. Scrope, utterly humiliated, bleated that two of his troopers had been 'left for dead' and one of his servants roughed up [96] but Buccleuch had clearly given orders there was to be minimal violence and no opportunistic pilfering. This was surgery not retribution: 'All sore astonished stood Lord Scrope/ He stood still as rock of stane/ He scarcely dared to trew his eyes/ When thro' the water they had gane' [97].

On 14 April Scrope wrote feverishly to Burghley, a long exculpatory epistle, blaming everyone but himself for the debacle. Buccleuch had apparently commanded five hundred riders and his 'proud attempt' was presented as some kind of full-scale attack which stormed the postern 'speedily and quietly'. It was all the fault of the watch who were either asleep on duty or had bunked off to get out of the rain [98]. According to the Shawfield MS, 'The Queen of England, having notice sent to her of what was done, stormed not a little' [99]; I think we can accept that as fact and a diplomatic hurricane blew up. King James was suitably apologetic but probably very far from being annoyed. Elizabeth wanted Buccleuch sent south to explain himself, along with Ker of Cessford the other 'Firebrand' [100].

After much procrastination Buccleuch handed himself in to Sir William Selby, Master of the Ordnance at Berwick [101]. George Ridpath gives only a brief account of the raid but confirms, 'at last to gratify Elizabeth it was found necessary to commit Buccleuch a prisoner in St. Andrews; and afterward to send him into England, where he did not continue long' [102]. A very light slap on the wrist and both hell-raisers were soon back on their own turf, but they'd seen the light and a map for the future with their own very reformed stances clearly marked.

As they spurred away to safety, Buccleuch's riders, his commando, might have felt pretty chipper. They'd done a very good job, no bloodshed and Scrope had egg all over his outraged face. What they didn't get, though their leader probably did, was that this was the last hurrah, the cowboy heroes riding off into the sunset or in their case a wet dawn, were cantering clear out of history. Many who rode with their dashing commander would be hanged by him later without a backward glance. Their present wasn't his future, and their time was pretty much up.

At the end of the American Civil War, the famous and pioneering photographer, Matthew Brady who'd chronicled the war with his striking images, laboriously captured on glass negatives, went bust. The nation had had its fill of war and the soulful dead scattered on battlefields and in trenches went out of vogue. Many of his million glass negatives were acquired by gardeners as glazing for their greenhouses and these priceless visions of a great nation torn by civil war simply and literally faded away in sunlight. The reivers were destined to go the same way. Their respective nations were jointly ashamed of them and their images, so frighteningly vivid in their day, would fade away to nothing in the bright strong light of a united realm. Like Brady's pictures, everyone had had enough.

NOTES:

[1] Troughend still stands, just past Otterburn heading north on the A68, the present house is much later dating from 1758.

[2] Marsden J., The Illustrated Border Ballads (London: Macmillan, 1990), pp. 36–37.

[3] Ibid., p. 44, there are two version of this ballad, one of which was collected by James Telfer, schoolmaster at Saughtree, recited to him by an ancient besom called Kitty Hall.

[4] Phillips, op. cit., p. 140.

[5] Ibid.

[6] Ridpath, op. cit., p. 355.

[7] Ibid., p. 358.

[8] Ibid.

[9] Hall, E., Chronicle (London: J. Johnson, 1809), p. 645.

[10] Lisle started well but went bad, ending up as a desperado for which he was eventually hanged.

[11] Phillips, op. cit., p. 144.

[12] Ibid., p. 145.

[13] Standard drill for such raids was for the strike force to establish a forward operating base and send out mounted commandos to harvest the loot.

[14] Phillips, op. cit., p. 46.

[15] Ridpath, op. cit., p. 371.

[16] 'Small' Beer was an essential as most water was unfit for consumption.

[17] Phillips, op. cit., p. 150.

[18] Ridpath, op. cit., p. 373.

[19] Ibid.

[20] Phillips, op. cit., p. 151.

[21] Ridpath, op. cit., p. 373.

[22] Hamilton Papers 1532–1543, ed. by J. Bain, vol. 1 (Edinburgh: Great Britain Register Office, 1890), p. xvi.

[23] Phillips, op. cit., p.152.

[24] State Papers & Letters of Sir Ralph Sadler, ed. by A. Clifford, vols 3 (Edinburgh: Constable & Co, 1809), vol. 1, p. 65.

[25] Hertford was plagued by a tricky younger brother Tom Seymour who'd married Queen Katherine Parr, a witless chancer whose head soon paid the price.

[26] Borland, Rev. R., Border Raids & Reivers (Glasgow: Thomas Fraser, 1910), pp. 63–64.

[27] Ibid., p. 68.

[28] Ridpath, op. cit., p. 231.

[29] Or 'Arquebus' a handgun, lighter and handier than a musket, though shooting a smaller ball with lesser charge.

[30] Ridpath, op. cit., p. 381.

[31] Borland, op. cit., p. 69.

[32] Ibid.

[33] Beaton was murdered on 29 May 1546, his body mutilated and hung from a window.

[34] These were Anne Boleyn and Katherine Howard.

[35] Ridpath, op. cit., p. 385.

[36] This was a new role which facilitated management of the army.

[37] Phillips, op. cit., p. 185.

[38] Cavalryman; half-armoured and armed with a lance.

[39] A troop of gentlemen bodyguards raised by Henry VIII in 1509, remained as an office until 1834.

[40] Patten, 'Expedition into Scotland etc', in Tudor Tracts, ed. by A. F. Pollard (London: Constable, 1903), p. 45.

[41] Ibid., p. 84.

[42] Ibid., pp. 71–78.

[43] Ibid., p. 90.

[44] Ibid., p. 90 & Ridpath, op. cit., p. 385.

[45] Ibid.

[46] Patten, op. cit., pp. 85–89.

[47] Most of the ground now is built over; see http://www.battlefieldstrust.com/media/682.pdf, accessed 12 July 2020.

[48] Ridpath, op. cit., p. 285.

[49] Patten constantly refers to these as 'Irish' but they were likely Highlanders.

[50] Ridpath, op. cit., p. 386 & Patten, op. cit., p. 102.

[51] Ridpath, p. 385, wrongly reports Home as being killed; see Patten, p. 102.

[52] Patten, p. 107 – known thereafter as 'Black Saturday'.

[53] Ibid., p. 108.

[54] Ibid., p. 115.

[55] Ibid., p. 116.

[56] Ibid., p. 112.

[57] Ibid., p. 123 – he claims Arran was the first to bolt, this may be apocryphal.

[58] Ibid.

[59] Roxburgh had been held by the English for decades during the fifteenth century.

[60] German pike or Arquebus armed mercenary soldier.

[61] Phillips, op. cit., p. 240.

[62] Ibid., p. 246.

[63] Sadler's State Papers, op. cit., p. 377.

[64] Lomas, op. cit., pp. 174–175.

[65] Ibid., p. 175, Carnaby lost that office in 1539.

[66] The 1569 Rebellion, ed. by Sir Cuthbert Sharp, 1840 (Durham: J. Shotton, 1975), p. xxi.

[67] Richard Norton, one of Northumberland's affinity, had been born in 1498, and out with the Pilgrimage of Grace, 30 years before.

[68] 1569 Rebellion, op. cit., p. xxii.

[69] Ibid., pp. xxi–xxii.

[70] Ibid., p. xxiii.

[71] Though he became 8th Earl, Harry later committed suicide in 1584, having been implicated in the Throckmorton Plot.

[72] 1569 Rebellion, op. cit., p. xxviii.

[73] Ridpath, op. cit., p. 435.

[74] Carey, R., The Stirring World of Robert Carey (Edinburgh: Constable & Co., 1808), p. 12.

[75] Ibid., p. 55.

[76] Ibid., p. 37.

[77] Ibid.

[78] Ibid., p. 57.

[79] Ibid., p. 60.

[80] Ibid., pp. 46–47.

[81] Ibid., p. 48.

[82] Ibid.

[83] The Shawfield Manuscript as quoted in Scott's Minstrelsy, p. 259.

[84] Ibid., p. 260.

[85] Ibid., p. 262.

[86] MacDonald Fraser, op. cit., p. 330.

[87] Ibid., p. 332.

[88] Ibid., pp. 125–126.

[89] Ibid., p. 338.

[90] Shawfield MS, op. cit., p. 261.

[91] MacDonald Fraser, op. cit., p. 335.

[92] Ibid., p. 338.

[93] Shawfield MS, op. cit., p. 261 – the source claims there were two hundred riders, but this is too many.

[94] Ibid.

[95] Ibid., p. 262, Will seems to have enjoyed privileges such as female company!

[96] CBP, ii, 252, p. 121.

[97] Marsden, op. cit., p. 175.

[98] CBP, ii, 252, p. 121.

[99] Shawfield MS, op. cit., p. 263.

[100] Pease, H., The Lord Wardens of the Marches of England and Scotland (London: Constable, 1913), p. 136.

[101] Ibid.

[102] Ridpath, op. cit., p. 472.

CHAPTER NINE: THOSE MIDDLE SHIRES

'They came too late and stayed too long'

The Wild Bunch directed by Sam Peckinpah (1969)

D'Artagnan himself couldn't have done better. Robert Carey, now in his early forties, was determined to be the one to bring this momentous news to James VI [1]; that he was now also James I of England and that Elizabeth I, 'Gloriana' was no more; tremendous tidings. Elizabeth had ruled for 45 years, and few could remember any other sovereign; she had attained near deified status [2]. Now she'd be succeeded by a King of Scots, the ultimate irony of the border wars – that after three centuries with Kings of England seeking to annex Scotland, the final score was exactly the reverse. Nor was this a conquest won by force of arms but a willing and sought after Protestant succession – the late Queen's eminence grise Robert Cecil had been a prime mover [3].

This wasn't just the usual succession, one ruler following another, it was in every sense a regime change and game-changer. The wild lads across the marches hadn't quite got it yet but this was the drafting of their obituaries. Things were about to change, and they'd find this process very painful, particularly for their necks.

James VI was by no means averse to seeing a good looking, strapping fellow in his bedroom, especially one who, on 26 March 1603, brought the news James had been waiting so long to hear. His hopes of 20 years were fulfilled and it was a thumping return on all the bribes he'd disbursed: 'I was quickly let in and carried up to the King's chamber. I kneeled by him and saluted him by his title of England, Scotland France and Ireland' [4]. Now the French bit was pushing it, as every toehold was long gone but England would do very nicely. James made all the usual noises of condolence; after all, the Queen was Carey's aunt. He promised him ample reward, (which was what he wanted to hear) and Carey made the point this was all on his own initiative and that the Council had tried to hold him back – just so the King knew who his friends were. Robert would be neither the first nor last to find out that the gratitude of princes spreads exceeding thin.

A BRAVE NEW WORLD?

And what did Robert Carey get from his ride? Rather less than he hoped for: 'Now I was to begin a new world: for by the King's coming to the crown I was to lose the best part of my living. For my office of wardenry ceased and I lost the pay of forty horse … Most of the great ones in court envied my happiness when I heard I was sworn of the King's bedchamber: and in Scotland I had no acquaintance. I only relied on God and the King. The one never left me, the other shortly after his coming to London deceived my expectation and adhered to those that sought my ruin' [5].

In fact, Carey's unauthorised ride cost him dear. He lost what friends he had in the administration and James had other concerns. It was through the capable conduct of his wife Elizabeth Trevanion [6] lady-in-waiting to Anne of Denmark that he began to climb back up the ladder. She looked after the weak and apparently backward Prince Charles (and future King), nurturing the stammering boy; she brought him out and on. Carey became the lad's governor in 1605, and six years later his Master of the Robes. Five years on he moved up to Chamberlain and in 1622 was elevated to Baron Carey of Leppington. Four years after that, he was created 1st Earl of Monmouth, dying a tolerably rich and revered elder statesman in 1639 when he was nearly 80 [7].

James' progress south was a PR stroke of some genius. He had, after all, had a long time to think about it but here he was, a King of Scotland marching on London with garlands and cheers: 'The King proceeding by easy journeys and being from time to time stopped by the hospitality and fondness of his new subjects, spent a whole month of his journey from Berwick to London. Ten days after his arrival in the capital he issued a proclamation requiring all those guilty of the 'foul and insolent' outrages lately committed on the borders to submit themselves to his mercy before 20th June on pain of being excluded from it forever' [8].

Just in case that wasn't plain enough he published a second blast a couple of days later: '… In consequence of which the bounds possessed by the rebellious borderers, should no more be the 'extremities' but 'The Middle' and the inhabitants thereof reduced to a perfect obedience' [9]. This was at the heart of James' cherished project. There would be no more Border. He was for the first time in history master of both realms; what had been the fringe was now the centre and it would come to heel or face consequences. What followed wouldn't be some warden's raid or even a judicial sweep; in modern terms it would amount to ethnic cleansing.

James VI of Scotland and I of England wasn't like his Stewart forebears. For one thing he'd lead a reasonably long life and die in his bed, having collectively reigned for nearly half a century and never seen a battlefield. He was physically unprepossessing, notoriously mean, and recoiled in terror at the sight of a drawn dagger, though Sir John Ramsay's knife had saved him from the Gowries [10]. He'd been horrified when Colquhoun widows presented their dead husbands' bloodied sarks (shirts) after a fracas with MacGregors in Glenfruin, though it was probably sheep's blood.

He was utterly determined to eradicate the old troublesome border then impose law and order at whatever cost to the inhabitants. To be fair and while expressions like 'The end justifies the means' may be more modern, the idea was the same and it's hard to see how it might have been done more tamely. Further south, his English subjects soon began to tire of their new king's horde of Scottish carpetbaggers, who flocked south in his wake, hungry for advancement and streets paved with other peoples' gold. The English 'soon began to treat the King and his countrymen with insolence and contempt' [11]. On this, even papists and puritans could agree.

King James was not to be deflected: 'The King in pursuance of his favourite purpose of extinguishing all memory of past hostilities between his kingdoms and if possible, of the places that had been the principal scene of these hostilities, prohibited the name of borders any longer to be used, substituting in its place, that of the Middle Shires' [12]. Well, reivers, you'd been warned.

He meant business: 'Soon after his arrival in London, he gave a commission to George Clifford Earl of Cumberland [13], a nobleman who had acquired high military fame in the wars of the late Queen; appointing him as Warden of the West and Middle Marches towards Scotland, with the most extensive powers and Lieutenant-General of the Counties of Cumberland, Northumberland, and Westmorland and of the town and county of Newcastle upon Tyne' [14]. That wasn't all; he was keeper of the upland Northumbrian dales, governor of Carlisle. He could appoint deputies and mete out justice. His wages and those of his officers were guaranteed. All he didn't get initially was the East March and Berwick where Sir John Carey was left in charge till the garrison was reduced.

Cumberland didn't win universal acclaim, John Graham (bit of a clue in the name) writing in the early twentieth century on the tribulations those of his name endured under the Earl's harsh governance was no fan: '[he] was not one of those [favourites] upon whose shoulder the King hung with maudlin infatuation – but one in whom he discovered transcendent merits unobserved by the world at large' [15]. And now for the Scottish side: 'at the end of July Alexander, Lord Hume was appointed Justiciar and Lord-Lieutenant over the three Marches' [16]. He had plenipotentiary powers, a free and unfettered commission and a thousand merks (marks) a year [in sterling] by way of salary. I doubt anybody was surprised that Hume did so well, after all his name had several centuries of form behind them.

TOUGH LOVE

John Graham doesn't much care for either of 'em: 'their government was simply an organised system of plunder, unchecked, un-reprimanded and unpunished' [17]. Despite the writer's bias, there is much truth in this. James, initially at last, wasn't minded to ask too many questions. It was results that mattered. Men such as Cumberland and Hume were as much occupiers as pacifiers and both had an eye to the main chance. Regions like the Graham heartland of Eskdale, unprofitable in endemic war, had much more to offer in peacetime, lush fertile ground ripe for exploitation. If only those annoying inhabitants could be got out of the way.

Who cared about the Grahams anyway, '[they] were represented as incorrigible criminals and oppressors and the very name of Graham was said to be a terror to all the country around' [18]. And yes, they were, it's easy to feel sorry for the Grahams if you'd not encountered them. If you had, you might well be cheering for the carpetbaggers. Meanwhile for the borderers themselves at the time of James' accession, it seemed like business as usual: 'Upon the report of the Queen's death the east border broke forth into great unruliness, insomuch as many complaints came to the King thereof' [19]. Robert Carey was still recovering from his head injury, sustained during his epic ride, and had to leave matters in the hands of his underlings. It's unlikely anyone on the frontier saw the tsunami approaching or had quite the measure of the man who was about to stir the waves.

James has never had the kind of romantic aura his very silly mother attained. George MacDonald Fraser, while admitting this might be harsh, picks up the general trend, describing him as 'a slobbering, goggling, pedantic pederast, stuffed with ill-digested scholarship, vain, cowardly and dishonest' [20]. He might have indeed been many of those things at times, but he was no fool, an arch-pragmatist and perhaps above all one who understood his borders. None of his predecessors on the English throne, except perhaps Richard III, had greater experience of border affairs. He knew how the Marches worked, and his desire to bring order to the border was intense and genuine; forget any mythic gloss, it needed doing.

There was an assumption, mere opportunism perhaps; that all law or such law as there was, on the Border was suspended between the death of one sovereign and the proclamation of a successor. It was certainly a handy fiction, and the riding names made the most of it – 'Ill-week', when a jolly good time was had by all bar their victims, would be their last loud hurrah. Hutcheon Graham of Cargo took up North Cumberland, sweeping as far down as Penrith, cheekily driving off the Bishop of Carlisle's herds whilst that worthy cleric fumed impotently from his battlements at Rose Castle (the Bishop's official residence from 1230–2009, 1 ½ miles (2.4 kilometres) from Dalston).

Similar crimes were re-enacted across the wide sweep of the marches and on both sides of the line. Clearly the reivers didn't get it; history had just overtaken them. Now it was unprecedented; there was one monarch in Edinburgh and the same one in London whose dearest project was their eradication. Bravado might be fun, but they were really just underscoring their own death warrants. Ironically, it was James himself who was pulling off the greatest foray of all, he'd bagged all England and his hungry train had plenty carpetbags. It would be English gold that did for the Steel Bonnets.

James' hopes were expressed in flowery, politic terms; he wanted amity to break out amongst his Scottish and English subjects and harmony to prevail. As the Venetian ambassador, the very worldly and cynical Giovanni Scaravelli, observed; 'such new and hopeful beginnings were mere wishful thinking, English and Scots would never be friends' [21]. James knew that too of course but he subscribed to that well tested dictum 'get them by the balls and their hearts and minds will follow'. Meanwhile, Cumberland's energetic deputy, the mercurial adventurer Sir Henry Leigh, was lucky to get out of a Graham ambush alive. It wouldn't all be one-sided.

Both Lieutenants-General had seasoned soldiers to lead their newly funded militias. Hume had Sir William Cranston; Cumberland chose Leigh. These were more Einsatzgruppen than UN peacekeepers. The old Marches were a real war zone. In no small degree they always had been but now the main players were a team not adversaries and they weren't necessarily taking prisoners. Some of those gentlemen bandits, who'd been star turns beforehand, experienced sudden and blinding epiphanies. Buccleuch recruited a force of two thousand light horsemen to serve in the Dutch wars [22] and became instantly zealous in his pursuit of domestic wrongdoers. James was canny enough to realise he needed allies in his fight and Scott's miraculous conversion earned him a peerage as 1st Lord Scott of Buccleuch in 1606.

Kerr of Cessford, equally drenched in blood, felt the same way and already Lord Roxburghe by 1600, was raised to an earldom 16 years later. Both did very well out of James; collaboration has its merits. Lord William Howard of Naworth, a son of the Duke of Norfolk who inherited the old Dacre lands by right of his wife and was known from his celebrated baldric as 'Belted Will', became another enthusiastic practitioner.

It would take James just four savage years, from 1603–1607 to achieve the bones of success, another three to consolidate. The Grahams would say this was a case of creating a desert and calling it peace and there was much of that, yet ultimately the medicine went down, and the patient recovered. In the early months of 1605, the King set up a Royal Commission to oversee pacification; ten sitting members, drawn equally from both realms and based at Carlisle, the nub of the border. Anybody who hoped this would just be another quick fix judicial sweep or beefed up warden's rode would be deluded. This was to be ethnic cleansing.

The list of sanctions was comprehensive:

All iron yettes to be removed from towers and Peles;

Weapons banned, beaten into ploughshares;

No man could own a horse worth more than £30.00 Scots – so working mounts only;

Known past offenders were effectively tagged and had to report in, they couldn't leave their homes for longer than 48 hours without authorisation;

The number of ale houses was to be reduced – even then the linkage between booze and banditry was noted;

Only an eldest son could inherit, so estates would not continually be diminished by sub-division;

Offenders, those who had offended or might or were thinking about it could be lawfully transported.

Just in case anyone still didn't get the message, Cranston descended mob-handed on Dumfries where he hanged 32 Armstrongs, Johnsons, and Batys [23]. Citizens of the town who were no strangers to scrapping turned on him and his troop had to hack their way out, losing several mounts [24]. This breed of mercenary cum officer practised what was known, with usual gallows humour, as 'Jeddart Justice' – the suspect was first hanged then tried thereafter, so proceedings tended towards the cursory. No need for too many tears though, as those who swung weren't innocent victims, most if not all were weighed down by more than their boots. Still, this was more terror than justice.

'Malefactors by the name of Graham' were a special mission for these commissioners. Of all the border names, they and the Armstrongs were most feared and hated. You can see why: 'A coroner's document of 1584 shows how some Grahams were killing others of the same name in a "miserable family dispute about land," and there was also a long and bloody feud between the houses of Richard of Netherby and Fergus of Mote. The Grahams were never friends of authority. In 1596, when a warden officer – assisted by ten Grahams and a bloodhound – overtook two Scottish cattle raiders that they had been chasing, the Grahams stood idly by while the thieves cut the officer down then stole both horse and dog' [25].

When Wattie, brother to Jock Graham of the Peartree, was on trial at Carlisle for horse-stealing, Jock kidnapped the sheriff's six-year-old son from outside the officer's home and used him as hostage to secure Wattie's release. In an attempt on the life of land-sergeant John Musgrave at Brampton, a group of Grahams set upon him and his followers with daggs [pistols] and guns and tried to burn him alive in a house. In 1592, Lord Maxwell complained against the Grahams of Netherby and other of Lang Will's descendants in respect of their "violent and masterful occupation" for 30 years past of Kirkandrews and Annandale, and 25 years similar oppression and exploitation of five other named districts.

In 1600 Lord Scrope compiled a long charge-sheet of the name's crimes, of which MacDonald Fraser writes: 'According to this, no fewer than sixty Grahams were outlaws, for murder, robbery and other crimes; they had despoiled above a dozen Cumbrian villages, sheltered felons, fought the warden's troops, murdered witnesses, extorted money from their enemies, and in one specific instance burned the house of one Hutcheon Hetherington to force him into the open so that they could cut him to pieces' [26]. It's a long list, which is much, much longer than this sample. These were a bad people, even by the elastic standards of their fellow borderers.

The King too singled out the Grahams for special attention in his proclamation of 1603: 'Forasmuch as all our Subjects in the North parts, who have felt the smart of the spoils and outrages done upon them at our first entry into this Kingdome by divers Borderers, but specially by the Greames, cannot be ignorant what care we have had that punishment should be done upon the offenders, having for that purpose to our great charge, maintained both Forces to apprehend them, and Commissioners to try them according to the Law, by whose travail, namely of our cousin the Earl of Cumberland our Lieutenant here, with assistance of other Commissioners, things are brought to that point, that the Offenders (but specially the Greames) confess themselves to be no meet [fit] persons to live in those Countries, And therefore have humbly besought us that they might be removed to some other Parts, where with our gracious favour, they hope to live to become new men, and deserve our Mercy. Although we do confess that we have rather inclined to this course of Mercy, as a thing more agreeable to our Nature, then the taking of so much blood as would be shed if we should leave them to the just censure of the Law' [27].

This was justification for what we'd term 'ethnic cleansing' which earned a justifiably evil reputation during the Balkan wars of the nineties: 'ethnic cleansing is rendering an area ethnically homogenous by using force or intimidation to remove from a given area persons of another ethnic or religious group' [28]. Now, our Jacobethan ancestors whilst they knew all about religious intolerance weren't necessarily bothered by what we'd called ethnicity. The Grahams weren't genetically different to anyone else around, but they were a distinct tribal group and I think that'll pretty much do.

In his 1993 article A Brief History of Ethnic Cleansing, published in the magazine 'Foreign Affairs', Andrew Bell-Fialkoff writes that the aim of the Serbian campaign in Bosnia during the terrible civil war of the 1990s was: 'The expulsion of an 'undesirable' population from a given territory due to religious or ethnic discrimination, political, strategic or ideological considerations, or a combination of those' [29]. On that basis I think the attempted removal of the Grahams counts as much as say the Death March of the Cherokee, both equally reprehensible. The Native Americans' only real offence was being in the wrong place, at the wrong time, and with the wrong skin tone.

If we are brutally objective, the Grahams had it coming. On 17 April 1605, a 150 were conscripted into the Dutch garrisons. Many more were rounded up but staged a successful mass-breakout from Carlisle. Many of these unwilling warriors deserted as quickly as they were recruited and more slunk back pretty soon after: 'For a considerable time no real progress was made in clearing the country of the condemned clan. The escapes from prison and returns from banishment were more numerous than the arrests' [30].

By now the Grahams, as born survivors, realised the game was changing radically and they needed to show some humility which they duly did, petitioning the King: 'that they, and others inhabiting within the bounds of Eske and Leven, being the borders of the realme of England against Scotland, are men brought up in ignorance, and not having had meanes to learne their due obedience to God, and your most excellent Majestie, of late, and immediately after the death of the Queen's most excellent Majestie, your Majestie's late dear sister, did disorderly and tumultuously assemble ourselves with all the warlike force and power that they could make, and being so disorderlie assembled, did invade the inlande part of the easte parte of the county of Cumberland, and spoiled many of your subjects of England with fire, sword, robbery, and reaving of their goods, and murthering and taking prisoners the persons of the same, which are misdemeanour; albeit we cannot excuse our ignorance, for that by the lawes of God we do knowe that all rebelling, reaving, and murthers are altogether forbidden, yet so it is, that some among us of evil and corrupt judgment did persuade us, that until your Majestie was a crowned kinge within the realme of England, that the law of the same kingdome did cease and was of no force, and that all acts and offences whatsoever done and committed in the meane tyme, were not by the common justice of this realme punishable by force, of the which malitious error put into our heads, as deceived men, and believing over reddy that grosse untruth, we did most injudiciously run upon your Majestie's inland subjectis, and did them many wronges, both by fyer, sword, and taking there goodes, in such sort as before we have acknowledged' [31]. Now, that's a long burst of grovelling but it was still too little and too late.

That same Hutcheon Graham, who'd so taunted the Bishop of Carlisle found his joke turn sour when he, with many others, was banged up. The list of charges he was facing was lengthy, and went back to the springing of Kinmont Will and the murder of Sir John Carmichael. The year 1606 witnessed a new year's hanging spree and every gaol was bursting. James had wanted results but even he began to feel a judicious tug away from overt connection to so much violent oppression. In January, he expressed a moue of concern, worried his officers were using methods that 'savoured of barbarism' [32]. Not too worried of course, Cranston was fully exonerated by the year's end and his robust defence was that any leniency now would smack of weakness and the borderers would take full advantage. It's hard to disagree.

Despite these barbarities, the Commissioners were still way behind on points and Graham survivors clung on tenaciously; after all they'd been doing just that for three centuries. No truly decisive outcome had yet appeared, and then: 'In the midst of his perplexity James received a suggestion from one Sir Ralph Sidley to transport the whole remnant of the Eskdale outcasts to Ireland where Sidley reckoned, he could, for a consideration, plant them upon certain land at his disposal in the County of Roscommon' [33].

Now here was a gift. If helpful Sir Ralph could offer resettlement, then so be it, for sure no one else was clamouring to have Grahams foisted on them. It was only necessary for the good gentry of the west to come up with the funds. It's hard to say if Sidley was being genuinely philanthropic or if he just saw an opportunity. Some £300.00 was raised from donations, well more of a levy really, James' commissioners were quick to lean on anyone who didn't cough up [34]. This might just be the making of a real resolution; transportation would be radical, but it was more humane than extinction. Ethnic cleansing might be nasty but genocide is that much worse but that was the only Plan B. Once the name was expunged then 'their lands may be inhabited by others of good and honest conversation' [35].

The King was already concerned at defections from the Dutch forts and wrote earnestly to his commissioners on 24 June 1606: 'We wish all means to be used for the apprehension of the Grahams who have returned from the Cautionary Towns [36]. It appears that divers of the Grahams and other surnames were formerly planted in the Province of Connaught, where they have grown to be men of good desert and quality ... Sir Ralph Sidley is well able to plant thirty of forty families there' [37].

In total it was around 50 families who were transported. If they expected to see any of the cash raised, they'd be disappointed, though being Grahams not surprised. Their 'land' was waste; water was scarce, so indeed labour and what there was came dear. If Sidley had held out any real hopes, these were soon dashed: 'The condition of the outcasts having become so wholly desperate many of them fled rather than face starvation and by some means found their way home to the border to the surprise and vexation of the authorities' [38].

Unsurprisingly, the native Irish didn't take to these newcomers, or they to the Irish. Borderers had served in Ireland before but hardly in peaceful roles. A few dumped there now made the best of it and signed on for local garrisons, the rest steadily began to defect. Legend has it that the passports they'd need to get back were easily faked and all in the name of 'Maharg', (Graham in reverse), which implies customs officials were either really daft or easily bribed. As late as 1614, James was still blasting out edicts stridently forbidding any to return: much good these did.

Ritchie Graham, son of his infamous father, was living in Brackenhill Tower. Cumberland tried to confiscate the place, but he'd overreached himself for once as young Ritchie was able to show good title, his estate having been bought fairly from Sir Thomas Dacre. Ritchie was sent to Ireland though soon came back and resumed residence but kept clear of the bad old ways. That lesson it seems had been learnt. Brackenhill still stands; it's on the north bank of the River Lyne four miles (6.4 kilometres) west of Longtown – now and perhaps ironically offered as an upmarket B &B.

Even more enterprising James Graham pointedly walked to London, as he couldn't now afford a horse, to press his claim directly on the King. James had many faults, but he was no tyrant and gave this young man a job – as Master of Horse to his favourite, the Duke of Buckingham. Honest toil proved more profitable than reiving and Graham prospered, so much so that Richard Graham was able to buy the estate of Netherby and Barony of Liddell from the Earl of Cumberland for cash and garnered a baronetcy in 1629. Sir Richard Graham of Esk stayed loyal to the Stuarts and fought bravely at Edgehill for Charles I in October 1642, being badly wounded. Now good honest men and true, the Grahams never looked back.

EMBERS

George MacDonald Fraser points out that at the time he was writing the Carlisle and Eden phone book was still crammed full of Grahams! Philip Walling Cumbrian farmer, barrister, and now author recalls a conversation he'd had with Graham of Netherby. The family had had to move out of the big house which was sold but Philip was told, they still owned peat cutting rights on the Solway Marshes which had been theirs since they came to Cumberland in the reign of Henry IV and the income was still enough to pay school fees to Eton for each laird's son!

It does seem that those in the west had it rougher than their contemporaries in Tynedale and Redesdale who'd been just as wild. The Redesdalers, Halls and Redes, didn't take too kindly to the kind of rough justice Leigh's officer Sir William Selby meted out, so they fought back vigorously enough for Leigh to think again. By now the Commission itself had been streamlined, pared back as the new measures, however tough, appeared at least to be producing some results.

Needless to say, Liddesdale merited close attention. Armstrong of Mangerton and Whithaugh together with Martin Eliott all swung for their innumerable crimes, and many towers were slighted. In September 1606 alone Hume, now elevated to Earl of Dunbar, hanged 140 suspects, with or without prior sentencing. Even five years on and the good work wasn't done, though Commissioners were claiming all, and everything was orderly, yet another 92 criminals were brought to book and just less than half of them danced at rope's end [39].

It wasn't just the Grahams who faced transportation, Ulster was in need of settlers, and it does seem many borderers, fearful of persecution at home, saw this as a lesser evil. They and their ancestors were noted as tough soldierly types and an awful lot of them feature in subsequent annals of empire. James also thought of Virginia, a new land where frontiersmen might do some good and it was an awful long way back. Fighting was after all what they were most proficient at and good news was, there was plenty still to be had. A company of Tynedale riders, captained by Andrew Grey, served in Bohemia (today's Czech Republic), and over three hundred more also went off to Ireland under one of their Charlton heidmen [40].

Criminality waned but it did not disappear, broken men also known, like the later Covenanting light cavalry, as Mosstroopers (and certainly at times the same men) rode as outlaw bands. Many still relied on their swords for resolving disputes: 'they expect no law but bang it out bravely, one and his kindred against the other and his; they will subject themselves to no justice but in an inhuman and barbarous manner, fight and kill one another' [41].

Godfrey Watson concludes his own account with the tale of Willie Armstrong of Westburnflat. Willie was something of a slow learner and failed take onboard that times had changed so reaved a dozen beasts from West Teviotdale. The law swiftly caught up with him and the posse sent him with his accomplices for trial at Selkirk Assizes. The verdict was never really in doubt and Will was sentenced to swing. By way of an appeal, he smashed free a heavy oak chair leg and brandished it aloft, calling on his team to fight their way clear, just like in the good old days. But these weren't the good old days anymore and none of his gang showed inclination to try the odds. They preferred, stoically, to accept their fate and dangle. And so, they did [42].

Just to show those grand old days weren't quite gone, and not all swords had been beaten into ploughshares: 'at the confluence of the Allan Water and the River Teviot, in (about April) 1627, 'Rattling Roaring Willie' fought a duel with and killed 'Sweet Milk'. William 'Willie' Henderson of Priesthaugh had been drinking at Newmill with a fellow traveller, ballad-maker and minstrel, William 'Sweet Milk' or 'Robert Rule' Elliot of either Cavers Parish or Rulewater. Both men were well-known in the district, but Willie in particular had a mean streak as a brawler, "his sword arm being dreaded as his bow arm was admired." Sweet Milk is recorded in the Cavers Parish records of 1623 and 1624 and was possibly related to "Dandie Ellot called Sweet Milk" whose name is recorded in association with complaints about raids into England in 1598' [43].

Following an argument, the two men spilled out onto the Heugh for a duel with swords, and Sweet Milk was slain. Willie fled to a hiding place near Crailing Dene on the Oxnam Water but rather rashly made a very public appearance on the day of the Rood Fair at Jedburgh. As Sweet Milk belonged to the Elliot family of reivers, it is said Willie was tracked down by Gilbert Eliott of Stobs – 'Gibbie wi' the gowden garters' and Archibald Elliot – 'Young Falnash' – and brought before the local sheriff. He was thereafter put on trial at the Court of Justice and Aire in Jedburgh and executed either on or before December 12, 1627. Jedburgh Presbytery records describe the "fearful and cruell slaughter" and the excommunication of Sweet Milk's assailant. A thorn tree planted to mark the spot of the duel could still be seen in the early 1800s [44].

The Steel Bonnets got no elegiac tributes till Scott came along and rewrote their history. Nor did they deserve any; their history was one of violence and savagery. Yes, they came from broken homelands, but it was mainly they themselves who did the breaking. Theirs was a dark and retrograde past, soon buried in obscurity. They had no apologists and fewer mourners. George Ridpath writing over a century later commented: 'The accession of James to the throne of England and both kingdoms thus devolving on one sovereign, was an event fruitful of blessings' [45]. It's most unlikely any borderer at the time necessarily agreed: 'The border which for many ages had been almost a scene of rapine and dissolution enjoyed, from this happy era a quiet and order which they had never before experienced' [46]. This was written after the Act of Union when Britain was busy forging a world empire and the ground had shifted immeasurably. One thing the riding names would have certainly understood – they wouldn't be missed.

NOTES:

[1] Carey, op. cit., pp. 66–67.

[2] Robert Cecil, 1st Earl of Salisbury, son of Lord Burghley and a prime mover in the Union of the Crowns.

[3] Carey, op. cit., p. 65.

[4] Ibid., p. 67.

[5] Ibid., p. 69.

[6] She may have been the model for Old Dame Bob in Jack & Jill.

[7] Carey's son inherited the title, but it became extinct when he died childless.

[8] Ridpath, op. cit., p. 483.

[9] Ibid.

[10] James had cause to be thankful to one dagger wielding page, John Ramsay, later knighted then raised to the peerage as 1st Earl of Holderness. Young John, and he'd be probably late teens, used his finely crafted Canongate ballock knife (so-called because of the suggestive pattern of the wooden grips, see above) in August 1600 to deal with the Earl of Gowrie who had apparently lured James up to see his etchings. Whether this was attempted murder, kidnapping or quite what hasn't been established but Ramsay's fast thinking and dexterity at arms ensured his advancement. Now I heard a tale that it was this same dagger that Ramsay lost in Paris a decade later, when it was stolen by one Francois Ravaillac after he'd passed out from drink and used by him to murder Henry IV. I also thought the knife had come back via purchase into the NMS collection, but a search failed to confirm this. It's still a good story.

[11] Ridpath, op. cit., p. 483.

[12] Ibid., p. 484.

[13] Somewhat unfortunately, Henry Clifford, Earl of Cumberland's grandson Sir George Wharton chose to fight a duel with Sir James Stuart. Both were well born and well-connected courtiers and it's ironic that Clifford's grandson should decide to settle matters in the old-fashioned way: 'George Wharton was the first that fell/Our Scotch Lord fell immediately/They both did cry to him above/To save their souls, for the boud [both] die[d]', see Minstrelsy, pp. 137–144.

[14] Ridpath, op. cit., p. 483.

[15] Graham, J., Condition of the Border at the Union (London: Routledge, 1907), p. 124.

[16] Ridpath, op. cit., p. 484.

[17] Graham, op. cit., p. 125.

[18] Ibid., p. 126.

[19] Carey, op. cit., p. 63.

[20] MacDonald Fraser, op. cit., p. 360.

[21] Ibid., p. 32.

[22] Elizabeth I had been happy to support the Dutch rebels in their fight against Spain.

[23] Baty = Beatty.

[24] MacDonald Fraser, op. cit., p. 365.

[25] MacDonald Fraser, op. cit., p. 365.

[26] https://www.pinterest.co.uk/haggishurler/grahams-of-the-border/, accessed 20 April 2020.

[27] By the King a proclamation for transplantation of the Greames. England and Wales, Sovereign (1603–1625: James I), James I, King of England, 1566-1625; imprinted at London: By Robert Barker, Printer to the Kings most Excellent Majestie, Anno 1603.

[28] United Nations definition.

[29] https://www.history.com/topics/holocaust/ethnic-cleansing accessed 16 April 2020.

[30] Graham, op. cit., p. 180.

[31] https://electricscotland.com/webclans/families/grahams_esk.htm, accessed 17 April 2020.

[32] MacDonald Fraser, op. cit., p. 368.

[33] Graham, op. cit., p. 186.

[34] MacDonald Fraser, op. cit., p. 371.

[35] Tait, J., Dick the Devil's Bairns: Breaking the Border Mafia (Kindle version: Amazon Media, 2018).

[36] These were Briel, Flushing, and Fort Rammeken on Walcheren.

[37] Graham, op. cit., p. 186.

[38] Ibid., p. 195.

[39] Watson, op. cit., p. 194.

[40] Ibid., p. 195.

[41] 'Survey of Newcastle', Harleian Miscellany, vol. iii, quoted in Gilpin's Life of Gilpin in 'Ecclesiastical Biography: Lives of Eminent Men (London: J. G. & F. Rivington, 1839), p. 273.

[42] Watson, op. cit., p. 196.

[43] From: The Death of 'Sweet Milk by Paul Greville Hudson (1876–1960), Hawick Museum.

[44] From: The Death of 'Sweet Milk by Paul Greville Hudson (1876–1960), Hawick Museum.

[45] A rather vapid adaption of the far better book by Glendon Swarthout.

[46] Ridpath, op. cit., p. 484.

CHAPTER TEN: REVOLUTION AND REINVENTION

'War is a womb big with many miseries'.

When Charles I of England raised his standard at Nottingham in August 1642, few could have foreseen that this quarrel between King and his Parliament would become as bitter and protracted as it did. William Cavendish, latterly Marquis of Newcastle, held the town of Newcastle [1] (city status wasn't granted until 1882) and county of Northumberland firmly for the crown. This was not to say Parliament was without supporters, a very influential Presbyterian clique existed. The town had, however already, had a taste, quite sufficient for most, of Scottish Covenanters two years earlier. For Newcastle civil war came early during the 2nd Bishops' War. King Charles had unwisely attempted to ram the Book of Common Prayer, Laud's Liturgy, down the throats of his northern subjects who had responded with force of arms.

Alexander Leslie, earl of Leven, a doughty old soldier who'd won his spurs and stellar reputation serving Gustavus Adolphus, led Scotland's well-structured army to an easy win at Newburn. Three and a half years later, he and his army, in the pay of England's Parliament, were back. They harried Cavendish back to the walls of York, then joined in the humbling of Prince Rupert at Marston Moor in July 1644. After that it was back to the old walls of Newcastle and a long, messy siege which ended when the place was finally stormed that October.

James Graham, Marquis of Montrose, led a doomed but spectacular crusade for the king during the 'Year of Miracles' till it ended in the mire at Philiphaugh. A first Civil War led to a second and the decimation of Scottish arms at Preston in 1648, this time fighting for King Charles. That disaster was compounded by two more at Dunbar on 3 September 1650 and then exactly a year later at Worcester when they fought for his son. Dunbar was followed by a ghastly death march as five thousand Scottish POWs were brutally herded down to Durham as re-saleable goods.

'Here lies John Hunter/Martyr who was cruelly/Murdered at Corehead/By Col. James Douglas/And his party for his adherence/To the word of God and/Scotland's Covenanted/Work of Reformation'.

Memorial in Tweedsmuir Church (erected 1726)

In the quarter century of his reign King Charles II never ventured into his northern kingdom. The throne of his ancestors was filled by a series of commissioners, latterly, his brother James, Duke of York, the future James VII. Initially the Committee of Estates, rudely interrupted by the capture of the members at Alyth in 1651, was reinstated. One of its early dictates was to forbid the holding of religious meetings or 'conventicles' without express royal authority. This was one measure of particularly sinister religious repression that ushered in a nasty asymmetric war in southwest Scotland which periodically spilled over. Then came the Jacobites, another of history's doomed causes, arguably the most over-romanticised of all and the north of England was briefly convulsed by Derwentwater's folly in 1715, an experience that coloured any hopes Bonny Prince Charlie may have had for support across the borders.

THE MAN WHO RE-INVENTED SCOTLAND

'We build statues out of snow and weep to see them melt'.

Sir Walter Scott

By a Royal Warrant dated 28 October 1817 'Prinny' still only regent, instructed Walter Scott to search for the lost Crown jewels of Scotland. They'd been used in the coronation of Charles II in 1660 and hauled out regularly for parliamentary sessions thereafter but by Scott's day they hadn't seen daylight for a century, and were stored in a chest within the deep bowels of Edinburgh Castle. With a typical flourish of showmanship, Scott, with a group of officers, 'found' and opened this magic casket and these emotive baubles were restored to the light. A keeper of the refreshed 'Scottish Regalia' (coincidentally a pal of Scott's) was appointed and a grateful Prince Regent rewarded Sir Walter, as he became, with his baronetcy [2].

Five years later Scott stage-managed a royal visit by, as he then was, George IV, a fat silly man, blinged up in ludicrous tartan who was paraded around as the great Scottish Hope. Daft as this might seem, it went down a storm and kick-started a national and indeed international tourist industry, one that has never faltered since. Politically it mattered and this was what got Scott his title. King George in straining kilt and the apparent homage to tradition cemented the House of Hanover as true rulers. Scott the pragmatist was working hand in hand with Scott the romantic and booting the Jacobites out of the premiership and down into a minor league. Any popular movement which is shunted off into the realm of romantic failure is no longer a threat.

His major contribution to nascent nationalism was the promotion of 'tartanry': that sense of identity expressed in an idealised, utterly romanticised Highland and borders legacy. Even the bourgeoisie of the lowlands, enthusiastic partners in a burgeoning empire and arch despisers of real Highlanders, had taken to the cult of Ossian and now went wholesale for tartanry. Ossian was reputed to be an ancient Gaelic bard who had recorded heroic tales of an earlier age, larger than life figures of myth on a par with those of the classics. Three books by James McPherson, published 1760–1773, purported to be collections, most probably drawn from oral traditions that still survived in the far north and much embroidered.

Scott rode the tartan wave, but he didn't spawn the craze. That was down to a pair of enterprising Polish spivs, John Sobieski Stolberg Stuart with his sibling Charles Edward and yes, they did claim to be Bonnie Prince Charlie's grandsons. With impeccable timing they reached Edinburgh in the run up to George's visit, ready equipped with a useful handbook on Scottish costume, Vestiarium Scoticum. This was apparently a long-lost ancient text, containing the secrets of clan dress. It might have been a con; it was indeed a con, but it worked, and the tartan industry has never looked back.

Tartanry has a lot to answer for. I recall talking to a group of young, fit looking Americans in Inverness all proudly sporting kilts of their very own family tartan (good news is if your family has lived in Mongolia for the last millennium, you'll have Scottish ancestry somewhere). As well as these improbable connections the lads were all wearing uniform white trainers. The bloke who'd sold them the kilts had advised that white trainers were de rigeur. Presumably he had shares in Sports Direct. The Stuart brothers would have smiled.

Sir Walter is the master spin doctor; his tartan revolution was a complete romantic makeover, and he did just the same, even more subtly, for the reivers. Mafia on prancing white chargers and natty hose aren't gangsters anymore, they're soap opera not organised crime, swashbucklers not ISIS, fit now for tea shops and tartanry, (neither of which they'd ever have dreamt of). Auld Wat would have been proud of his descendant; it was the finest deception the riding names ever pulled off.

Scott was born in Edinburgh, ninth child (only three survived infancy) of a successful lawyer who had connections to the Border Scotts. At the age of two young Walter contracted the polio that would leave him lame. Physically, he'd never be the Errol Flynn of his own fiction. Still, every cloud and all that; to recuperate he was packed off to his grandfather's farm at Sandyknowe directly beneath the solid finger of Smailholm tower, perched so dramatically on its gnarled crag, the ancient peel seeming to spring directly from the living rock and still yelling 'who dare meddle wi' me' to the world. This wasn't the only inspiration; his aunt Jenny acted as teacher and mentor, steeped in the old lore – she'd light a spark that would flash around the globe.

Young Walter survived his illness and was given a good education, it was naturally intended he'd follow his father into the law. He went up to university aged 12 before being articled to his dad three years later. He moved in the bright light of an Edinburgh society enriched by the glow of Enlightenment. His friend Adam Ferguson's father hosted glittering literary soirees where Scott met Burns, their only encounter. He was an assiduous lawyer, admitted into the faculty of Advocates in 1792. His desire for martial glory was granted by Bonaparte and Scott volunteered for the Edinburgh Light Horse, Dad's Army with saddles, stupendously fashionable as gentlemen kitted themselves out in well-tailored uniforms and preened, waiting for an invasion that, happily, never happened.

It wouldn't be true though to say he never saw action, he 'brassed up' some annoying miners at Cross causeway and rattled his un-blooded sabre at equally insolent mill-workers. After Waterloo, he was an early battlefield tourist, socialising around Paris now the French had been hammered, still in his yeomanry get-up. He even managed to wangle an invite to kiss the Tsar's hand. Impressed with both his pristine uniform and noticeable limp, HRH asked in what engagement he'd been wounded. Unabashed, Walter described his riot control duties 'some slight actions'. Happily, his host was none the wiser [3].

Scott both married and prospered and in the final year of the eighteenth century picked up a lucrative and handy office as Sheriff-Depute for the county of Selkirk, based in the Burgh. He was on the rise, his poetry and writing were already being noticed and starting to sell, his law practice was doing well, and his wife had her own income. He owned a spacious trendy town house in Edinburgh and kept a cottage at Lasswade to satisfy the residency qualification for his judicial post. In 1796, his friend James Ballantyne had established a press in Kelso, and it was he who first published Scott's verse. In less than a decade his Lay of the Last Minstrel boosted a rapidly expanding reputation. Marmion in 1810 went, as we say, viral. By then Ballantyne had moved his house to Edinburgh and Scott accepted a partnership in the publishing firm.

He soon decided to try his hand at fiction, then very much a junior branch of literary endeavour. A succession of romantic and dramatic novels, with suitably Scottish themes followed. He made the White Cockade Hollywood; the sleet shrouded horror of Culloden was already too far back to have an impact, besides Scott's Tory and Presbyterian credentials were unassailable. He was now the 'Wizard of the North' feted and admired. Ivanhoe in 1819 was a move away from Scotland and an international bestseller – one of my Children's TV treats in the early 1960s was Roger Moore in the small-screen series!

The bad news was that during an economic slump in 1825 his publishing house went bust and Scott applied his titanic energies to paying off the debt. These were substantial, the best part of ten million quid in today's money. His great house at Abbotsford and all his income were put into what today would be termed a voluntary arrangement and he prepared to write his way out of debt. He didn't quite make it but did work himself to death in the process. Yet the very attempt is surely a mark of his greatness, the heroic course, what other could the author of Marmion, Ivanhoe & Rob Roy adopt?

I adore the house, it is pure Scott, grand without being overly pretentious – not all agree, his biographer feels that 'although Abbotsford [4] is architecturally unpretentious by the standards of the age … it was in more senses than one a folly. The gaslight caught the jewels of Soldier's wives and duchesses; but it also transformed the coarse complexions of gentry' families into cheeks and lips that looked as cold and wan as Emily in the Mysteries of Udolpho; behind the table laden with hideous Coalport China, champagne glasses and newly bought cutlery lurked the armoury' [5]. Personally, I revere the armoury but then I would, and one could be reminded of a failed officer in one of the Sharpe novels whose house is crammed with trophies of battles he'd never fought in, rows of muskets and swords he'd run away from.

THAT ETTRICK SHEPHERD

It was Scott's genius and that of his sometimes friend and collaborator James Hogg, (1770–1835) 'the Ettrick Shepherd', which re-branded the old borderers and created a whole new mythology, even though it was based on the old. Neither collaborator, in spite of the mighty weight of their combined genius, created the border ballads, some of which are of impressive lineage (see appendix two) but they did record, conserve, and make them widely available. Some might say they rewrote many completely.

Their friendship spanned two decades but was frequently sparky, as Hogg himself recounts: 'I called on him after his return from the Parliament House, on pretence of asking his advice about some especially important affair, but in fact to hear his sentiments of my new work. His shaggy eyebrows were hanging very low, a bad prelude which I knew too well. "I have read your new work Mr. Hogg", said he, "and I must tell you downright plainly, as I always do, that I like it very ill – very ill indeed … it is a false picture of the times and the existing characters, altogether an exaggerated and unfair picture". Ouch! Hogg was just as blunt as his defence of his work '… in no one instance have I related a story of cruelty or a murder which is not literally true. An' that's a great deal more than you can say ….' [6].

Though the two men came from vastly different social strata, Hogg could always give as good as he got. The Ettrick Shepherd was the son of a minor tenant farmer, but his mother Margaret was a noted collector of border ballads. Her maiden name was Laidlaw and her father had been something of a mystic, able to talk to the fairies, something that could have got him either an award today or a stay in a long-term institution. He did get to attend school, but his education was interrupted by his father's bankruptcy and her had to seek whatever work he could get, shepherd or farm labourer.

His continuing education was provided by his mother and uncle. He had talent with the fiddle and saved hard to buy one. Despite a grinding life of tough manual work, he taught himself to read and pursued a shepherd's life, working for a paternalistic relation Laidlaw of Blackhouse. The farmer allowed him free rein of his own library. Hogg composed songs and formed a literary group among his own fraternity of shepherds. In the circumstances of his time and class, this was remarkable stuff.

By now Scott, already well established was collecting material for his Minstrelsy and from 1802 they began their active collaboration. Hogg wanted a farm of his own and visited the highlands – set his heart on a place; this was on the Isle of Harris but was unable to complete. He wrote a series of letters to Scott on his travels, and these were published in Scots Magazine. Hogg was successful with women, if less so in business and his creditors began to press. It was in 1810 when he'd have been about 40 (his exact date of birth unclear) that he made the move to Edinburgh and a career writing full time. He wobbled for a while but became established. He met Wordsworth and Buccleuch gave him a farm for life, rent free. His output was consistent and sold well but money troubles persisted.

In 1817 he collaborated with the publisher William Blackwood and set up Edinburgh Monthly Magazine, soon re-branded as Blackwood's Magazine. And it was this which made him famous. Blackwood, as a high Tory, openly courted controversy and built a circle of partisan writers able to supply his ammunition. Hogg was, for a while, a leading light but was forced onto the back benches and finally into a split. Lampooned by his fellow scribes as the Ettrick Shepherd caricature in their columns, he went to work for the competition. His money worries didn't dissipate in fact they continued to multiply. He met Scott for the last time in 1830 and died five years later, his death hastened by injuries sustained in a fall through ice while out curling.

Scott's Minstrelsy of the Scottish Border – published in three volumes 1802/1803, was still a triumph, even if one conditioned by his own time and his own agenda. Without him and Hogg, the ballads would probably, or at least possibly, have disappeared. If the reiver he magicked up was a charlatan and the chivalric era he painted a chimera, at one level it doesn't matter, the strand was preserved and his take on the stories becomes part of them. Eminent as they were, Scott and Hogg were not the only compilers: Francis James Child anthologised several hundred from the borders, both sides together with their American descendants, arranged in five volumes [7].

KING COAL

'Six hundred years of sweat and toil/ In that deep and dark abyss/ The entrepreneur has spoken/ Blown a tasteless goodbye kiss' [8].

And then there was coal. During the medieval period, all coal was referred to as 'sea' coal. This may have been because the coal was delivered out of the Tyne to London by ship or because erosion of the exposed coal outcrops along the Tyne and Northumberland coast produced frequent quantities on beaches. The Northumbrian coastal measures outcropped along the coast unlike in Durham where the seams were much deeper, thus the Durham measures opened up much later.

In the thirteenth century Newcastle was considered primarily a source for leather hides and manufactured goods but the trade was damaged by the long years of the Border wars and the reduction of the ready supplies of hides from Northumbrian beasts. Coal was being mined at Whickham and Winlaton by the mid to late thirteenth century and mines were soon being dug at Elswick, Heworth, and on the Town Moor. By the mid-fifteenth century 'keelmen' were already becoming an established monopoly. Following the Dissolution of the Established Church by Henry VIII and the rise of a new urban middle class, the mines flourished.

By 1787, over 7,000 miners worked in and around Newcastle. Early mines were shallow drifts or bell pits. Many accidents occurred, men died at Whickham and Thrislington, for instance, as early as 1329. Causes of accidents tended to be collapse, gas explosions, and flooding. The miners were lowered up and down in buckets and if the shafts spread too far outwards the weight of the roof and gear might produce a collapse. By the late sixteenth century mines were being sunk far deeper and horse-drawn engines 'gin-gans' were employed to pump out excess water. Newcommen's 'fire' engines were being built after 1715 and Watt perfected his steam engine in 1769 [9].

Mechanical means could be harnessed to raise the coal and in 1753 Michael Menzies of Chartersheugh Colliery near Washington (now Tyne & Wear) developed his own version – the 'Menzie'. As mines became ever deeper, concerns over safety multiplied. As early as 1662 a petition signed by over 2,000 subscribers was submitted to parliament petitioning for improved means of ventilation; gas was always a killer and in the eighteenth century more and deadlier accidents occurred [10].

There was a time, through the nineteenth century, when Newcastle was the powerhouse of the world, a vast, sprawling industrial giant, inhabited by a race of titans; Stephensons, father and son, Swan, Hunter and Armstrong, several generations of engineering and entrepreneurial talent that changed Tyneside, Britain, and the world. Dobson and Grainger created a cityscape to match this dynamic outpouring of innovation, and the population multiplied exponentially; the outlines of that old medieval centre were subsumed if not fully erased. Railways sprang up over the city and county like a monstrous web; the railway and Central Station altered the whole visual amenity, slashing relentlessly across contours of time in a breathless race for modernity.

Steam was the driver, quite literally, of change. By 1814 the first steam-powered ferry Tyne Steam Packet (later renamed as Perseverance) was sailing between Newcastle and Shields. The use of steam tugs which followed soon after ended a centuries' long tradition of closing the collieries for two of the winter months. Iron was now beginning to replace timber in ships and Prince Albert the first to be built on Tyneside slid into the water in 1842. As industry began to boom, so mining began to decline, at least in the local context. Some new pits were opened but the High Main seam was becoming exhausted. From the 1820s new seams were being opened in County Durham and mining investment began to shift towards the east of that county.

In the pantheon of figures unique to Newcastle, a breed as distinctive (and often as contentious) as the reivers were the keelmen. A 'keel' was a form of fat bellied, single-masted, open longboat, which was oval-shaped and purpose built for the sole job of ferrying coals. Both keels and keelmen were spawned by King Coal and the tradition endured for centuries till dredging and maritime expansion in the mid-nineteenth century did away with them, and their trade passed into history and legend.

I've a connection with this remarkable race as my great-great-great-grandfather and several known generations beforehand worked as keelmen.

Typically, the boat was crewed by the master, two seamen and a junior, known as the 'Pee-dee'. Though essentially inshore their trade demanded both strength and seamanship. They rowed their laden vessels, each groaning under around 20 tons of coal, out to colliers waiting in the deeper channel. Each cargo had to be loaded and unloaded by hand, back-breaking work, pace dictated by the ebb and swell of the tide [11].

FROM THE SHEEP'S BACK

Wool was the key to wealth and industry in the Scottish Marches, though linen production came first. This was part of a conscious effort by a quango, the Board of Trustees for Manufacture, whose role was to encourage and stimulate native industries in Scotland [12]. Growing flax was encouraged via subsidies but by the end of the eighteenth century this was being displaced by the emerging woollen industry, centred then on Galashiels. Before it passed into terminal decline, the linen industry gave us the term 'heckler' [13]. In 1777 the Manufacturers' Corporation of Galashiels was set up with fewer than two dozen members yet the first mill was up and running by the close of that century [14].

Swiftly the market took off and then boomed. Checked cloth, the 'shepherd's plaid', became a bestseller as did the emerging glut of tartans – the industry had Scott to thank for both. Fat King George, posturing in tartan that would make the most enthusiastic US Gael-seeker blush, fuelled the spate. A London-based Scottish trader James Locke is credited with invention of the word 'tweed' after, it is said, he'd just misread the word 'tweel' (twill) and wrote asking for tweed. It's a nice story but Locke as a tailor himself probably already knew better. More likely this was clever marketing, linking to the River Tweed and all things Walter Scott.

Hawick developed a burgeoning capacity for producing fine quality hosiery at about the same time. John Hardie, the resident magistrate, introduced the use of stocking frames, a step towards mass production in 1771. Napoleon did his bit as well. His imperialism certainly fuelled the success of our nation of shopkeepers or more precisely manufacturers and those long wars from 1793 on and off, mainly on, till 1815 massively boosted demand. Inevitably, there was a post-war slump but by mid-century Hawick was producing a million pairs of stockings each year.

Throughout the nineteenth century the Borders woollen industry established a raft of successful brands which filled upmarket niches. Hawick moved from stockings to underwear and fortunes were built on the backs of sheep. It was a tough environment for the workers, perhaps less dangerous than mining but hours were long and the work hard. The early shift, 'lamp-lighters', usually clocked on at say 05.45 and the workforce was expected to be cracking on by 06.00. If not, you were locked out, you'd work for six days a week with only the Sabbath off. Forget any holiday pay as well [15].

Fleeces came into the mill in their raw state, courtesy of the previous four-legged owner. There was no screening for ticks or parasites. The raw product was re-sorted and that depended on maintaining levels of consistency in the blending process. Thereafter, the material was rgani and carded to convert core fibre into workable strands which went on firstly to the spinners and then weavers. Woven cloth was then returned to the mill for finishing. Mills, not necessarily dark and satanic, dominated the border towns and their economies; their spirit still does at least in part even if now virtually all are transformed into retail outlets. Galashiels and Hawick still have the feel of run-down mill towns. By and large, none have any real traces of the reivers, but the woollen legacy still resonates [16].

WEAPONS OF MASS DESTRUCTION

For most of August 2019 I appeared at Bamburgh Castle in the guise of no lesser genius than William George Armstrong, First Baron of Cragside (1810 –190), I even grew the sideburns! On several mornings, with a fine screen of haze, luminous after drenching overnight rain, I stood on the gun terrace next to a Napoleonic 32-pounder and marvelled at the breadth of both the man's scientific genius and his entrepreneurial flair.

All this led to the dawn of an era of Industrial War, conflict on a scale never imagined, where competing technologies ratcheted up levels of human suffering to unimagined heights. This began with the American Civil War (1861–1865) and led to the conflagration of 1914 where Armstrong's factories provided vast quantities of arms and matériel; small arms, machine-guns, quick firing artillery, aircraft, tanks, and vast leviathans, warships which carried his guns that could throw a shell for 20 miles and more. William, Lord Armstrong was a game-changer who bestrode the international arms trade like a colossus and whose sprawl of factories at Elswick employed tens of thousands of workers. Making guns is no longer respectable even if just as necessary but Armstrong was nonetheless the epitome of a genuinely great innovative industrialist.

All this vast mass production would be needed, and industrial warfare was about to come suddenly it seemed and horribly of age. As the great man, in his dotage, supervised the wonderful medieval fantasy he was creating or re-creating at Bamburgh, even he could not have foreseen what was to come. By and large neither did anyone else as the world's empires stumbled into chaos and slaughter – men and women of the borders' region would do more than play their part and they'd pay a very heavy price indeed. Irony indeed that it would be an Armstrong, wildest of the wild reiver names that would take the world into an age of mass destruction. I've a nagging feeling his ancestors would probably have applauded.

LEGACY

'At one moment when President Richard Nixon was taking part in his inauguration ceremony, he appeared flanked by Lyndon Johnson and Billy Graham. To anyone familiar with border history it was one of those historical coincidences which send a little shudder through the mind: in that moment, thousands of miles and centuries in time away from the Debatable Land, the threads came together again …' [17].

As events would prove, there was more irony in this than MacDonald Fraser could have appreciated at the time as Nixon turned out as devious and underhand as the trickiest of border heidmen. They'd probably have approved of his actions but not that he was daft enough to get caught.

In 2020, just before lockdown bit, I was lecturing to the Towton Battlefield Society near Tadcaster on the Steel Bonnets' participation during the Wars of the Roses (this was sporadic but as ever, enthusiastic, and brutal). The mainly Yorkshire audience took a view that we northerners (i.e., north of Yorkshire) were just plain hard, always had been, and still were. Is this our legacy? Probably, Newcastle upon Tyne has a reputation for a hard drinking and frequently brawling culture, and you've never really played rugby till you've been up against Hawick. The northern English and border regiments contributed more battalions than almost any others to the cauldron of the Great War, one of these was the Piper of Loos.

AND THE PIPER PLAYED ON

Daniel Logan Laidlaw VC [18], dubbed the Piper of Loos, was born in Berwickshire into a military family. It was an older brother who both taught young Dan the pipes and persuaded him to transfer from the Durham Light Infantry ("DLI") into the King's Own Scottish Borderers ("KOSB"). A reservist by 1914 he re-enlisted and reached the rank of acting-corporal in 15 KOSB, taking part in the battle of Loos during September 1915. It was Laidlaw whose legendary courage, calmly walking along the parapet, reminiscent of Caesar's 10th Legion standard bearer during the tricky landing off the south coast of England in 55 BC, that inspired his comrades to go over the top and keep moving forwards. He kept playing till he was hit.

His citation reads: 'For most conspicuous bravery prior to an assault on German trenches near Loos and Hill 70 on 25th September 1915. During the worst of the bombardment, when the attack was about to commence, Piper Laidlaw, seeing that his company was somewhat shaken from the effects of gas, with absolute coolness and disregard of danger, mounted the parapet, marched up and down and played the company out of the trench. The effect of his splendid example was immediate, and the company dashed out to the assault; Piper Laidlaw continued playing his pipes till he was wounded' [19]. I was fortunate enough on the 90th anniversary of his feat to be piped across the same ground by his great-grandson – a highly evocative experience, happily, the Germans weren't firing but the vin blanc was flowing.

He received his VC from the King himself at Buckingham Palace in early 1916 and later gained a Croix de Guerre. Twice promoted he survived the war and was demobbed in April 1919. Look at a picture of Laidlaw, every inch an NCO, formidable bristling moustache, no-nonsense face, and granite eyes. He couldn't be anything other than a borderer. If we want to imagine what kind of face snarled from beneath a steel bonnet, his will surely fit.

But is it true? Are we borderers a harder, more contentious breed? It's hard to say and even if correct this may not be the sole legacy of the riding names. We must remember those northern English and southern Scots who served in both World Wars came, in many cases from backgrounds of hard industrial labour or agriculture, another tough taskmaster. Coal mines and shipyards, harsh border hills, steelworks, and factories toughened young men as much, if not more than reiving. And the Steel Bonnets were by no means a majority of border inhabitants. It is a fact though that army recruiting does well in the border counties; regiments such as the Rifles recruit heavily here, soldiers though, not necessarily officers!

One thing that does stand out, at least to those here who are influenced by such things is the abundance of our heritage and how much, in a largely unchanging landscape, has been preserved. We are blessed in that we can see the place as it was. George MacDonald Fraser aptly describes grim Hermitage in Liddesdale as 'sod off in stone'. And he's right. There are plenty more, Lordly Bamburgh, massive on its volcanic spur, Hollows Tower, bastles such as Black Middings, Gatehouses and scores of others, looking as though their stubby, cyclopean stones spring up from the ground. Yet there are more recent traces too; the World Wars also left their mark!

REIVERS RULE OK

What does this all amount to in terms of a reiver heritage? Does such a thing exist? That the northern English and southern Scottish characters are different to the rest of their countrymen and women is accepted but to what extent did Johnnie of Gilnockie, Bold Buccleuch and Kinmont Will contribute? I suspect the answer must be at best undecided. The Steel Bonnets blazed a nasty trail through their corner of history and then vanished into the hole of black legend. The version Scott so brilliantly created was, for the most part, pure fiction. Young Lochinvar never existed; he's Scott's version of Mel Gibson's William Wallace – Braveheart, great cinema, just a shame about the history.

Echoes come down to us through the ballads and we hear about the reivers' many misdeeds through official records but they themselves stay silent, even Robert Carey, though he knew them, wasn't of them, he was more like an imperial district officer in some far-flung corner of empire – honest, decent, and brave but still a foreigner. As L. P. Hartley so memorably began, 'the past is like a foreign country, they do things differently there'.

That applies profoundly to the riding names, we know remarkably little about them as individuals, and we can't begin to understand the harsh realities of their daily lives. George MacDonald Fraser, one who certainly comes close, once described them as being free in a way we can't understand. But he's a glorious romantic beneath the gruff pragmatism and we love him for it. Freedom wasn't really free at all and what measure of liberty they enjoyed came at a very high price. Plain fact is, they weren't much loved, and they certainly weren't missed. And that they would certainly have understood. We can't recreate their lives or begin to understand them; maybe a survivor from the hideous Balkan wars of the 1990s would get it, but the rest of us can't. Romance aside, that's our good fortune, there was nothing good about the good old days and the best part of the narrative was probably when the song was ended.

NOTES:

[1] Cavendish (1593–1676) was a man of vast wealth, much of which he owed to the King's patronage, his wife Margaret 'Mad Madge' was something of a polymath and way ahead of her time.
[2] Wilson, A. N., The Laird of Abbotsford (London: Pimlico, 2002), p. 78.
[3] Ibid., p. 39.
[4] See: https://www.scottsabbotsford.com/?gclid=EAIaIQobChMIlKPon_Ch6QIVzO3tCh0dvAACEAAYASAAEgKaQ_D_BwE
[5] Wilson, op. cit., p. 56.
[6] Ibid., p. 110.
[7] Scott, Sir W., Minstrelsy of the Scottish Border (London, Henry Stevens Son & Stiles 1904).
[8] The Last Northumbrian Coal Mine by John Robison.
[9] https://englandsnortheast.co.uk/CoalMiningandRailways.html accessed 6 May 2020.
[10] Ibid.
[11] Middlebrook, op. cit., pp. 84–85.
[12] Board of Trustees for Fisheries, Manufactures and Improvements in Scotland (1727–1906); this was an rganization set up to stimulate the Scottish economy whilst avoiding direct competition with England.
[13] A heckler, the word now used to describe someone who disrupts a meeting meant s textile worker whose role was to draw fibres from flax though a 'heckle'.
[14] http://www.bbc.co.uk/legacies/work/scotland/borders, accessed 6 May 2020.
[15] Ibid.
[16] Ibid.
[17] Southern Reporter 2 November 1916. [8] https://www.historic-uk.com/HistoryUK/HistoryofBritain/Devils-Porridge/, accessed 15 January 2021.
[18] He spent most of his later life as postmaster at Norham.
[19] He did retell the story to a BBC audience in the sixties, he saw nothing remarkable in what he did, 'whey Ah just played me pipes….'

GLOSSARY

'Backsword' – a form of weapon with one sharpened cutting edge and the other flattened and blunt, primarily a horseman's weapon designed for the cut.

'Barbican' – a form of defended outer gateway designed to shield the actual gate itself.

'Bartizan' – a small corner turret projecting over the walls.

'Bastion' – projection from the curtain wall of a fort usually at intersections to provide a wider firing platform and to allow defenders to enfilade (flanking fire) a section of the curtain.

'Batter' – outward slope at the base of a masonry wall to add strength and frustrate mining efforts.

'Battery' – a section of guns, may be mobile field artillery or a fixed defensive position within a defensive circuit.

'Breast and back' – body armour comprising a front and rear plate section.

'Breastwork' – defensive wall.

'Broadsword' – a double-edged blade intended for cut or thrust, becoming old-fashioned though many would do service, often with an enclosed or basket hilt.

'Broken man [men]' – outlaw(s).

'Buff Coat' – a leather coat, long skirted and frequently with sleeves, fashioned from thick but pliant hide, replaced body armour for the cavalry.

'Caliver' – a lighter form of musket, with greater barrel length than the cavalry carbine (see below).

'Cannon' – heavy gun throwing a 47 pound ball; a demi-cannon fired 27 pound ball; cannon-royal shot a massive 63 pound ball.

'Captain' – the appointed guardian of an area, perhaps a more defensive role.

'Carbine' – a short-barrelled musket used primarily by cavalry.

'Case-shot' – Also referred to as canister this was a cylindrical shell case, usually tin, sealed in beeswax and caulked with wooden disks, wherein a quantity of balls were packed and filled with sawdust. A cartridge bag of powder was attached to the rear and, on firing the missile had the effect of a massive shotgun cartridge, very nasty.

'Casement' – a bomb proof chamber or vault within the defences.

'Cleared' – innocent of charges made.

'Commission of Array' – this was the ancient royal summons issued through the lords-lieutenants of the counties to raise militia forces, in the context of a civil war such an expedient was of dubious legality as clearly unsanctioned by Parliament.

'Committee of Both Kingdoms' – this was brought into being as a consequence of two parliamentary measures (16 February and 22 May 1644) to ensure close cooperation between the English and Scots. Cromwell, Manchester, and Essex were all members of the Committee which sat at Derby House.

'Constable' – a leader of tenantry group on demesne lands who could be mustered both for defence and offense.

'Cornet' – a pennant or standard and thus also the junior officer who carried it.

'Corselet' – this refers to a pikeman's typical harness of breast and back, with tassets for the thighs.

'Cuirassier' – these were heavy cavalry wearing three quarter harness, something of an anachronism. Sir Arthur Hesilrige's 'Lobsters' were the most famous example; as the wars progressed reliance upon armour decreased considerably.

'Culverin' – a gun throwing a 15 pound ball; mainly used in siege operations the guns weighed an average of 4,000 lbs. the lighter demi-culverin threw a nine pound ball and weighed some 3,600 lbs.

'Dagg(s)' – Wheelock horseman's pistols, usually carried in saddle holsters.

'Dragoon' – essentially mounted infantry, the name is likely derived from 'dragon' a form of carbine; their roles was to act as scouts and skirmishers and they could fight either mounted (rare) or dismounted.

'Ensign' (or 'Ancient') – a junior commissioned officer of infantry who bears the flag from which the name derives.

'Falcon' – light gun firing a 2 ¼ pound ball.

'Falconet' – light gun throwing a 1 ¼ pound shot.

'Field-works' – a system of improvised temporary defensive works employed by an army on the march or protecting an encampment.

'Flintlock or 'firelock' – a more sophisticated ignition mechanism than match; the flint was held in a set of jaws, the cock which when released by the trigger struck sparks from the steel frizzen and showered these into the pan which ignited the main charge.

'Foot' – infantry.

'Free Quarter' – troops paying for food and lodgings by a ticket system, requisitioning or outright theft in practice.

'Fusil' – this was a form of light musket usually carried by gunners and latterly by officers, hence 'fusilier'.

'Gabion' – wicker baskets filled with earth which formed handy building blocks for temporary works or sealing off a breach.

'Glacis' – a sloped earthwork out from the covered way to provide for grazing fire from the curtain.

'Grayne' – sept of a riding name.

'Guns' – artillery.

'Halberd' – a polearm, outdated in war but carried as a staff of rank by NCOs.

'Harquesbusier' – an archaic term describing the cavalryman armed with carbine, sword and brace of pistols, the latter sometimes still referred to as 'daggs'.

'Heidman' – leader/chieftain of a riding name or grayne.

'Horse' – cavalry.

'Insight' – household goods and effects liable for plunder.

'Land-Sergeant' – an officer responsible for a defined 'patch', subordinate to and appointed by the warden.

'Linstock' – a staff having a forked end to hold match – used for discharging cannon.

'Lunette' – flanking walls added to a small redan (see below) to provide additional flanking protection and improved fire position; a 'demi-lune' is a crescent or half-moon structure built projecting from the curtain to afford greater protection.

'Magazine' – bomb proof vault where powder and shot are stored.

'Main Gauche' – literally left hand; this was a form of dagger used in conjunction with the rapier.

'Matchlock' – the standard infantry firearm, slow and cumbersome, prone to malfunction in wet or wind, it was nevertheless rugged and generally reliable. When the trigger was released, the jaws lowered a length of lit cord 'match' into the exposed and primed pan which flashed through to the main charge, where the charge failed to ignite this was referred to as 'a flash in the pan'.

'Matross' – a gunner's mate, doubled as a form of ad hoc infantry to protect the guns whilst on the march.

'Meutriere' – or 'murder-hole' space between the curtain and corbelled out battlements enabling defenders to drop a variety of unpleasant things onto attackers at the base of the wall.

'Minion' – gun shooting a 4-pound ball.

'Morion' – infantry protective headgear, the morion was a conical helmet with curving protective brim and central ridged comb intended to deflect a downwards cut.

'Mosstrooper' – an outlaw 'broken man' or in the later Civil Wars context irregular light cavalry.

'Musket' – the term refers to any smooth-bored firearm, regardless of the form of lock, rifled barrels were extremely rare, though not unknown at this time.

'Nolt' – cattle.

'Ordnance' – artillery.

'Pike' – a polearm with a shaft likely to be between 12 and 18 feet in length, finished with a diamond-shaped head.

'Plump Watch' – a tactical unit designed to keep watch for raiders.

'Postern' ('Sally Port') – a small gateway set into the curtain allowing resupply and deployment of defenders in localised attacks on besiegers.

'Pricker' – mounted scout or forager.

'Rapier' – a slender, long bladed thrusting weapon, more likely to be owned by gentry, bespoke and more costly than a trooper's backsword.

'Ravelin' – a large V shaped outwork, beyond the ditch or moat, intended to add protection to a particularly vulnerable point.

'Redoubt' – a detached, square, polygonal or hexagonal earthwork or blockhouse.

'Reiver' – one of the riding names of the border, a raider whose primary objective was cattle stealing.

'Riding Name' – one of the primarily upland dales families on either and both sides of the border.

'Robinet' – light field gun firing a 1 ¼ pound shot.

'Rode' – raid.

'Scarp' – inner wall of ditch or moat.

'Sconce' – a small, detached fort with projecting corner bastions.

'Snap' – cold rations carried in a 'snapsack'.

'Swine-Feather' – also known as Swedish feathers – a form of metal-shod stake that could be utilised to form an improvised barrier against an enemy.

'tasset' – a section of plate armour hinged from the breastplate intended to afford protection to the upper thigh.

'Tercio' – a Spanish term for the military formation, derived from the Swiss model which dominated renaissance warfare, and developed into a more linear formation after the reforms of the Swede Gustavus Adolphus, essentially a brigade.

'Touch-hole' – the small diameter hole drilled through the top section of a gun barrel through which the linstock ignites the charge, fine powder was poured in a quill inserted into the touch-hole.

'Train' – a column of guns on the move, the army marches accompanied or followed by the train.

'Trained Bands' – local militia.

'Wheel-lock' – more reliable and much more expensive than matches, this relied upon a circular metal spinning wheel wound up like a clock by key. When the trigger was released, the wheel spun and the jaws lowered into contact and fitted with pyrites, showered sparks into the pan.

Bibliography

Manuscripts and Archive Sources

National Archives, Blackett Family Records, NCRO, ZBK

———, Delaval Family Records, NCRO, 1DE & 2DE

Tyne & Wear Archives, Chamberlain's Accounts, TW 543/18

———, NCA Chamberlain's Accounts, 1642–45, TW543/27

Primary Sources

A Continuance of Certain Special and Remarkable Passages No. 2, 03 – 10 January 1644

'A letter from the Corporation of Newcastle upon Tyne to the Mayor and Aldermen of Berwick', ed. by J Raine, Archaeologia Aeliana 1.2 (1832), 366

A True experimentall and exact relation upon that famous and renowned Siege of Newcastle, William Lithgow (Edinburgh: Printed by Robert Bryson, 1645)

An English Chronicle of the reigns of Richard II, Henry IV, Henry V and Henry VI, ed. by J. S. Davies (London: Camden Press, 1866)

An Ordinance with Severall Propositions 1643 (Richardson, Reprints; Oxford: Oxford University Press, 2005)

Andrews, G., Acts of the High Commission Court within the Diocese of Durham, vol. 34 (Durham: Surtees Society, 1858)

Anglo-Saxon Chronicle (London: George Bell & Sons, 1880)

Baillie, J., Impartial History of the Town and County of Newcastle upon Tyne (Newcastle: Vint & Anderson, 1801)

Bede, Ecclesiastical History of England (London: George Bell & Sons, 1880)

Benet, J., 'John Benet's chronicle for the years 1400 to 1462', ed. by G. L. Hariss and M. A. Harriss, in Camden Miscellany vol. XXIV (London: Royal Historical Society, 1972)

Brut Chronicle, ed. by F. W. D. Brie, 2 vols (London: Kegan Paul, 1906)

By the King a proclamation for transplantation of the Greames.
   England and Wales, Sovereign (1603-1625: James I), James I, King of England, 1566-1625 (imprinted at London: By Robert Barker, Printer to the Kings most Excellent Majestie, Anno 1603)

Calendar of Fine Rolls: Edward IV; Edward V; Richard III, 1471 – 1485 (London: HMSO, 1961)

Calendar of Patent Rolls, Edward IV 1467 – 1477, Edward IV, Edward V, Richard

III. 1476 – 1485 (London: HMSO, 1899–1901)

Calendar of Documents relating to Scotland, vol. IV 1357–1509, ed. by J. Bain (London: HMSO, 1888)

Calendar of State Papers and Manuscripts existing in the Archives and Collections of Milan, ed. and trans. by A. B. Hinds (London: HMSO, 1912)

Chastellain, G, 'Chronique des derniers Ducs de Bourgoyne', in Pantheon Literaire iv

Sir Herbert Maxwell of Monteith, Chronicles of Lanercost 1272–1346 (Glasgow: James MacLehose & Sons, 1913)

Christ ruling in midst of his enemies; or, Some first fruits of the Churches deliverance, budding forth out of the crosse and sufferings, [microform] and some remarkable deliverances of a twentie yeeres sufferer, and now a souldier of Jesus Christ; together, with Secretarie Windebanks letters to Sr. Jacob Ashley and the Maior of Newcastle, through which the violent prosecutions of the common adversaries to exile and banishment, are very transparent. Wherein also the reader shall find in severall passages, publike and particular, some notable encouragements to wade through difficulties for the advancing of the great designe of Christ, for setting up of His kingdome, and the ruine of Antichrist, by Lieutenant Colonel, John Fenwicke London (printed for Benjamin Allen in Pope's-head Alley, 1643)

Chronicles of London, ed. by C. L. Kingsford (Oxford: Clarendon Press, 1905)

Como, D. R., 'Women, Prophecy, and Authority in Early Stuart Puritanism', The Huntington Library Quarterly, 61.2 (1998), 203–222

Complaynt of Scotland written in 1548, (Edinburgh: Constable, 1801)

Copies of Letters from Francis Anderson and Others (Richardson Reprints)

Croyland Abbey Chronicle, ed. by H. T. Riley (London: Bohn, 1854)

The Croyland Chronicle Continuation 1459–1486, ed. by N. Prona and J. Cox (London: Richard III and Yorkist History Trust, 1986)

The Cotton MS, the British Library

Davies, R., York Records of the Fifteenth Century (Gloucester: Gloucester Reprints, 1976)

Diary of Mr. Robert Douglas when with the Scots Army in England (Edinburgh: Edinburgh University Press, 1833)

English Historical Documents, vol. 5 1327–1484, ed. by A. R. Myers (London: Eyre & Spottiswood, 1969)

Extracts from the Newcastle Council Minute Book 1639–1656, ed. by M. H. Dodds, Newcastle upon Tyne Record Series, vol. 1 (Newcastle upon Tyne: Northumberland Press, 1920)

'Favver', The Siege and Storming of Newcastle (Newcastle upon Tyne: T & G Allan, 1889)

Froissart's Chronicles, ed. by G. Brereton (London: Penguin, 1968)

Grey's 'Chorographia' (Newcastle upon Tyne: n. pub., 1649)

Furnivall, F. J. and H. W. Hales, ed., Bishop Percy's Folio Manuscript, vol. 3 (London: Trubner, 1868)

Hall, Edward, The Union of the Two Noble and Illustre Famelies of Lancastre and York (London: n. pub., 1548)

Hamilton Papers 1532–1543, ed. by J. Bain, vol. 1 (Edinburgh: Great Britain Register Office, 1890)

Hammond, P. W. and R. Horrox, The Harleian Manuscripts, 4 vols British Library Harleian Manuscripte (London: British Library, 1979–1983)

'Hearne's Fragment', in Chronicles of the White Rose, ed. by J. A. Giles (London: James Bohn, 1834)

His Majesties Passing through the Scots Army (pamphlet, 1644)

Historie of the Arrivall of King Edward IV in England and the final Recoverye of his Kingdomes from Henry VI A.D. 1471, ed. by J. Bruce (London: Camden Society, 1838)

Lindsay of Pitscottie, Chronicles of Scotland, volume II (Edinburgh: George Ramsay, 1814)

Kingsford, C. L., ed., The Song of Lewes (Oxford: Clarendon Press, 1890)

Kirby, J. L., ed., Calendar of Signet Letters of Henry IV and Henry V 1399–1422 (London: HMSO, 1978)

Knyghthode and Bataile, ed. by R. Dyboski and Z. M. Arend (London: Early English Texts Society, 1935)

Letters and Papers, Foreign and Domestic, of Henry VIII, 1519–23 cited in Second to None: A History of Coldstream (Coldstream: Coldstream and District Local History Society, 2010)

Mancini, Dominic, The Usurpation of Richard III, ed. by C. A. J. Armstrong (Oxford: Oxford University Press, 1969, reprinted Gloucester 1984)

Machiavelli, Niccolo, The Art of War (New York: Northwestern University Press, 1965)

Major, John, History of Greater Britain (Edinburgh: Scottish History Society, 1892)

Monopoly of the Tyne (Newcastle upon Tyne: Society of Antiquaries of Newcastle upon Tyne, 1978)

More, Sir Thomas, The History of Richard III Complete Works, ed. by R. S. Sylvester, vol. II Yale edition. 11 (London: Yale, 1963)

Northumberland Lay Subsidy Roll 1296, ed. by C. M. Fraser (Newcastle upon Tyne: Society of Antiquaries of Newcastle upon Tyne, 1968)

Pedigrees recorded at the heralds' visitations of the counties of Cumberland and Westmorland: made by Richard St. George, Norry, king of arms in 1615, and by William Dugdale, Norry, king of arms in 1666 (Newcastle upon Tyne: Browne and Browne, 1891)

Phillip De Commynes, The Memoirs of the Reign of Louis XI 1461–1463, trans. M. Jones (London: Hardpress,1972)

'Plumpton Letters', ed. by T. Stapleton (London: Camden Society, 1839)

Vergil, Polydore, Three Books of Polydore Vergil's English History, ed. by H. Ellis (London: Camden Society, 1844)

Fabyan, Robert, The New Chronicles of England and France, ed. by H. Ellis (London: Camden Society, 1809)

'Rose of Rouen', Archaeologia XXIX, pp. 344–347

Rotuli. Parliamentorum, ed. by J. Strachey & others, 6 vols (London: n. pub., 1767–1777)

Rous, J., Historiae Regum Anglicae, ed. by T. Hearne (Oxford, 1716)

Rous, J., The Rous Roll, ed. by C. Ross and W. Courthope (Gloucester: Alan Sutton, 1980)

Sadler's State Papers, ed. by A. Clifford, 3 vols (Edinburgh: Constable, 1809)

Scottish Exchequer Rolls vii Ramsay ii, held by National Records of Scotland

Shielings & Bastles (London: Royal Commission on Historic Monuments, 1970)

Short English Chronicle, ed. by J. Gairdner (London: Camden Society New Series xxviii, 1880)

Talhoffer, Hans, Manual of Swordfighting, trans. & ed. by M. Rector, facsimile edn (London: Greenhill, 2000)

The Household of Edward IV, ed. by A. R. Myers (Manchester: Manchester University Press, 1959)

The Great Chronicle of London, ed. by A. H. Thomas and I. D. Thornley (London: George W. Jones, 1938)

The Journal of Sir William Brererton 1635 in North Country Diaries, ed. by J. C. Hodgeson (Durham: Surtees Society, 1915)

The Parochial Chapelries of Earsdon and Horton, H. H. E. Craster (Newcastle upon Tyne: Andrew Reid & Co., 1909), http://www.archive.org/stream/historyofnorthum09nort/historyofnorthum09nort_djvu.txt

The Paston Letters 1422–1509, ed. by J. Gairdner, 3 vols (London: Edward Archer, 1872–1875)

The Priory of Hexham, vol. i (Durham: Surtees Society, 1864)

The Register of Freemen of Newcastle upon Tyne from the Corporation, Guild and Admission Books chiefly of the Seventeenth Century, M. H. Dodds, Newcastle upon Tyne Record Series, vol. 3 (Newcastle upon Tyne: Northumberland Press, 1923)

http://www.archive.org/details/pedigreesrecorde00sainrich

The Stirring World of Robert Carey (London: Ripping Yarns Com, 2004)

The Taking of Newcastle or Newes from the Army (Edinburgh: n. pub., 1644)

http://www.archive.org/details/pedigreesrecorde00sainrich

The Visitation of Northumberland in 1615, R. St George, ed. by George W. Marshall (London: n. pub., 1878)

'The Year Book de Termino Paschae 4 Edward IV', in The Priory of Hexham, vol. 1 (Durham: Surtees Society, 1864)

Three Fifteenth Century Chronicles, ed. by J. Gairdner (London: Camden Society 1880)

Vita Sancta Wilfrithi (Cambridge: Cambridge University Press, 1985)

Warkworth, John, A Chronicle of the First Thirteen Years of the Reign of Edward IV 1461–1474, ed. by J. O. Halliwell (London: Camden Society Old Series X, 1839)

Waurin, Jean de, Recueil des Chroniques D'Angleterre, ed. by W. Hardy & E. L. C. P. Hardy 1891

Whethamstede, J., 'Registrum' in Registra quorandum Abbatum Monasterii S. Albani, ed. by H. Riley, 2 vols Rolls Series (London: Longman, 1872–1873)

William Gregory's 'Chronicle of London', in Historical Collections of a Citizen of London in the Fifteenth Century, ed. by J. Gairdner C.C New Series xvii (London: Camden Society, 1876)

William of Worcester, 'Annales Rerum Anglicarum', in Liber Niger Scaccarii, ed. by J. Hearne, 2 vols (Oxford: n. pub., 1728)

SECONDARY SOURCES

A Biographical Dictionary of Eminent Scotsmen in Four Volumes, vol. III, ed. by R. Chambers and rev. by T. Thomson (Glasgow: Blackie & Son, 1855), available at: http://www.archive.org/stream/biographicaldict04chamiala#page/n7/mode/2up.

Adams, M., Admiral Collingwood: Nelson's Own Hero (London: Head of Zeus, 2005)

———, King in the North (London: Head of Zeus, 2013)

Allen, K., The Wars of the Roses (London: Jonathan Cape, 1973)

Allmand, C., Henry V (London: Methuen, 1992)

Arch Aeliana, vol. xiv

Allsop, B. & U. Clark, Historic Architecture of Northumberland & Newcastle upon Tyne (Northumberland: Oriel Press, 1977)

Anderson-Graham, P., Highways & Byways in Northumberland (London: MacMillan, 1920)

Archer, R. E. C., Government and People in the Fifteenth Century (Gloucsester.: Alan Sutton, 1995)

Armstrong, P., Dark Tales of Old Newcastle (Newcastle upon Tyne: Newbridge Studios, 1990)

Armstrong, R. B., History of Liddesdale, Eskdale, Ewesdale, Wauchopedale & the Debatable Land (Edinburgh: David Douglas, 1883)

Ashley, M., The English Civil War (London: Thames & Hudson, 1978)

Ashworth, N. & M. Pegg, History of the British Coal Industry (Oxford: OUP, 1986)

Bagley, J. J., Margaret of Anjou, Queen of England (London: H. Jenkins, 1948)

Bain, J., ed., Calendar of Documents Relating to Scotland 1108—1509 (London: Scottish Records Office, 1881–1884)

Banks, F. R., Scottish Border Country (London: Batsford, 1951)

Barbour, R., The Knight and Chivalry (London: Sphere Books, 1974)

Barr, J., Border Papers, ed. by Revd. J. Stevenson and A. J. Crosbie, 2 vols (Edinburgh: Publisher, 1894)

Barriffe, W., Militaries Discipline; or the Young Artilleryman (6th edn 1661; Partizan Press, 1988)

Barrow, G. W. S., Robert Bruce (Edinburgh: Edinburgh University Press, 1965)

———, The Kingdom of Scots (Edinburgh: Edinburgh University Press, 1973)

Bartlett, C., The English Longbowman 1313—1515 (Oxford: Osprey, 1995)

Bates, C. J., History of Northumberland (London: Elliot Stock, 1895)

Bean, J. M. W., 'The Percies and their Estates in Scotland', Archaeologia Aeliana, 4th Series, 35 (1957), 91–99

———, The Estates of the Percy Family (Oxford: Historical Series, 1958)

Beckensall, S., Life and Death in Prehistoric Northumberland (Newcastle upon Tyne: Frank Graham, 1976)

Behrens, C. B. A., Merchant Shipping and the Demands of War (London: HMSO, 1955)

Bennett, H. S., The Pastons and Their England (Cambridge: Cambridge University Press, 1932)

Bingham, C., The Stewart Kings of Scotland 1371–1603 (London: Weidenfeld & Nicolson, 1974)

Blackmore, H. L., The Armouries of the Tower of London - Ordnance (London: HMSO, 1976)

Blair, C., European Armour (London: Batsford, 1958)

Boardman, A. V., The Battle of Towton 1461 (Gloucester: Alan Sutton, 1996)

———, The Medieval Soldier in the Wars of the Roses (Gloucester: Alan Sutton, 1998)

———, Hotspur (Gloucester: Alan Sutton, 2003)

Bogg, E., The Border Country (Newcastle upon Tyne: Mawson Swan & Morgan, 1898)

Borland, Reverend R. R., Border Raids & Reivers (Dalbeattie: Thomas Fraser, 1910)

Bourne, H., the History of Newcastle upon Tyne; or the ancient and present state of that town (Newcastle upon Tyne: John White, 1736)

Boyes, J., 'The Blue Streak Underground Launchers', Airfield Research Group Review, 140 (2013)

———, 'Blue Streak Underground Launchers', Royal Air Force Historical Society Journal, 58 (2013)
Brand, J., History of Newcastle upon Tyne, 2 vols (London: H. White & Son, 1789)

Breeze, D. J. & B. Dobson, Hadrian's Wall, 4th edn (London: Penguin, 2000)

Brenan, G., The House of Percy, 2 vols (London: Freemantle & Co, 1898)

Brockett, J., A Glossary of North Country Words (Newcastle upon Tyne: T. & J. Dinsdale, 1849)

Brooke, C., Safe Sanctuaries (Edinburgh: John Donald, 2000)

Brown, M., The Black Douglases (Edinburgh: John Donald, 1999)

Brown, P., The Great Wall of Hadrian (London: Heath Cranton, 1932)

———, The Friday Books, 4 vols (Newcastle upon Tyne: Bealls, 1934–1946)

Burne, Colonel A.H., Battlefields of England (London: Methuen, 1950)

———, More Battlefields of England (London: Methuen, 1952)

Burne, Colonel A.H., & P. Young, The Great Civil War 1642–1646 (London: Eyre & Spottiswoode, 1959)

Byrd, E., Flowers of the Forest (London: Macmillan, 1969)

Caldwell, D. H., The Scottish Armoury (Edinburgh: John Donald, 1979)

Campbell, J., 'England, Scotland and the Hundred Years War', in J. R. Hale et al (eds.), Europe in the Later Middle Ages (London: Faber and Faber, 1965)

Campbell, D. B., Siege Warfare in the Roman World 146 BC – AD 378, illustrated by Adam Hook (Oxford: Osprey, 2005)

———, Roman Auxiliary Forts 27 BC – 378 AD (London: Osprey, 2009)

Carpenter, C., The Wars of the Roses: Politics and the Constitution in England c.1437–1509 (Cambridge: Cambridge University Press, 2002)

Cathcart King, D. J., Castellarium Anglicanum, vol. 2 (New York: Kraus International, 1983)

Chadwick, H. M., Early Scotland (London: Octagon Press, 1974)

Chalmers, M. & W. Walker, 'The United Kingdom, Nuclear Weapons, and the Scottish Question', The Non-proliferation Review (Spring 2002)

Charlesworth, D., 'The Battle of Hexham', Archaeologia Aeliana, 4th Series, 30 (1952), 57–68

———, 'Northumberland in the Early Years of Edward IV', Archaeologia Aeliana, 4th Series, 31 (1953), 69–81

Charleton, R. J., A History of Newcastle upon Tyne (London: Walter Scott Publishing, 1894)

Charlton, B., Upper North Tynedale (Northumberland: National Park Authority, 1987)

Charlton, J., Hidden Chains – the Slavery Business and North East England 1600–1865 (Newcastle upon Tyne: Tyne Bridge, 2008)

Chesterton, G. K., A Short History of England (London: Biblio-Bazaar, 2008)

Child, F. J., The English and Scottish Popular Ballads, vol. 1 (New York: Dover Publications, 1965)

Clark, P., Where the Hills Meet the Sky (Northumberland: Glen Graphics, 2000)

Collingwood Bruce, J., Handbook to the Roman Wall, 11th edn (Newcastle: Andrew Reid, 1957)

Colvin, H. M., D. R. Ransome & J. Summerson, History of the King's Works III 1485–1660, Part 1 (London: HMSO, 1975)

Collins, R., & M. Symonds, Hadrian's Wall 2009–2019 (Newcastle upon Tyne: Society of Antiquaries, 2019)

Cowan, R., Roman Legionary 58 BC – 69 AD, illustrated by Angus Macbride, Osprey Men-at-Arms series (Oxford: Osprey, 2003)

Cook, D. R., Lancastrians & Yorkists, The Wars of the Roses (London: Longman, 1984)

Corfe, T., Riot: The Hexham Militia Riot 1761 (Northumberland: Hexham Community Partnership, 2004)

Cross, R., & B. Charlton, Then and Now – a Snapshot of Otterburn Training Area (London: Defence Estates, 2004)

Crow, J., 'Harbottle Castle, Excavations and Survey 1997–1999', in Archaeology in Northumberland National Park, ed. by P. N. K. Frodsham (York: Council for British Archaeology, 2004)

Cruft, K., J. Dunbar & R. Fawcett, Borders, Pevsner Architectural Guides: The Buildings of Scotland (London: Yale, 2006)

Crumlin-Pedersen, O., The Skuldelev Ships I (Stockholm: Viking Ship Museum and the National Museum of Denmark, 2002)

Cunliffe, B., The Ancient Celts (London: Penguin, 1999)

Davies, H., A Walk along the Wall (London: Frances Lincoln, 1974)

De Fonblanque, E. B., Annals of the House of Percy: From the Conquest to the opening of the nineteenth century, vol. 1 (London: R. Clay & Sons, 1887)

De Groot, Jerome, 'Chorographia: Newcastle and Royalist Identity in the late 1640s', The Seventeenth Century, 8.1 (2003), 61–75

Deary, T., Dirty Little Imps – Stories from the DLI (Durham: County Record Office, 2004)

Dent, J. & R. McDonald, Warfare & Fortifications in the Borders (Newton St. Boswells: Scottish Borders Council, 2000)

Devine, T. M., The Scottish Nation 1700–2000 (London: Allen Lane, 1999)

Dickinson, F., The Reluctant Rebel (Newcastle upon Tyne: Cresset Books, 1996)

Divine, D., The North-West Frontier of Rome (London: Macdonald & Co, 1969)

Dixon, D. D., Whittingham Vale (Newcastle upon Tyne: Robert Redpath, 1895)

———, Upper North Coquetdale (Newcastle upon Tyne: Robert Redpath, 1903)

Dixon, P. W., Fortified Houses on the Anglo-Scottish Border: A study of the Domestic Architecture of the Upland Area in its Social and Economic Context (PhD thesis, Oxford University, 1976)

Dockray, K. R., 'the Yorkshire Rebellions of 1469', The Ricardian, 6.82 (December 1983)

———, Chronicles of the Reign of Edward IV (Gloucester: Alan Sutton, 1983)

Dodds, J. F., Bastions & Belligerents (Newcastle upon Tyne: Keepdale, 1996)

Drummond Gould, H., Brave Borderland (Edinburgh: Thomas Nelson, 1936)

Ducklin, K., & J. Waller, Sword Fighting (London: Robert Hale, 2001)

Duncan, A. A. M., Scotland, the Making of a Kingdom (Edinburgh: Oliver & Boyd, 1975)

Durham, K., Strongholds of the Border Reivers, Osprey 'Fortress' Series (London: Osprey, 2008)

———, Border Reiver 1513–1603, Osprey 'Warrior' Series (London: Osprey, 2011)

Eddington, A., Castles & Historic Houses of the Border (Edinburgh: Oliver & Boyd, 1926)

Elliot, G. F. S., The Border Elliots and the family of Minto (Edinburgh: privately published, 1897)

Ellis, J., Eye deep in Hell (London: Crook Helm, 1976)

Eyre Todd, G., Byways of the Old Scottish Border (London: Macmillan, 1913)

Falkus, G., The Life and Times of Edward IV (London: Weidenfeld & Nicolson, 1981)

Ferguson, J., The Flodden Helm and events linked to the death of Thomas Howard in 1524 (Berwick on Tweed: privately published, 2009)

Fiorato, V., A Boylston & C. Knussel, eds., Blood and Roses: The Archaeology of a Mass Grave from the Battle of Towton AD 1461 (Oxford: OUP, 2000)

Fisher, A., William Wallace (Edinburgh: John Donald, 1986)

Foster, J., Guns of the North-East Coast (Barnsley: Pen & Sword, 2004)

Frodsham, P. & P. Ryder, et al Archaeology in Northumberland National Park (York: Council for British Archaeology, 2004)

Furgol, E., A Regimental History of the Covenanting Armies (Edinburgh: John Donald, 1990)

Gardiner, S. R., History of the Great Civil War 1642–1649 (London: Longmans, 1886–1891)

Gaunt, P., The Cromwellian Gazetteer (Gloucester: Tempus, 1987)

Gerrard, C. M., P. Greaves, A. R. Millard, R. Annis & A. Caffell, Lost Lives, New Voices: Unlocking the

Stories of the Scottish Soldiers from the Battle of Dunbar 1650 (Oxford: Oxbow Books, 2018)

Gillingham, J., The Wars of the Roses (London: Weidenfeld & Nicolson, 1981)

Given-Wilson, C., Chronicles of the Revolution 1397–1400 (Manchester: Manchester University Press, 1993)

Goldsworthy, A., The Complete Roman Army (Sale: Phoenix Press, 2003)

———, Roman Warfare (Sale: Phoenix Press, 2007)

———, Hadrian's Wall (London: Profile, 2018)

Good, G. L. & C. J. Tabraham, 'Excavations at Threave Castle, Galloway, 1974-78', Medieval Archaeology 25 (1981), 90–140

Graham, J., Condition of the Border at the Union (London: George Routledge, 1907)

Grant, A., 'Richard III in Scotland', in The North of England in the Reign of Richard III, ed. by A. J. Pollard (London: St. Martin's Press, 1996)

Grant, A., Henry VII (London: Methuen, 1985)

Gravett, C., Medieval Siege Warfare (London: Osprey, 1990)

Greig, A., Fair Helen (London: Riverrun [Quercus], 2014)

Griffith, G., The Viking Art of War (London: Greenhill Books, 1995)

Griffiths, R. A., 'Local Rivalries and National Politics: The Percies, the Nevilles and the Duke of Exeter 1452–1455', Speculum, 43.4 (1968), 589—632

———, The Reign of King Henry VI (Los Angeles: University of California Press, 1981)

———, ed., Patronage, the Crown and the Provinces in Later Medieval England (Gloucester: Sutton, 1981)

———, The Making of the Tudor Dynasty (Gloucester: Sutton, 1985)

———, Kings and Nobles in the Later Middle Ages (Gloucester: Sutton, 1986)

———, King and Country: England and Wales in the Fifteenth Century (Gloucester: Sutton, 1991)

Gully, Reverend M., Letters of C.J. Bates (Kendal: Titus Wilson, 1906)

Haigh, P. A., The Military Campaigns of the Wars of the Roses (Boston: Da Capo Press, 1995)

Hall, E., Chronicle (London: J. Johnson, 1809)

Hallam, E., The Plantagenet Encyclopedia (London: Colour Library Direct, 1990)

———, ed., the Chronicles of the Wars of the Roses (London: Colour Library Direct, 1988)

Hammond, P. W., Richard III – Lordship Loyalty and Law (Spalding: Richard III & Yorkist History Trust, 1986)

Harrison, W.J., The Geology of Northumberland (proof notes 1879)

Hartshorne, C. H., Memoirs Illustrative of the History and Antiquities of Northumberland volume 2, Feudal and Military Antiquities of Northumberland and the Scottish Borders (London: Bell & Daldy, 1852)

Hayes-McCoy, W. A., Irish Battles (Belfast: Appletree Press, 2009)

Haythornthwaite, P., The English Civil War 1642–1651 (London: Weidenfeld Military, 1994)

Heald, H., Magician of the North (Carmathen: McNidder & Grace, 2010)

Hearse, G. S., The Tramways of Northumberland (Durham: George S. Hearse, 1961)

Heeney, S., Beowulf (London: Faber, 1999)

Hepple, L. W., A History of Northumberland and Newcastle upon Tyne (Newcastle upon Tyne: Phillimore, 1976)

Hermann, R., R. J. Crellin & M. Uckleman, Bronze Age Combat (Oxford: British Archaeological Reports, 2020)

Hewitson, T. L., Weekend Warriors from Tyne to Tweed (Gloucester: Tempus, 2006)

Hicks, M. A., 'Edward IV, the Duke of Somerset and Lancastrian Loyalism in the North', Northern History, 20.1 (1984), 23–37

Higham, N. J., The Kingdom of Northumbria 350–1100 (Gloucester: Alan Sutton, 1993)

Hodges, C. C. & J. Gibson, Hexham & its Abbey (Northumberland: Hexham Abbey, 1919)

Hodgson, J., Northumberland, Part II vol. 1 (Newcastle upon Tyne: Frank Graham, 1973)

Hogg, J., Songs by the Ettrick Shepherd (Edinburgh: William Blackwood, 1831)

Homer, Iliad, Rouse translation (Edinburgh: Thomas Nelson & Sons, 1938)

Hope Dodds M., ed., A History of Northumberland, vol. 15 (Newcastle upon Tyne: Northumberland County History Committee, 1940)

Horrox, R., Richard III and the North (Cambridge: Cambridge University Press, 1986)

———, Fifteenth Century Attitudes (Cambridge: Cambridge University Press, 1994)

Howell, R., Newcastle upon Tyne and the Puritan Revolution: A Study of the Civil War in North England (Oxford: Oxford University Press, 1967)

Howitt, W., Visits to Remarkable Places, 2 vols (Philadelphia: Carey and Hart, 1842)

Hudson, R., 'Re-thinking change in old industrial regions: reflecting on the experiences of North East England', Environment and Planning A, 37.4 (2005), 581–596

Hugill, R., Castles and Peles of the English Border (Newcastle upon Tyne: Frank Graham, 1970)

Hunter Blair, C. H., 'Harbottle Castle', History of the Berwickshire Naturalists Club, 28 (1932–1934)

———, Mayors & Lord Mayors of Newcastle upon Tyne (Newcastle upon Tyne: Society of Antiquaries, 1940)

Hunter Blair, P., Roman Britain & Early England (Edinburgh: Thomas Nelson & Sons, 1963)

Jackson, D., The Northumbrians (London: Hurst, 2019)

Kapelle, W. E., The Norman Conquest of the North (North Carolina: Croom Helm, 1979)

Keegan, Sir J., The Face of Battle (London: Penguin, 1976)

Keen, M., English Society in the Later Middle Ages 1348–1500 (London: Penguin, 1990)

———, ed., Medieval Warfare – a History (Oxford: Oxford University Press, 1999)

Kendall, P. M., Warwick the Kingmaker (New York: W. W. Norton, 1957)

Keppie, L., The Making of the Roman Army from Republic to Empire (Oklahoma: University of Oklahoma Press, 1998)

Kightly, J., Flodden and the Anglo-Scottish War of 1513 (London: Almark, 1975)

Kinross, J., Walking and Exploring the Battlefields of Britain (London: David & Charles, 1988)

Lander, J. R., Crown and Nobility 1450–1509 (London: Edward Arnold, 1976)

Lander, J. R., The Limitations of English Monarchy in the later Middle Ages (Toronto: University of Toronto Press, 1989)

Lang, J., Stories of the Border Marches (New York: Dodge, 1916)

Leadman, A. D., 'the Battle of Towton', Yorkshire Archaeological Journal, 10 (1889), 287–302

Leighton, Reverend A., Wilson's Tales of the Borders, 8 vols (Newcastle upon Tyne: Gall & Inglis, [undated])

Loades, M., Swords & Swordsmen (Barnsley: Pen & Sword, 2017)

Logan Mack, J., The Border Line (Edinburgh: Oliver & Boyd, 1924)

Lomas, R., North-East England in the Middle Ages (Edinburgh: John Donald, 1992)

———, Northumberland – County of Conflict (Edinburgh: Tuckwell Press, 1996)

Long, B., The Castles of Northumberland (Newcastle upon Tyne: Harold Hill, 1967)

Loyd, A., 'My Afghan Diaries', Saturday Times Magazine, 2 May 2020, 42

Lynch, M., Scotland a New History (London: Pimlico, 1992)

McCutcheon, C., Home Guard Manual 1941 (Gloucester: History Press, 2007)

Macdonald, A. J., Border Bloodshed (Edinburgh: Tuckwell, 2000)

MacDonald Fraser, G., The Steel Bonnets (London: Barrie & Jenkins, 1971)

MacDougall, N., James III: A Political Study (Edinburgh: John Donald, 1982)

———, James IV (Edinburgh: John Donald, 1989)

Mackenzie, E., History of Northumberland (Newcastle upon Tyne: Mackenzie & Dent, 1825)

MacLauchlan, H., Survey of the Roman Wall (London: [imprint unknown], 1858)

———, Old Roman Roads in Northumberland (London: [imprint unknown], 1867)

McFarlane, K. B., 'The Wars of the Roses', Proceedings of the British Academy, 50 (1964)

———, The Nobility of Late Medieval England (Oxford: Oxford University Press, 1975)

———, England in the Fifteenth Century, ed. by G. L. Harris (London: Hambledon Press, 1981)

McIvor, I., A Fortified Frontier (Gloucester: Tempus, 2001)

Mackay, J., Braveheart (Edinburgh: Mainstream, 1995)

McNamee, C., The Wars of the Bruces: Scotland, England and Ireland (Edinburgh: Birlinn, 1997)

McNeil, E., Flodden Field: A Novel (London: Severn House, 2007)

Mabbit, J., Archaeology, Revolution and the End of the Medieval English Town: Fortification and Discourse in Seventeenth Century Newcastle upon Tyne (Newcastle upon Tyne: Tyne Bridge, 2010)

Manning, O., Fortunes of War Trilogy (London: Penguin/Random House, 2014)

Marsden, J., The Illustrated Border Ballads (London: Macmillan, 1990)

———, Northanhymbre Saga (London: BCA, 1992)

———, Fury of the Norsemen (New York: St. Martin's Press, 1995)

Mayer, L., Capability Brown and the English Landscape Garden (Oxford: Oxford University Press, 2011)

Maxwell-Irving, A., The Border Towers of Scotland; the West March (Stirling: Maxwell-Irving, 2000)

Meade, D. M., The Medieval Church in England (Worthing: Churchman, 1988)

Meikle, M., A British Frontier (Edinburgh: Tuckwell, 2004)

Middlebrook, S., Newcastle upon Tyne, its Growth and Achievement (Newcastle upon Tyne: Newcastle Chronicle & Journal, 1950)

Moat, D.D., The North West Borderland (Newcastle: Frank Graham, 1973)

Moffat, A., The Borders (Selkirk: Deerpark Press, 2002)

———, Arthur & the Lost Kingdoms (Edinburgh: Birlinn, 2012)

Moffat, A. & G. Rose, Tyneside; a History of Newcastle and Gateshead from Earliest Times (Edinburgh: Mainstream Publishing, 2009)

Moranville, H., ed., Chronographia Regum Francorum, iii (Paris: Librairie Renouard, 1897)

Morgan, A., A Fine and Private Place, Jesmond Old Cemetery (Newcastle upon Tyne: Tyne Bridge, 2004)

Morris, M., Edward I – a Great and Terrible King (London: Random House, 2008)

———, Castle; a History of the Buildings that Shaped Medieval Britain (London: Random House 2012)

Moses, H., The Fighting Bradfords (Durham: County Durham Books, 2003)

Murray's Handbook for Travellers in Durham & Northumberland (London: John Murray, 1890)

Murray Kendall, P., Warwick the Kingmaker (London: Phoenix, 2002)

Myers, A. R., ed., The Household of Edward IV: The Black Book and the Ordinance of 1478 (Manchester: Manchester University Press, 1959)

Nef, J. U., The Rise of the British Coal Industry (London: Routledge, 1932)

Neillands, R., the Hundred Years War (London: Routledge, 1990)

———, The Wars of the Roses (London: Routledge, 1992)

Nicolle, D., Medieval Warfare Source Book (London: Brockhampton, 1999)

Nicholson, H., Tom Fleck (Online: YouWriteon.com, 2011)

Norman, A. V. B. and D. Pottinger, English Weapons and Warfare 449–1660 (London: Dorset Press, 1966)

Oakeshott, R. E., A Knight and his Castle (London: Dufour Editions, 1996)

———, A Knight and his Weapons (London: Dufour Editions, 1997)

———, A Knight and his Horse (London: Dufour Editions, 1998)

———, A Knight and his Armour (London: Dufour Editions, 1999)

Oliver, N., A History of Ancient Britain (London: Weidenfeld & Nicolson, 2012)

Oliver, S., Rambles in Northumberland and on the Scottish Border (London: Chapman & Hall, 1835)

Oman, Sir Charles, The Art of War in the Middle Ages, vol. 2 (London: Greenhill, 1924)

Osprey, New Vanguard 108, English Civil War Artillery 1642–1651

———, Campaign 119, Marston Moor 1644

———, Elite 25, Soldiers of the English Civil War (1) Infantry

———, Elite 27, Soldiers of the English Civil War (2) Cavalry

———, Fortress 9, English Civil War Fortifications 1642–1651

———, Essential Histories 58, The English Civil Wars 1642–1651

———, Men-at-Arms 14, The English Civil War Armies

———, Men-at-Arms 331, Scots Armies of the English Civil Wars

Patten, W., 'Expedition into Scotland etc' in Tudor Tracts, ed. by A. F. Pollard (London: Constable, 1903)

Paterson, J., Autobiographical Reminiscences (Glasgow: Maurice Ogle & Co, 1876)

Paul, Sir J. B., The Scots Peerage (Edinburgh: David Douglas, 1905)

Pearson, H., Achtung Schweinehund (London: Abacus, 2008)

Pease, H., The Lord Wardens of the Marches of England and Scotland (London: Constable, 1913)

———, The History of the Northumberland (Hussars) Yeomanry 1819–1923 (London: Constable, 1924)

Pegler, M., Powder and Ball Small Arms (Wiltshire: Crowood Press, 1998)

Percy Folio of Ballads and Romance, ed. by J. W. Hales and F. J. Furnival (London: De La Mare Press, 1905–1910)

Percy, Bishop Thomas, Reliques of Ancient English Poetry, ed. by H. B. Wheatley (New York: Dover, 1906)

Percy Hedley, W., Northumberland Families, vol. 1 (Newcastle upon Tyne: Society of Antiquaries, 1968)

Percy, Thomas, Reliques of Ancient English Poetry, ed. by J. V. Pritchard, Book One: I 'Chevy Chase' (London: J. Dodsley, 1775)

Perry, R., A Naturalist on Lindisfarne (London: L. Drummond, 1946)

Pevsner, N. & E. Williamson, Durham, The Buildings of England Series (London: Penguin, 1985)

Pevsner, N. & I. Richmond, Northumberland, The Buildings of England Series (London: Penguin, 1992)

Phillips, G., The Anglo-Scots Wars 1513–1550 (Woodbridge: Boydell Press, 1999)

Philipson, J., Whisky Smuggling, and Illicit Distillation on the Middle March of Northumberland (Newcastle upon Tyne: Society of Antiquaries, 1991)

Pitcairn, R., Criminal Trials in Scotland 1488–1624, ed. by William Tait (Edinburgh: the Maitland Club, 1833)

Platt, W., Stories of the Scottish Border (London: Harrap, 1919)

Pollard, A. J., 'Characteristics of the Fifteenth Century North', in Government, Religion and Society in Northern England 1000–1700, ed. by C. Appleby and P. Dalton (Oxford: Oxford University Press, 1977)

———, North-eastern England during the Wars of the Roses: War, Politics and Lay Society, 1450-1500 (Oxford: Oxford University Press, 1990)

———, 'Percies, Nevilles and the Wars of the Roses', History Today (September 1992)

———, The Wars of the Roses (London: St. Martin's Press, 1995)

———, North of England in the Reign of Richard III (Gloucester: Sutton, 1996)

Prestwich, M., Armies and Warfare in the Middle Ages (New Haven: Yale University Press, 1996)

Proceedings of the Society of Antiquaries of Newcastle upon Tyne, 9

Rambles in Northumberland and on the Scottish border; interspersed with brief notices of interesting events in border history, William Andrew (London: Chapman and Hall, 1835), pp. 234–236, https://books.google.co.uk/books?id=PO4-AAAAYAAJ&printsec=frontcover&source=gbs_ge_summary_r&cad=0#v=onepage&q&f=false, accessed 1 April 2020

Ramsay, Sir J. H., Lancaster and York, 2 vols (Oxford: Clarendon Press, 1892)

Ransome, C., 'The Battle of Towton', English Historical Review, 4.15 (1889), 460–466

Reid, N. H., 'Alexander III; the Historiography of a Myth' in Scotland in the Reign of Alexander III 1249 – 1286, ed. by N. H. Reid (Edinburgh: John Donald, 1990)

Reid, S., All the King's Armies – A Military History of the English Civil War 1642–1651 (Gloucester: History Press, 2007)

Richardson, D., The Swordmakers of Shotley Bridge (Newcastle upon Tyne: Frank Graham, 1973)

Richardson, M. A., The local historian's table book, of remarkable occurrences, historical facts, traditions, legendary and descriptive ballads [&c.] connected with the counties of Newcastle upon Tyne, Northumberland and Durham (London, J. R. Smith 1846), available at https://books.google.co.uk/books?id=yhcHAAAAQAAJ&pg=PP7#v=onepage&q&f=false

Ridpath, G., The Border History of England and Scotland (Edinburgh: Mercat Press, 1979)

Rissik, D., The DLI at War – History of the DLI 1939–1945 (Durham: DLI, 1952)

Ritchie, C. I. A., 'Cumbrian Sleuth Hounds', Cumbria Lake District Life, 35.8, 474.

Robb, G., The Debatable Land (London: Picador, 2018)

Robson, R., Rise and Fall of the English Highland Clans: Tudor Responses to a Medieval Problem (Edinburgh: John Donald, 1989)

Rogers, Col. H. C. B., Artillery through the Ages (London: Military Book Society, 1971)

Rollaston, D. & M. Prestwich, eds., The Battle of Neville's Cross 1346 (Lincolnshire: Studies in North-eastern History, 1998)

Rose, A., Kings in the North (London: Phoenix, 2002)

Ross, C., Edward IV (London: Eyre Methuen, 1974)

Ryder, P. F., Harbottle Castle – a short historical and descriptive account (Northumberland: National Park Authority, 1990)

Sadler, D. J., Battle for Northumbria (Newcastle upon Tyne: Bridge Studios, 1988)

———, War in the North – The Wars of the Roses in the North East of England 1461–1464 (Leigh-on-Sea: Partizan Press, 2000)

———, Border Fury – The Three Hundred Years War (London: Longmans, 2004)

———, Dunkirk to Belsen (London: JR Books, 2009)

———, The Red Rose & The White (Harlow: Longman/Pearson, 2010)

———, The Field Gun Run (London: Royal Military Tournament, 2010)

———, Blood on the Wave (Edinburgh: Birlinn, 2010)

Sadler, D. J. & R. Serdiville, Siege of Newcastle upon Tyne 1644 (Gloucester: History Press, 2011)

———, Little Book of Newcastle upon Tyne (Gloucester: History Press, 2011)

———, The Battle of Flodden 1513 (Gloucester: History Press, 2013)

———, Tommy at War 1914 – 1918 (London: Biteback, 2013)

———, Ode to Bully Beef (Gloucester: History Press, 2013)

———, Cromwell's Convicts (Barnsley: Pen & Sword, 2020)

Sadler, D. J. & A. Speirs the Battle of Hexham 1464 (Northumberland: Ergo Press, 2007)

Saklatvala, B., Arthur, Roman Britain's last Champion (Newton Abbot: David & Charles, 1967)

Salter, V., High Lives and Low Morals – the Duel that shook Stuart Society (London: Pimlico, 2000)

Sawyer, P., Oxford Illustrated History of the Vikings (Oxford: Oxford University Press, 1997)

Scotland's Secret Bunker 1951 – 1993; A Guide and History (St. Andrews: Scotland's Secret Bunker Guide, 2007)

Scott, Sir Walter, Border Antiquities, 2 vols (London: Longmans, 1814)

———, Minstrelsy (London, Ward Lock 1892 edition)

Scofield, C. L., The Life and Reign of Edward the Fourth, 2 vols (London: Routledge, 1967)

Second to None: A History of Coldstream (Coldstream: Coldstream and District Local History Society, 2010)

Seward, D., Henry V as Warlord (London: Sidgwick & Jackson, 1987)

———, The Wars of the Roses (London: Robinson, 2013)

———, Richard III – England's Black Legend (London: Pegasus, 2017)

Seymour, W., Battles in Britain, vol. 1 (London: Sidgwick & Jackson, 1989)

Simons, E. N., Reign of Edward IV (New York: Barnes & Noble, 1966)

Sinclair, Sir, J., General Report on the Agricultural State and Political Circumstance of Scotland (Edinburgh: Constable & Co., 1814)

Sitwell, Brigadier W., The Border (Newcastle upon Tyne: Andrew Reid, 1927)

Skene, W. F., Four Ancient Books of Wales, vol. 1 (Edinburgh: Edmonston and Douglas, 2007)

Smout, T. C., History of the Scottish People (London: Fontana, 1969)

Smout, T. C. with A. J. S. Gibson, Prices, Food and Wages in Scotland 1550–1780 (Cambridge: Cambridge University Press, 1994)

Smurthwaite, D., The Ordnance Survey Guide to the Battlefields of Britain (London: Michael Joseph, 1984)

Society of Antiquaries of Newcastle upon Tyne, Pilgrimage of the Roman Wall June 26th July 3rd 1886 (South Shields: Society of Antiquaries of Newcastle upon Tyne, 1886)

Spaven, M., Fortress Scotland; a Guide to the Military Presence (London: Pluto Press, 1983)

State Papers & Letters of Sir Ralph Sadler, ed. by A. Clifford, 3 vols, vol. 1 (Edinburgh: Constable & Co, 1809)

Steel of Aikwood, Lord, Against Goliath (London: Pan Macmillan, 2008)

Stewart, G., & J. Sheen, Tyneside Scottish (Barnsley: Pen & Sword, 1999)

Stewart, R., The Marches (London: Jonathan Cape, 2016)

Storey, R. L., 'The Wardens of the Marches of England towards Scotland 1377–1489', English Historical Review, 72.285 (1957), 593–615

———, End of the House of Lancaster (Gloucester: Sutton, 1999)

Stow, G. B., ed., Historia Vitae et Regni Ricardi Secundo introduced (Pennsylvania: University of Pennsylvania Press, 1977)

Summerson, H., 'Carlisle and the English West March in the Late Middle Ages', in The North of England in the Reign of Richard III (Oxford: Wiley-Blackwell, 1996)

'Survey of Newcastle', Harleian Miscellany, vol. iii, quoted in Gilpin's Life of Gilpin in Ecclesiastical Biography: Lives of Eminent Men (London, J. G. & F. Rivington, 1839)

Sykes, J., Remarkable Events, 3 vols (Berwick upon Tweed: Sykes, 1866)

Tabraham, C. J., Hermitage Castle (Edinburgh: Historic Scotland, 1996)

———, Scotland's Castles, revised edn (London: Batsford, 2005)

———, Smailholm Tower (Edinburgh: Historic Scotland, 2007)

Tait, J., Dick the Devil's Bairns: Breaking the Border Mafia (Kindle version, Amazon media, 2018)

Terry, C. S., The Life and Campaigns of Alexander Leslie (London: Longmans, 1899)

———, 'The Scottish Campaign in Northumberland and Durham Between January and June, 1644', Archaeologia Aeliana new Series, 21 (1899), 146–179

———, 'The Siege of Newcastle by the Scots in 1644', Archaeologia Aeliana, new series, 21 (1899), 180–258

———, The Army of the Covenant, 2 vols (Edinburgh: Scottish History Society, 1917)

The Baronetage of England, or the History of the English Baronets, and such Baronets of Scotland, as are of English families; with genealogical tables, and engravings of their armorial bearings, vol. 4, Revd. William Bethan, Miller, (1804), https://www.worldcat.org/title/baronetage-of-england-or-the-history-of-the-english-baronets-and-such-baronets-of-scotland-as-are-of-english-families-with-genealogical-tables-and-engravings-of-their-armorial-bearings-collected-from-the-present-baronetages-approved-historians-public-records-authentic-manuscripts-well-attested-pedigrees-and-personal-information/oclc/71617621, accessed 1 April 2020

The 1569 Rebellion, ed. by Sir Cuthbert Sharp (Durham: J. Shotton, 1975)

The Death of Sweet Milk by Paul Greville Hudson (1876-1960), Hawick Museum.

Thrupp, S. L., 'The problem of replacement Rates in Late Medieval English Population', Economic History Review, 18.1 (1965), 101–119

Tomlinson, W. Weaver, A Comprehensive Guide to Northumberland (Newcastle upon Tyne: Robinson, 1863)

———, Sixteenth Century Life in Northumberland (Newcastle upon Tyne: Robinson, 1866)

Tough, D. L. W., The Last Years of a Frontier (Oxford: Oxford University Press, 1928)

Tranter, N., Fortalices & Early Mansions of Southern Scotland 1400–1650 (Edinburgh: Moray Press, 1935)

Traquair, P., Freedom's Sword: Scotland's Wars of Independence (London: Harper Collins, 1998)

Trevelyan, G. M., English Social History; a Review of Six Centuries – Chaucer to Queen Victoria (London: Ghose Press, 1946)

———, A History of England (London: Penguin, 1975)

Treece, H., & E. Oakeshott, Fighting Men (Leicester: Brockhampton Press, 1963)

Tuck, A., Border Warfare (London: HMSO, 1979)

———, Crown and Nobility, 1272–1462 (New York: Barnes & Noble, 1985)

Veitch, J., History and Poetry of the Scottish Border (Edinburgh: William Blackwood & Sons, 1893)

Wagner, P. & S. Hand, Medieval Sword and Shield (California: Chivalry Bookshelf, 2003)

Ward, S. G. P, Faithful: The Story of the Durham Light Infantry (London: Thomas Nelson & Sons, 1969)

Warwicker, J., Churchill's Underground Army (Barnsley: Pen & Sword, 2008)

Warner, P., Sieges of the Middle Ages (Barnsley: Pen & Sword, 2005)

Watson, C., 'The Battle of Sauchieburn', Battlefield Trust Magazine, 24.4 (Spring 2020)

Watson, F., Under the Hammer (East Linton: Tuckwell Press, 1998)

Watson, G., The Border Reivers (Newcastle upon Tyne: Sandhill, 1974)

Weiss, H., 'A Power in the North? The Percies in the Fifteenth Century' in The Historical Journal, 19.2 (1976), 501–509

Welford, R., A History of Newcastle & Gateshead, 3 vols (London: Walter Scott, 1884)

———, 'Newcastle Householders in 1655; Assessment of Hearth or Chimney Tax', Archaeologia Aeliana 3rd Series, 7 (1911), 49

White, R., History of the Battle of Otterburn 1388 (Newcastle upon Tyne: Emerson Charnley, 1857)

Wilcox, P., Rome's Enemies (2) Gallic and British Celts, illustrated by Angus Macbride, Osprey Men-at-Arms series (Oxford: Osprey, 1985)

Williams, T., The Viking Longship (London: British Museum, 2014)

———, Viking Britain (London: William Collins, 2018)

Wills, F. A., ('the Vagabond') Rambles of Vagabond (Newcastle upon Tyne: Chauhau 1936)

———, Fifty Weekend Walks Around Newcastle on Tyne (London: Hodder & Stoughton, 1951)

Wilson, A. N., The Laird of Abbotsford (Oxford: Oxford University Press, 1980)

Wise, T., The Wars of the Roses (London: Osprey, 1983)

———, Medieval Heraldry (London: Osprey, 2001)

Woolgar, C. M., The Great Household in late Medieval England (London: Yale University Press, 1999)

Wrightson, K., 'Continuity, Chance and Change; the Character of the Industrial Revolution in England: Elements of Identity; the Remaking of the North East', in Northumberland, History and Identity, ed. by R. Collis (Gloucester: Tempus, 2007)